AF361282

DEFINING AND DEFYING BORDERS

Lationamericana

1 Stephanie M. Pridgeon, *Revolutionary Visions: Jewish Life and Politics in Latin American Film*

2 Cecily Raynor and Rhian Lewis (eds.), *Digital Encounters: Envisioning Connectivity in Latin American Cultural Production*

3 Kathleen Ann Myers, Beth T. Boyd, Pablo García Loaeza, Cara Anne Kinnally, and Alejandro Mejías-López, *Contemporary Colonialities in Mexico and Beyond*

4 Vanessa Marie Fernández, *Defining and Defying Borders: Tracing Hispanism across Literary Magazines*

Defining and Defying Borders

Tracing Hispanism across Literary Magazines

VANESSA MARIE FERNÁNDEZ

UNIVERSITY OF TORONTO PRESS
Toronto Buffalo London

Toronto Buffalo London
utorontopress.com
Printed in the USA

ISBN 978-1-4875-4862-9 (cloth)
ISBN 978-1-4875-4912-1 (EPUB)
ISBN 978-1-4875-4915-2 (PDF)

Latinoamericana

Library and Archives Canada Cataloguing in Publication

Title: Defining and defying borders : tracing Hispanism across literary magazines / Vanessa Marie Fernández.
Names: Fernández, Vanessa Marie, author.
Series: Latinoamericana (Toronto, Ont.)
Description: Series statement: Latinoamericana | Includes bibliographical references and index.
Identifiers: Canadiana (print) 20230501192 | Canadiana (ebook) 20230501370 | ISBN 9781487548629 (cloth) | ISBN 9781487549152 (PDF) | ISBN 9781487549121 (EPUB)
Subjects: LCSH: Journalism and literature – Spain – History – 20th century. | LCSH: Journalism and literature – Latin America – History – 20th century. | LCSH: Spanish literature – History and criticism – Periodicals – History – 20th century. | LCSH: Spanish American literature – History and criticism – Periodicals – History – 20th century. | LCSH: Spain – Intellectual life – 20th century. LCSH: Latin America – Intellectual life – 20th century.
Classification: LCC PN5317.L6 F47 2024 | DDC 860.9/006–dc23

Cover design: Louise OFarrell
Cover image: iStock.com/Pillon

We wish to acknowledge the land on which the University of Toronto Press operates. This land is the traditional territory of the Wendat, the Anishnaabeg, the Haudenosaunee, the Métis, and the Mississaugas of the Credit First Nation.

This book has been published with the assistance of San José State University Department of World Languages and Literatures.

University of Toronto Press acknowledges the financial support of the Government of Canada, the Canada Council for the Arts, and the Ontario Arts Council, an agency of the Government of Ontario, for its publishing activities.

Canada Council for the Arts | Conseil des Arts du Canada

Funded by the Government of Canada | Financé par le gouvernement du Canada

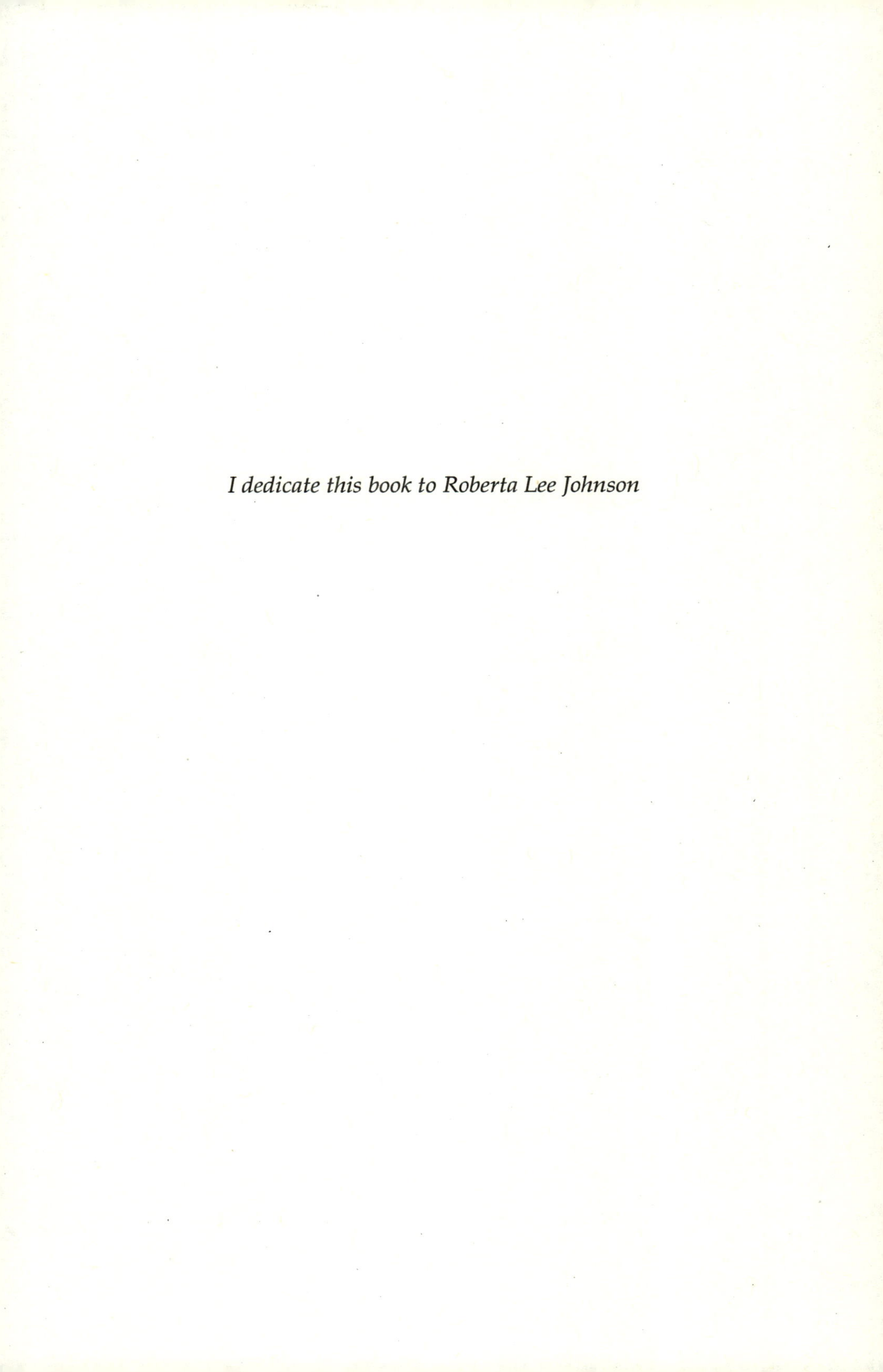

I dedicate this book to Roberta Lee Johnson

Contents

Acknowledgments

This book has evolved significantly since its earliest iterations, and I am therefore owing to many for their support, especially Roberta L. Johnson, who has been a part of the entire journey. Initiating this project would not have been possible without the visionary partnership that Roberta and Michelle Clayton forged in order to guide my work. In this initial phase, I am also appreciative of Maarten Van Delden, Efraín Kristal, Maite Zubiaurre, and Andrea Loselle. Further development of this work would not have been possible without insight from a number of colleagues whose feedback, whether at conferences, surrounding related publications, or through informal discussions, significantly contributed to shaping this work; Brenda Ortiz-Loyola, Silvia Bermúdez, Patrick Collier, Ignacio M. Sánchez Prado, Javier Krauel, Robert Patrick Newcomb, José Díaz-Garayúa, Beatriz González Stephan, Alejandro Mejías López, Lori Cole, Ruby Ramírez, Avizia Long, María del Pilar Blanco, Gayle Rogers, Alma Heckman, Leslie Harkema, Evelyn Scaramella, Mark Amengual, Lucía Osa-Melero, Cristina Tortora, Michael Kaufman, Renée Fox, Nikki Yeboah, Magdalena Barrera, Marcos Pizarro, Jordi Aladro, Teresa Estrabao, Almut Wolf, Carmen Alicia Martínez, Norma Klahn, Lilly Pinedo Gangai, and Isabelle Ramos.

Support from the College of Humanities and the Arts and the Department of World Languages and Literatures at San José State University enabled this book's completion. In particular, I am profoundly grateful for Dean Shannon Miller and Katherine D. Harris. Lisa Vollendorf, Damian Bacich, Roula Svorou, Jason Aleksander, and Kristine Adams have also played indispensable roles in helping this project move forward. I would also like to acknowledge my colleagues Chunhui Peng, Jean-Luc Desalvo, Romey Sabalius, Cheyla Samuelsom, Keach Inaba, Yasue Yanai, Michiko Uryu, and Anne Fountain. For their inquisitive and engaging perspectives, I thank Spanish graduate students at

San José State, in particular those in the "Decolonizing Borderlands" seminars. This work's progress is also owing to support I received at Duquesne University from Dean James Swindal, Edith Krause, and Mary Ann Hess. From the Center for Latin American Studies at the University of Pittsburgh, I am grateful to Karen Goldman. At Rice University I thank Dr. Lane Kaufmann, Dr. José Aranda, and Dr. Gisela Heffes.

Early grants that propelled this study were sponsored by the UCLA Department of Spanish and Portuguese, Mr. and Mrs. Ben and Rue Pine, the UCLA Graduate Division, the UCLA Latin American Institute, the Mellon Foundation, and the Program for Cultural Cooperation between Spain's Ministry of Culture and United States Universities. Grants sponsored by Duquesne University include a National Endowment for the Humanities Research Grant, and a Presidential Scholarship Award. At San José State, RSCA fellowships, Artistic Excellence Programming Grants, and Dean's Professional Development Grants provided indispensable support.

Archival work for this project was possible thanks to many libraries across Spain, Mexico, Argentina, and the United States. In Spain, I thank the Residencia de Estudiantes and librarians Alfredo Vlaverde Lavado, Rosa Martín López, Mar Santos Fernández, and Susana Sueiro Ortiz de Cantonad. At the Fundación Ortega y Gasset, I wish to thank Begoña Paredes, María Isabel Ferreiro, and Javier Zamora Bonilla. I would also like to thank librarians and staff at the Biblioteca Nacional de España in Madrid and at the Hemeroteca Municipal de Madrid, at Conde Duque. In Mexico, I would like to thank the many people who helped me at the Instituto de Investigaciones Filológicas at the UNAM, including Lic. María Magdalena Miranda and Lic. Enrique Hernández at the Hemeroteca at the Biblioteca Rubén Bonifaz Nuño, and Dr. Aurora M. Ocampo and Dr. Carlos Rubio Pacho. I must also thank the staff at the Hemeroteca Nacional de México. I am especially grateful to Dr. Alicia Reyes Mota and Eduardo Mejía Muñiz at the Capilla Alfonsina, and to Lic. María Angélica Navarrete at *El Universal*'s Hemeroteca. I also thank Dr. Aimer Granados at the UAM, Cuajimalpa and Dr. Rose Corral Jorda at the Colegio de México. In Argentina, I thank Emilio Bernini at the Instituto de Literatura Argentina Ricardo Rojas as well as Dr. Noé Jitrik and Luciano Carloti at the Instituto de Literatura Hispanoamericana, at the Universidad de Buenos Aires. Thank you to Victoria Viau at Villa Ocampo. At the Academia Argentina de Letras I thank Lic. María Adela Di Bucchianico, Dr. Alejandro E. Parada, Lic. Clara E. Cantone, Bib. Carmen Mirta Apreda, and Bib. Fabiana Luppino. I thank Dr. Marta M. Campomar at the Fundación Ortega y Gasset Argentina and Dr. Patricia Artundo. In the United States, at the University of Texas, Austin,

I thank T-Kay Sangwand for her assistance at the Nettie Lee Benson Latin American Collection and the staff at the Harry Ransom Center. I am also grateful for University of California, Los Angeles, librarians Cynthia Danielle McCullough, I Reynoir, Valerie Rom-Hawkins, Davis S. Poepoe, Antonia Osuna-García, George Nicholas, Rodrigo Carlo Medina, Marta D. Martínez, Jennifer C. Lee, Antigone Kutay, Kelly L. Jue, Diane Howell, Cindy Hollmichel, Sandra Farfan-García, Eudora Loh, and Jennifer Osorio.

At the University of Toronto Press, I am deeply appreciative of Mark Thompson, Stephanie Mazza, and the very generous reviewers who evaluated my work with such care, offering feedback that improved this manuscript exponentially. For their immeasurable support throughout this entire process, I am profoundly grateful to my family: my parents, Susan and Ivan; my siblings, Alina and Michael; my Los Angeles parents, Dale and Virginia; and my grandmother, Wanda D. Frey. Lastly, this book would not have been possible without the incalculable patience, enthusiasm, love, and smiles that my husband, Jorge Francisco, and our son, Jorge Andrés, have generously shared with me every step of the way.

DEFINING AND DEFYING BORDERS

Introduction

La revista anticipa, presagia, descubre, polemiza. El escritor de revistas es el guerrillero madrugador, el 'pioneer' que zapa terrenos intactos. La revista es vitrina y es cartel. El libro ya es, en cierto modo, un ataúd.

[The journal anticipates, predicts, discovers, debates. A journal contributor is an early rising warrior, the pioneer who excavates unchartered territories. The journal is a shop window and a billboard. The book is, in a sense, a coffin.]

Guillermo de Torre, "Modelos de estación,"
(Seasonal Models) *Síntesis*, July 1928

On 1 September 1927, Ernesto Giménez Caballero, founder and director of Madrid's *La Gaceta Literaria* (Madrid 1927–31), enthusiastically praised a recent Mexican novel for displaying "la virginidad que le pedíamos a América" [the virginity we were asking for from America] (101). Albeit condescendingly, he applauded how the novel simultaneously incorporated "Un paisaje de figuras y pasiones: prognato, exótico, milenario, supersticioso, primitivo" [A landscape of figures and passions, prognathous, exotic, millenary, superstitious, primitive] with "los reflejos de una civilización audaz y piadosa como la española" [the reflexes of a daring and compassionate civilization like the Spanish one] (101). Thus, in Giménez Caballero's estimation, the novel's strength rested in its ability to portray Latin America as "exotic" in a literary work that, as he saw it, proudly belonged to the Spanish literary tradition. In his estimation, employing modern narrative techniques, this novel succeeded in securing a space for Latin America in European aesthetic discussions, while at the same time putting Spanish American literature on the international map. Taken out of its context, Giménez Caballero's laudatory description of a distinctly Latin American novel that employed modern narrative techniques thereby situating Latin America on an international literary field, might easily be attributed to a novel from the Latin American Boom of the 1960s, such as Colombian Gabriel García Márquez's *Cien años de soledad* [One Hundred Years of Solitude] (1967). However, the Spanish writer was in fact describing Mexican Mariano Azuela's *Los de abajo* [The Underdogs] (1915), a novel that portrayed the visceral tragedy of the revolutionary war.

Entitled "Un gran romance mexicano" [A Great Mexican Romance], Giménez Caballero's review appears alongside a fragment of Mariano Azuela's *Los de abajo*. Together, they occupy the bottom third of the third page in *La Gaceta Literaria*'s 1 September 1927 issue. This positioning's importance will be explained later in this introduction. The fragment is *Los de abajo*'s fifteenth chapter, which details a party with lively drinking and singing followed by the revolutionaries' continued journey across arduous terrain. Featuring colloquial dialogues and detailed descriptions of the Mexican landscape, this particular selection illustrates why Giménez Caballero would paternalistically praise the novel's "mexicaness," "es el mejicano con alma precolombina: bravía, infantil, noble y sin sentido" [it's the Mexican with a pre-Colombian soul, brave, infantile, noble, and senseless] (3). Yet, despite his accolades on the novel's unique ability to exemplify Mexican culture, for Giménez Caballero, the novel is part of a Castilian literary tradition, "un poema de guerrilleros castellanos" [a poem from Castilian warriors], akin to works by late nineteenth- and early twentieth-century Spanish authors Pío Baroja, Benito Pérez Galdós, and Ramón del Valle Inclán and very much part of "el ciclo de habla española" [the Spanish-speaking cycle]. In situating this novel of the Mexican revolution within a broader Spanish literary field, Giménez Caballero thus undermines the Mexican national identity he claimed to praise, a contradictory position that repeatedly appears in this piece.

Anachronistically, Giménez Caballero's review presented *Los de abajo* as the counterpart in prose to Rubén Darío's late nineteenth-century movement *modernismo* that had transformed Spanish American poetry: "Se puede hacer sin miedo la afirmación: desde los poemas de Rubén Darío, nada comparable a esta novela" (101) [One can fearlessly affirm: since Rubén Darío's poems, nothing is comparable to this novel]. If Darío's *modernismo* had conquered "lo fácil: el verso, el lirismo" [what is easy, verse, lyricism], Azuela had mastered a more sophisticated genre, the novel: "Lo difícil en América seguía siendo la novela. Tanto en Massachusetts como en las Pampas" [The difficult (genre) in America, continued to be the novel. In Massachusetts as in the Pampas] (101). Furthermore, in Giménez Caballero's estimation,

Darío had merely translated European styles, specifically French artistic techniques, into Spanish. Azuela's accomplishment was far greater because he had infused his text with what Giménez Caballero believed was a distinctly Latin American aesthetic. Although he acknowledged that Chilean Eduardo Barrios, author of *El niño que enloqueció de amor* [The Little Boy Driven Mad by Love] (1915), and Argentine Ricardo Güiraldes, author of *Don Segundo Sombra* [Mr. Segundo Sombra] (1926), had made great strides in developing the novel, Giménez Caballero maintained that their work was still excessively European: "había todavía demasiado perfil, demasiada europeidad, cierto sabor de antigua cepa" [too much profile, too much Europeaness, a certain taste of ancient sap, still lingered] (101). Azuela's *Los de abajo*, by contrast, was "esencialmente mexicano" [essentially Mexican] (101). Yet, again, notwithstanding his insistence on *Los de abajo*'s "mexicanness" as one of the novel's most positive attributes Giménez Caballero also described it as part of a Spanish literary tradition: "es un romance. Un género mediévico, infante, balbuceador" [it is a Romance. A medieval genre, infantile, babbling] (101). Giménez Caballero concludes his evaluation of *Los de abajo* with a discussion on the novel's value as a marketable product, which suggests an underlying interest in gaining a foothold in the Latin American literary market.

Giménez Caballero's review of *Los de abajo* in *La Gaceta Literaria*'s 1 September 1927 issue illustrates how journals, magazines, and newspapers allow scholarship to easily chart the continued development of the Spanish American transatlantic field of cultural production that Alejandro Mejías López outlined in *Inverted Conquest: The Myth of Modernity and the Transatlantic Onset of Modernism* (2009). While Giménez Caballero's review provides evidence that transatlantic literary discussions were taking place between Spain and Latin America, its content displays continued tensions within this field as Spain and Latin American independent nations negotiated a postcolonial relationship. As noted above, although *Los de abajo* was valued as a symbol of a distinctly Mexican national literature in Mexico, Giménez Caballero's review reveals Spanish intellectuals' tendency to consider the former colony's cultural production to be a part of a broader Spanish field. While, in theory, Giménez Caballero praised a distinct Mexican culture, in practice, viewing it through empire's lens, he did not respect its boundaries. Moreover, read alongside other content in the issue, Giménez Caballero's imperial purview is even more telling. The article above Giménez Caballero's review of *Los de abajo*, "Un debate apasionado: Campeonato para un meridiano intelectual" [A Passionate Debate: Championship for an Intellectual Meridian] was part of the well-known emblematic

1927 *polémica del meridiano intelectual* [intellectual meridian polemic]. This debate, described in chapter 3, began when *La Gaceta Literaria* proposed Madrid as the intellectual centre for Spain and Latin America in April 1927. Reading the editorial as an attempt to gain control over their cultural capital, most Latin Americans, and primarily Argentine intellectuals writing in Buenos Aires's *Martín Fierro* (1924–7), proclaimed that the proposal threatened the former colonies' cultural independence from Spain. Although the main transatlantic exchanges over the controversial Madrid meridian idea took place between *La Gaceta Literaria* and *Martín Fierro*, other journals from across Latin America and Europe participated in the "Passionate Debate."

The tensions in Spain and Latin America's postcolonial relationship illustrated in the articles briefly described above are not unique to *La Gaceta Literaria*. As this book will show, just like Giménez Caballero's review of *Los de abajo*, articles, editorials, and other contributions to journals, magazines, and newspapers across Spain and Latin America during the early twentieth century offer exceptional insight into the underlying transatlantic tensions between the European country and its former colonies. And, although the *polémica del meridiano intelectual* might have been one of the most expansive and enduring debates, it was certainly not the only one that took place in Spanish and Latin American journals, magazines, and newspapers at the time. These debates and exchanges taking place in transatlantic Hispanic print culture thus offer scholarship a unique opportunity to contextualize literary texts in a more nuanced manner, one that surpasses national boundaries. Benedict Anderson argued that periodicals aided in the creation of nationalisms and played an important role in fostering "imagined communities." Nineteenth-century regional newspapers published different types of political and social news and information, organizing events from disparate areas into a single textual space. In doing so, print culture created the impression that a particular territory formed a community bound by the written word. Like Anderson, scholarship on print culture has primarily evaluated journals, newspapers, and magazines as sites on national formation. The research presented in this book expands this notion to demonstrate that literary journals created intellectual communities – "naciones intelectuales" [intellectual nations], as Ignacio M. Sánchez Prado described them for the Mexican context – of the critical imagination that actually traversed national borders, fostering a more cosmopolitan imaginary that comprised not just one country but several.

Journals, magazines, and newspapers are a unique medium because they simultaneously outline boundaries and traverse borders.

Especially during the early twentieth-century avant-garde era, this type of print media often embodied, in form and content, a particular aesthetic style, theme, nationalistic or cultural perspective, thereby defining clear confines. As Spanish avant-garde novelist Benjamín Jarnés put it at the time, journals are "un libro colectivo cuyas páginas han de estar sutilmente ligadas por una eléctrica red de generosidades y vehemencias, si se quiere obtener de ella un fruto eficaz" [a collective book. If one wants to obtain from it an effective fruit, its pages must be subtly linked by an electric web of generosities and vehemence] (263). Within these limits, however, Jarnés explains, they are a space for experimentation, acting like a show room or display window in a store, "La buena revista es como una antesala donde todo novicio creador de parcelas nuevas de arte, ha de detenerse algún tiempo hasta ver definitivamente admitida o rechazada su frágil mercancía" [A good journal is like an entryway where every novice creator of new art parcels must spend some time in order to know whether the fragile merchandise will be admitted or rejected] ("Revistas Nuevas" [New Journals] *Revista de Occidente* 15 263). In this sense, then, just as Giménez Caballero's review of Mariano Azuela's *Los de abajo* demonstrates, a journal has the power to determine the validity of a work of art and its aesthetic value to a cultural field "las revistas ... nos ayudan a tasar, a comparar, a justipreciar de algún modo los valores, porque toda revista es un escaparate de valores" [journals ... help us somehow rate, compare, appraise values, because every magazine is a storefront of values] ("Revistas Nuevas" [New Journals] *Revista de Occidente* 15 263). Precisely because they were part of a cosmopolitan avant-garde, these "collective books" that were also a "space for experimentation," and a "storefront of values" to use Jarnés's descriptors, were hospitable spaces that hosted transnational contributions and encouraged discussions and debates within their prescribed limits. They published contributions from a plurality of geographies, nations, genres, and disciplines. Within that same issue of *La Gaceta Literaria* described above, for example, articles on Spanish painters Maruja Mallo and Pablo Picasso appeared alongside pieces on Argentine poet Francisco Luis Bernárdez. Within their outlined boundaries, journals, magazines, and newspapers like *La Gaceta Literaria* thus traversed many types of borders.

As collective books, spaces of experimentation, storefronts of values, and hospitable spaces, journals, magazines, and newspapers play a critical role in shaping cultural fields. This book explores how they charted the Spanish American field of cultural production during the early twentieth century, offering scholarship an invaluable resource within which to situate literary texts. Providing a distinct, visual example of print culture's importance to the field, Giménez Caballero published his "Universo de la literatura española contemporánea" [Contemporary Spanish Literature Universe] in *La Gaceta Literaria* on 15 July 1927. This sketch, which I will delve into further in chapter 3, depicts planets, stars, and comets representing prominent literary figures and artists (primarily from Madrid, although Mexican Alfonso Reyes and Catalans Eugeni D'Ors and Joan Miró make the cut) alongside journals. The most prominent journals are Madrid-based *Revista de Occidente* (1923–36), *Revista de las Españas* (Madrid 1926–36), and, of course, *La Gaceta Literaria*, placed near leading vanguard prose writer Ramón Gómez de La Serna's Madrid tertulia [gathering] "Pombo." Publications from other areas, such as Murcia's *Verso y Prosa* (1927–8), Huevla's *Papel de Aleluyas* (1927–8), and Sevilla's *Mediodía* (1926–9), are smaller and relegated to the periphery of the "universe." Similarly, Giménez Caballero's subsequent article "Cartel de la nueva literatura" [New Literature's Poster] (*La Gaceta Literaria* April 1928), also discussed in chapter 3, is accompanied by a diagram depicting a pentagon, "tres triángulos netos y uno en preforma" [three distinct triangles and one taking shape], with coordinates (alpha, omega, beta, each representing an area) that hierarchically organize literary networks in Spain. Describing his sketch, Giménez Caballero emphasizes that journals (like his own, of course) are the best coordinates, "el núcleo absoluto donde se insertan numeradores y denominadores" [the absolute nucleus where nominators and denominators are inserted], for determining the construction of a Spanish literary field.[1] Pointing to a network of exchange, Giménez Caballero details how other countries, such as France and Italy, influence Spanish journals and highlights that *La Gaceta Literaria* breaks through longstanding traditions/influences to connect languages and fields of cultural production, including Spanish America. At the same time, celebrating Spain's cosmopolitan presence in a Western cultural field, Giménez Caballero emphasizes that all foreign journals include at least one Spanish contributor in their roster.

Spanish poet and member of *La Gaceta Literaria*'s editorial board Guillermo de Torre penned the epigraph that opens this chapter in his "Modelos de estación" [Seasonal Models] (July 1928), one of two articles he published on the topic in the Buenos Aires journal *Síntesis* (Buenos Aires 1927–30). Coinciding with Jarnés's assessment of the medium, de Torre puts forward that "La revista anticipa, presagia, descubre, polemiza. El escritor de revistas es el guerrillero madrugador, el 'pioneer' que zapa terrenos intactos. La revista es vitrina y es cartel" [The journal anticipates, predicts, discovers, incites polemics. The journal is a store window and a poster] (231).[2] This quality, in de

Torre's estimation, makes journals more timely, up to date, and "alive" than books, which de Torre deems to be coffins. Describing numerous journals, de Torre, like Giménez Caballero, offers a lengthy description of the Spanish literary field. He claims that "mi objetivo preferente se orienta, en esa enumeración de jóvenes revistas, a evidenciar el proceso de descentralización literaria española y a señalar el auge de la periferia" [in enumerating so many new magazines, my goal is to evidence Spanish literature's decentralization, pointing to a boom coming from the periphery] (232). Of course, de Torre does clarify that peripheral journals were undoubtedly influenced by the centre, meaning Madrid. De Torre penned a second article on the topic, that also appeared in *Síntesis*, "A través de las revistas" [Through Journals] (April 1929). Here he focuses on surveys conducted in three journals, one in Spain (*La Gaceta Literaria*), one in Italy (*La Fiera Letteraria: lettere, scienze, arti* Milano 1925–7), and the other in France (*Les Nouvelles Littéraires* Paris 1922–85). Albeit from a Eurocentric perspective, the Spanish intellectual points out that, despite being from very different nations, the surveys in each journal are similar, suggesting that this medium illustrated generational commonalities across borders.

Jarnés, Giménez Caballero, and de Torre were journal editors and therefore particularly aware of their medium's crucial role in outlining fields of cultural production. They were also acutely conscious of their own influence across this medium and used it to engage, often provocative, transatlantic debates in the Spanish American field. For instance, as we have seen thus far, Giménez Caballero overtly presented his Castilian-centred perspective in his review of *Los de abajo*, in his "Universo," and in his "Carteles." He would also defend *La Gaceta Literaria* in the *polémica del meridiano intelectual*. A particularly controversial figure, de Torre instigated the *polémica del meridiano intelectual* with his 15 April 1927 editorial entitled "Madrid, Meridiano intelectual de Hispanoamérica" [Madrid, Hispanic America's Intellectual Meridian] which this book considers in chapter 3, and also, as chapter 4 recounts, debated Chilean Vicente Huidobro on the origins of *ultraísmo* [Ultraism], an avant-garde poetic movement. Jarnés similarly engaged aesthetic discussions and debated Mexican novelist Jaime Torres Bodet over Spanish philosopher José Ortega y Gasset's essay "La deshumanización del arte" [Th Dehumanization of Art] in Spanish and Argentine journals. As chapter 4 explains, the dialogue between Jarnés and Torres Bodet played out across journals but concluded in the Mexican writer's novel *Margarita de niebla* [Misty Margarita] (1927).

While Giménez Caballero, de Torre, and Jarnés participated in very different transatlantic disputes, the overarching theme was similar;

how to define Spain and Latin America's postcolonial relationship. Most Latin American intellectuals were open to a transatlantic relationship that crossed borders but also respected hard-won national identities while, as we have already seen in Giménez Caballero's review of *Los de abajo*, many Spanish figures still perceived Latin America's cultural production as part of a field still dominated by Spain. Describing how borders and boundaries were contested within a medium that simultaneously crossed borders and defined boundaries, each chapter in this book addresses the different types of debates and exchanges that emerged in journals, magazines, and newspapers surrounding this ongoing point of contention between Spain and Latin America. In some cases, as chapter 4 demonstrates, cultural products, such as novels, were directly in the crossfire of these disputes. Yet, this book will show that these transatlantic frictions, whether peripherally or directly, influenced all cultural production in the Spanish American field. Present scholarship must therefore use this map of exchanges provided by journals, magazines, and newspapers when contextualizing cultural products under scrutiny. In the field of Hispanism specifically, this resource is invaluable in helping us better articulate literary historiography.

Hispanists have already drawn attention to journals, magazines, and newspapers, theorizing this medium as a resource for scholarship. Beatriz Sarlo, for example, has pointed out that unlike individual books, journals uniquely contextualize a period ("Intelectuales y revistas" [Intellectuals and Magazines] 10). She further underscores that they chart power struggles and cultural nuances, "informan sobre las costumbres intelectuales de un período, sobre las relaciones de fuerza, poder y prestigio en el campo de la cultura" [inform about a period's intellectual customs, about strength, power, and prestige relationships in the cultural field] (15). Additionally, journals, magazines, and newspapers "son un lugar y una organización de discursos diferentes, un mapa de relaciones intelectuales, con sus clivajes de edad e ideologías, una red de comunicación entre la dimensión cultural y política" [are a place and an organization of different discourses, a map of intellectual relationships, with their age-related and ideological cleavages between cultural and political dimensions]. Each journal is therefore, in itself, a map charting multiple cultural fields that intersect, uniquely contextualizing each piece published within any given volume and the broader field. In line with Sarlo, Roxana Patiño and Jorge Schwartz's introduction to their 2004 special edition of *Revista Iberoamericana* highlights that journals are "constructoras informales de genealogías y proyectos culturales" [informal builders of genealogies and cultural projects] (648). Specifically, each journal issue provides scholarship with insight into cultural development and formation as texts dialogue with each other on its pages (648).

Adding to Sarlo, Patiño, and Schwartz's observations, in her evaluation of the journal *Cuadernos Americanos* (Mexico 1942–86), Liliana Weinberg has highlighted that journals create intellectual networks. She thus explains that scholarship stands to benefit from "meterse en los entresijos que conducen a redes intelectuales, proyectos editoriales, reglas de sociabilidad, formas explícitas e implícitas de polémica y tomas de posición" [delving into cruxes that drive intellectual networks, editorial projects, social norms, explicit and implicit polemics and position-taking] (n.p.). Moreover, Weinberg observes that each journal volume belongs to a series that is also part of the "little magazine" genre, interwoven into a seemingly borderless fabric of publications that transcended regional, cultural, political, and national borders. Thus, as this book establishes, tracing the seams woven by 1920s Spanish and Latin American print culture re-contextualizes and offers new insight into our understanding of literary historiography across a Spanish American cultural field. In line with Eric Bulson's view of the "little magazine" as a "world form," which I will return to, this book maintains that print culture's transnationalism requires relinquishing nation-based traditions in favour of a more pluralistic vision that supports emerging lines of inquiry in Hispanism, such as Iberian Studies and Transatlantic Studies. As objects of study, just as Sarlo, Schwartz, Patiño, and Weinberg have pointed out, journals' multinational and multigeneric content demands that our scholarship traverse borders and fields of inquiry. In "Hispanic Studies and the Legacy of Empire," his contribution to Akiko Tsuchiya and William G. Acree Jr.'s volume *Empire's End: Transnational Connections in the Hispanic World*, Alejandro Mejías López emphasizes that within Hispanist scholarship:

> over two centuries of literary relationships, conflict, exchange, encounters, and confrontation have remained mostly unexplored in any systematic way that might have opened up a more sophisticated understanding of the trajectories of the literatures written in Spanish, expanding their two often unidirectional relationship with the North Atlantic, decentering and perhaps dismantling Hispanism as a concept and as a field, and stimulating new, more complex paradigms from which to think through the ever problematic division between monolithic centers and peripheries. (208)

Literary journals, magazines, and newspapers allow us to delve into these uncharted pathways to reconfigure our field of study. This book demonstrates that print culture not only enables but demands that we reorient our view of Hispanic literary historiography. Transgressing borders and disputing boundaries, journals, magazines, and newspapers provide a concrete map of an indisputably complicated, often contradictory, Spanish American cultural field that does not easily fit into neatly divided Hispanist categories, namely, Latin Americanism vs. Peninsularism. Translating texts and traversing borders, print culture invites us to utilize more pluralistic approaches, such as Transatlantic Studies and Iberian Studies.

Print culture reveals that literary studies, particularly in the early twentieth century modernist era I address in this book, need to be transnational and transatlantic. As Eric Bulson argues in *Little Magazine: World Form*, the little magazine "enabled the formation of an increasingly interconnected (but not totalizing) global infrastructure" (3). It therefore "provides an alternative model of the literary field that emerged during and after modernism, one that was *decommercialized, decapitalized, and decentered*" (14; emphasis in original). He explains that a "long critical tradition has cordoned off little magazines by nation or language," which has significantly limited scholarship on a medium that, in its very form, resists such limitations: "This kind of mononational thinking about the magazine has had the unfortunate effect of limiting the kind of comparative approach that can let us see the relevance it has, if any, outside the more tightly regulated national and transcontinental paradigms already in place" (12). For Bulson, therefore, despite appearing in different languages and in different nations, little magazines shared a common form, style, and intent that brings them together as a genre.

Turning back to Hispanism, then, in as much as print culture forged networks across borders and strengthened national boundaries, it makes clear that, by and large, our scholarly purview has been too narrow. First, the traceable network in journals, magazines, and newspapers illustrates that the idea of Latin America generated a transnational field of inquiry within Latin America and across the Atlantic.[3] As this book explains, Latin Americanism (identified as *hispano/ibero/latino americanismo*) and its implications for culture, nation, and empire were broadly contested across early twentieth-century little magazines. Such debates have also contributed to the development of Latin Americanism within Hispanism, a topic that Fernando Degiovanni has assiduously evaluated in *Vernacular Latin Americanisms* (2018). Second, the debates and exchanges in 1920s journals, magazines, and newspapers consistently question centre-periphery paradigms rooted in outdated imperial models. More inclusive paradigms that are at once able to transcend borders, acknowledge national boundaries, and account for empire are thus necessary to investigate postcolonial literary and cultural production across Spain and Latin America. Currently, although still widely contested, Transatlantic and Iberian Studies are promising options. The examples in this book illustrate that applying print culture's lens to literary historiography necessitates relinquishing outdated dichotomies that continue to weigh down our field. A key step is coming face to face with empire.

Addressing Hispanism's roots in empire, scholars have evaluated the field's origins and how it was shaped by both the US empire and the defunct Spanish empire. Joan Ramon Resina has pointed out that, in Spain, the nineteenth century constituted "the period of nation building as well as the rise of Hispanism" that produced an "Impoverishing monolinguism and the atomization of Iberian cultures into a number of mutually exclusive national philologies" (2). This form of nineteenth-century Hispanism, as James Fernández has detailed, was transported to US academia. The Castilian-centred purview persisted well into the twentieth century (a topic discussed extensively by Anne J. Cruz and Sebastiaan Faber among others) and has driven the tensions between Latin Americanism and Peninsularism that, unfortunately, continue to this day in US Hispanism. Sebastiaan Faber explains that, as of the 1898 Spanish American War, when Spain lost its last colonies across the Atlantic, Cuba, Puerto Rico, and the Philippines to the United States, US Hispanism began to see Latin America as a legitimate field of study in higher education (Fantasmas 319). And, by 1916, Stanford's Alfred Coester had published *The Literary History of Spanish America* (Faber Fantasmas 321). Fernando Degiovanni delves deeply into this topic in the previously mentioned *Vernacular Latinamericanisms*, where he focuses on figures such as Coester and Spanish intellectual and Columbia University professor Federico de Onís to describe how Latin Americanism, within Hispanism, emerged as a discipline in the United States and across Latin America. Throughout the twentieth century, as Sebastiaan Faber has outlined in "Fantasmas hispanistas y otros retos trasatlánticos" [Hispanist Ghosts and Other Transatlantic Challenges] Latin Americanism gained a foothold in academic departments in the United States and by the 1960s, especially with the inauguration of organizations like the Latin American Studies Association (LASA), shifted the power dynamic. Latin Americanism overcame the "de facto hegemony within academic Hispanism of the Peninsular over the Latin American" (Faber Economies 18). Since then, Latin Americanism has grown larger than Peninsularism and continues to dominate Hispanism.

Akiko Tsuchiya and William G. Acree Jr.'s volume *Empire's End: Transnational Connections in the Hispanic World* features contributions from Peninsularists and Latin Americanists from multiple disciplines (historians, literary and cultural critics), that "debate productively the problem of empire and its cultural impact on the Spanish-speaking world" (6). Bookending the compilation, Sebastiaan Faber's "Hispanism, Transatlantic Studies, and the Problem of Cultural History" opens the collection and Alejandro Mejías López's "Hispanic Studies and the Legacy of Empire" provides a conclusion. Both articles advocate Transatlantic Studies as a means of overcoming Hispanism's staunch adherence to empire. Faber underscores the field's attachment to nationalisms and, most prominently, a Castilian–Spain-centred focus. Addressing the "ghosts of empire" in Hispanic Studies, Mejías López proposes a transatlantic perspective that examines "over two centuries of literary relationships, conflict, exchange, encounters, and confrontation" can lead to "a more sophisticated understanding of trajectories of the literatures written in Spanish" and incite "stimulating, new, more complex paradigms from which to think through the ever problematic division between monolithic centers and peripheries" (208). Acknowledging critics such as Abril Trigo and Joan Ramon Resina, Mejías López points to their legitimate apprehension that the field could potentially reproduce the same hegemonic dynamics it intends to overcome. Yet, Mejías López maintains that, as this book illustrates, a transatlantic perspective allows for a deeper understanding of postcolonial power dynamics that enhance scholarship on both sides of the Atlantic. In charting a Spanish American field of cultural production, journals, magazines, and newspapers map Hispanism as a transnational and transatlantic field ripe with tensions surrounding geographical borders and national boundaries. This medium thus proves that Hispanism's current division between Latin Americanism and Peninsularism does not accurately depict the field. As a result, approaches, such as Transatlantic and Iberian Studies offer scholarship a more effective approach into "literary phenomena, which not only transgress boundaries, but also originate in the frontiers between languages and nations," as Santiago Pérez Isasi observes in *Looking at Iberia: A Comparative European Perspective* (2013, 21).

Situating debates over Transatlantic and Iberian studies, Cecilia Enjuto-Rangel, Sebastiaan Faber, Pedro García Caro, and Robert Patrick Newcomb's recent volume *Transatlantic Studies: Latin America, Iberia, and Africa* (2020), investigates "the continuities and fractures between Latin America, the Iberian Peninsula, and Spanish-and Portuguese-speaking Africa" (1). I propose that, offering unique insight into empire's role in cultural production while charting "continuities and fractures," print culture supports the visions set forth for Transatlantic Studies in

Empire's End and *Transatlantic Studies*. This medium outlines a narrative that has been obscured by the hegemony that has historically structured United States Hispanism. Closely examining debates and exchanges that took place across journals, magazines, and newspapers allows scholars to trace aesthetic developments, and the tensions surrounding them, as they unfolded and within the complex transnational and transatlantic field within which they actually took place.

Transatlantic Studies includes contributions from scholars who see the value of Transatlantic and Iberian Studies, such as Joseba Gabilondo, José del Valle, Julio Ortega, and Mario Santana, alongside those who are entirely opposed to these approaches, such as Joan Ramon Resina and Abril Trigo. Scholars who favour Transatlantic and Iberian studies don't necessarily agree on whether this type of scholarship is an approach, a critical model, or a new field, but coincide overall in seeing the value that the more pluralistic and nuanced lens has to offer their research and teaching. On the other side of the debate, opposition is more clear cut. Resina, as Enjuto-Rangel, Faber, García Caro, and Newcomb put it in their introduction, "sees Transatlantic Studies as an opportunistic attempt to shore up the hegemony of the Spanish language as the basis for Iberian and pan-Hispanic identities" (2), and Trigo "questions the need for a new disciplinary umbrella in the first place" (8). Interestingly, these debates and exchanges within Hispanism surrounding the validity, value, and usefulness of Transatlantic and Iberian Studies have much in common with the controversial transnational and transatlantic discussions taking place across Spanish and Latin American journals a century ago. And both point to the richness and complexity of Hispanism that, as Mabel Moraña has pointed out, "has functioned as a dominating political force, as an interpretive and representational cultural model, and as an epistemological paradigm throughout the entire development of Spanish America's and Spain's cultural histories" (*Ideologies of Hispanism* ix). Hispanism can thus only benefit from these self-reflective continued dialogues as we critically examine how we map literary historiography and cultural developments. This book proposes that, as a medium that both transcends borders and defines boundaries, journals, magazines, and newspapers provide a map that invites us to critically re-examine Hispanism's empire-driven structures and position-takings. Transnational, transatlantic, and interdisciplinary, print culture requires that Hispanism employ more pluralistic and inclusive modalities like Transatlantic and Iberian Studies.

My work on print culture builds upon pioneering research in Anglo-modernism and in Hispanism. In Anglo-modernist studies, as early as 1976, Malcolm Bradbury and James Walter McFarlane devoted a chapter to the question in their *Modernism: 1890–1930*. Since then, Scholes and Wulfman's *Modernism in the Magazines* (2010) and Eric Bulson's *Little Magazine: World Form* (2016) examine print culture as a genre that relocates modernism's coordinates. Vital to these studies are efforts such as The Modernist Journals Project, a comprehensive online archive of digitized modernist magazines organized by Brown University and the University of Tulsa, and Oxford University Press's *Critical and Cultural History of Modernist Magazines*, which includes volumes on Britain and Ireland (2009), North America (2012), Europe (2013), and a forthcoming one on Latin America.

Gayle Rogers's *Modernism and the New Spain: Britain, Cosmopolitan Europe, and Literary History* (2012) explores the intersections between Spanish and British Modernism, casting new light on these literary traditions by examining Spanish and English literary journals, bilingual anthologies, translations, and biographies to prove that Spain participated in early debates forging modernism. Traversing the Atlantic in another direction, my reading shows that Spain's dialogue was not only with *North* but also with *Latin* America. Patricia Novillo Corvalán's *Modernism and Latin America: Transnational Networks of Literary Exchange* (2017) investigates Latin America's previously overlooked influence on modernist studies and questions the longstanding London, Paris, New York axis. However, this book gives little attention to print culture's participation in forging the networks it investigates.

Since the latter part of the twentieth century, Hispanists have also paid attention to print culture as instrumental in creating networks. In Spain, scholars include Andrés Soria Olmedo, María del Rosario Rojo, César Antonio Molina, Evelyn López Campillo, and Rafael Osuna.[4] Notably, in *Barcelona and Madrid: Social Networks of the Avant Garde* (2012) Aránzazu Ascunce Arenas uses journals to trace connections between Madrid and Barcelona's literary and artistic circles. On the other side of the Atlantic, Saúl Sosnowski's *La cultura de un siglo: América Latina en sus revistas* [A Century's Culture: Latin America in Its Magazines] (1999) has been updated by Aimer Granados's *Las revistas en la historia intelectual de América Latina: redes, política, sociedad y cultura* [Journals in Latin America's Intellectual History: Networks, Politics, Society, and Culture] (2012).[5] John King, Nélida Salvador, Patricia Artundo, Beatriz Sarlo, Hector René LaFleur, Sergio D. Provenzano, Pedro Alonso, and Nora Pasternac have contributed significant studies on Argentine journals.[6] In Mexico, Fernando Curiel, Carlos Ramírez, and Antonio Sierra have indexed twentieth-century cultural journals, and the Fondo de Cultura Económica (FCE) has continued to update its collection of facsimiles.[7] In addition, Pedro Ángel Palou, Guillermo Sheridan, and Luis Mario

Schneider have all referenced journals in their studies on the avant-garde groups *Contemporáneos* and *Estridentistas*.[8]

Emilia de Zuleta and Carmen Alemany Bay are among the first scholars to focus on literary magazines and journals as a vehicle for the transatlantic exchange of aesthetic ideas between Spain and Latin America. Emilia de Zuleta's *Relaciones literarias entre España y la Argentina*[Literary Relations between Spain and Argentina] (1983) surveys the presence of Spanish authors in Argentinean journals, starting with *Nosotros* (Buenos Aires 1907–43) in 1907 and concluding in 1949 with the magazine *Realidad* (Buenos Aires 1947–9). Published in 1998, Carmen Alemany Bay's *La polémica del meridiano intelectual de hispanoamérica* [The Hispanic American Intellectual Meridian Polemic] *(1927)* is a critical edition of the articles involved in *la polémica del meridiano intelectual*, which I examine in chapter 3. Adela Pineda Franco's *Geopolíticas de la cultura finisecular en Buenos Aires, París y México: Las revistas literarias en el modernismo* [Turn of the Century Geopolitics in Buenos Aires, Paris, and Mexico: Literary Journals in *Modernismo*] (2006) offers an unusually broad geographical scope, tracing the development of Rubén Darío's *modernismo* in Argentinean, French, and Mexican literary journals. Her work is significant for its re-evaluation of *modernismo* as a transatlantic and transnational movement that was modern, cosmopolitan, and Latin American. Furthermore, her use of journals as a means of more thoroughly understanding *modernismo* is unprecedented. However, her study focuses on Paris rather than on Madrid as a transatlantic counterpart. Alejandro Mejías López's *The Inverted Conquest: The Myth of Modernity and the Transatlantic Onset of Modernism* (2009) expands upon Pineda Franco's re-evaluation of *modernismo.* Framing his study with Pierre Bourdieu's notions of symbolic capital and literary field, Mejías López argues that "*modernismo* created a continental Spanish American literature, actively engaged in the international, cultural, and political arena, and became the only post-colonial literature to wrest cultural authority from its former European metropolis" (4). He therefore proposes a renewed understanding of this Latin American movement as a "groundbreaking postcolonial literary project" that affirmed Latin America's cultural independence from Spain and claimed its legitimate place in the international field of cultural production (12).

Hispanist scholarship, such as Marina Pérez de Mendiola's *Bridging the Atlantic: Toward a Reassessment of Iberian and Latin American Cultural Ties* (1996) has also been increasingly evaluating Spain and Latin America's transatlantic relationship during the early twentieth century. Featuring correspondence between figures such as Spaniard Miguel de Unamuno, Peruvian Ricardo Palma, and Argentine Manuel Ugarte,

Claudio Maíz's *Constelaciones unamunianas: Enlaces entre España y América (1898–1920)* [Unamunian Constellations: Connections between Spain and America (1898–1920)] (2009) explores the existence of a transatlantic "patria intelectual" [intellectual homeland].[9] Underscoring connections between Cuba, Brazil, and Spain, Rachel Price traces the interconnected development of concrete poetics between 1868 and 1968 in *The Object of the Atlantic: Concrete Aesthetics in Cuba, Brazil, and Spain, 1868–1968* (2014). Emphasizing translation's crucial role in constructing transatlantic poetic networks, Ignacio Infante's *After Translation: The Transfer and Circulation of Modern Poetics across the Atlantic* (2013) sketches a web of reciprocity across Europe and North and South America. And further exploring translation's role in establishing networks, Gayle Rogers's *Incomparable Empires: Modernism and the Translation of Spanish and American Literature* (2016) uncovers how modernist translations expose "interimperial dynamics and cross-linguistic traffic," that resituate longstanding imperial paradigms on both sides of the Atlantic (11). Disrupting canonical narrations of Spanish and American literary histories, translations reveal that these competing empires cross-pollinated and enriched each other. While Maíz, Price, Infante, and Rogers's studies employ different mediums to outline complex transatlantic/transnational maps, their investigations coincide in pointing to the importance of acknowledging empire's role in shaping networks of exchange. Likewise, the debates and exchanges that I explore across journals, articulate the continuation of a battle for cultural prestige that began with *modernismo* and played out throughout the 1920s as Spain and its former colonies renegotiated their relationship.

The characteristics that make journals, magazines, and newspapers an invaluable resource for scholarship also present a series of challenges. A space where fragmented texts from a plurality of genres centring on multiple topics intersect, journal pages offer seemingly endless possibilities for intellectual inquiry. Moreover, working with a medium that both defies borders and defines boundaries requires selecting nodes of articulation in order to make the study's scope manageable. I therefore outlined a triangular network across Spain, Mexico, and Argentina. During the 1920s, when Spain's Silver Age was at its peak in Madrid, Buenos Aires and Mexico City were emerging as important centres for Latin American intellectual and cultural activity, specifically surrounding the avant-garde. Although other regions in Spain and Latin America, such as Barcelona and Cuba, were also critical, this study focuses the strong triangular network that developed between Madrid, Buenos Aires, and Mexico City, where, as the following section outlines, avant-garde cultural production was rapidly developing. Mexico's and Argentina's cultural prosperity at this time had much to do with their ports, which enabled transatlantic correspondence with Europe, and Madrid in particular as a Spanish-speaking nexus in the Old World. Additionally, their political trajectories positioned them – Mexico City in the north and Buenos Aires in the south – as major cultural and cosmopolitan centres. Mexico's revolution would inspire Latin American countries to embrace their Mesoamerican past. At the same time, Buenos Aires's intellectual class, bolstered by massive European immigration, began to challenge Madrid and other European centres for cultural prestige. Meanwhile, as the exchanges and debates occurring across print culture detailed in this book illustrate, Spanish intellectuals sought to maintain cultural hegemony over former colonial nations. Not surprisingly, however, these overtures were most often met with opposition from Latin America, pointing to a polemical postcolonial relationship. Yet, as this book details, such tension created a triangular network of exchange that prompted significant cultural and socio-political progress on both sides of the Atlantic.

Employing journals, magazines, and newspapers to revise our understanding of the Hispanic Vanguard Era during the 1920s and 1930s, this book is structured around four main topics: postcolonialism, social reform, the literary market, and aesthetics. Chapter 1, "Negotiating Nationalism and Empire," centres on debates surrounding the ideological and practical implications of the terms *ibero/hispano-americanismo*. Race, culture, language, and history are featured topics in these polemics surrounding notions of empire and national identity. Chapter 2, "Transcultural Solidarity: Generational Shifts and Social Reform in Print Culture," expands upon the analysis set forth in chapter 1. This chapter offers two examples of how a younger generation in Spain and Latin America managed to create new transatlantic relationships based on solidarity surrounding social reform. Their focus on socio-political issues, such as educational reform and amnesty, enabled them to forge relationships despite colonialism's legacy and hard-won national identities. If, in chapter 1, the debates and exchanges described resulted in a recurring lack of consensus on the purpose, significance, and usefulness of the terms *ibero/hispano-americanismo*, in chapter 2, we see how solidarity over social reform managed to circumvent this impasse. Chapter 3, "Cultural Capital: Postcolonial Networks and the Literary Market," examines how, despite contradictions and shortcomings, *La Gaceta Literaria* garnered a position of prestige in transatlantic and Iberian fields, which, in turn, enabled its successful entrance into the Latin American and Iberian literary markets. Within and beyond its own borders, the journal generated trans-Iberian, transatlantic, and trans-European interactions that successfully transgressed geographical and national boundaries, generating discussions and mobilizing key cultural stakeholders, including, authors, publishers, and booksellers. Illustrating how debates and exchanges in journals, magazines, and newspapers directly impacted aesthetic production, chapter 4, "Vying for Aesthetic Capital," offers examples of debates centring on authorship and cultural prestige that shaped avant-garde poetry and prose. Adding to ongoing revisions of long-held imperialist misconceptions that relegate Latin American nations to a peripheral position in the West, the postcolonial negotiations that I chart in journals, magazines, and newspapers across a Spanish American field of cultural production further prove that not only did Latin American intellectuals not assume that they occupied a marginal position within Western intellectual geography, but instead felt that, coming from young, modern nations, they inhabited a privileged space within it.[10] I conclude this book with a brief Epilogue reflection on "A Medium, a Process, and a Path Forward."

Chapter One

Surpassing Colonialism: Negotiating Nationalism and Empire in Print Culture

Y bien, a fin de cuentas, ¿qué es la hispanidad [*sic*] Ah, si yo supiera ... Aunque no, mejor es que no la sepa, sino que la anhele, y la añore, y la busque, y la presienta, porque es el modo de hacerla en mí.

Miguel de Unamuno "Hispanidad"
(Hispanicity) *Síntesis*, 6 November 1927

Opening the Buenos Aires journal *Síntesis*'s sixth issue, Spanish writer Miguel de Unamuno laid out a reflection on "Hispanidad" [Hispanicity], which, as the above quote illustrates, he was unable to define in the end, "And well, in sum, ¿what is *hispanicity*? Ah, if I knew ... Although, it is best that I not know, that I instead long for it, and look for it, and intuit it, because that is how to make it in myself" ("Hispanidad" 310).[1] Unamuno's sense of *hispanidad* as an indefinable intuition, something that is inherent to each individual, yet difficult to explain, points to why the term has been, and continues to be, subject to many interpretations and employed for many different purposes. In broad strokes, Hispanidad can be understood as a cultural identity marker originating in Spain and inherited by the Americas through colonization. As such, this term is tied to the politics of empire and subjugation, making it, understandably, controversial. Current debates on Hispanism in US academia and on terminology such as Hispano(a)/Hispanx, Chicano(a)/Chicanx, and Latino(a)/Latinx demonstrate that consensus on Hispanidad/Hispanicity/Hispanic remains aspirational. However, delving into attempted articulations of the term, or terms such as *Hispanoamericanismo* and *Iberoaemericanismo*, often used interchangeably as we will see in 1920s Spanish and Latin American journals, magazines, and newspapers, offers unique insight into present dialogues.[2] Topics such as race, culture, language, and history featured prominently in these polemics surrounding notions of empire and national identity. Therefore, charting these debates that both created and transcended borders, much like the very medium in which they played out, allows us to critically reconsider how Hispanism is constructed and practised today. Contextualizing the debates, the first section in this chapter reviews turn-of-the-century Spanish and Latin American perspectives on race, culture, empire, and nationalism in Miguel de Unamuno's *En torno al casticismo* [On Casticism] (1895), José Enrique Rodó's *Ariel* (1900), and José Vasconcelos's *La raza cósmica* [The Cosmic Race] (1923). The second section focuses transcontinental debates in Latin America surrounding *hispano/ibero-americanismo*. Expanding this scope, the third section explores transatlantic debates that took place across journals, magazines, and newspapers in which Spain and Latin America negotiated nationalism and empire in efforts to define a postcolonial relationship. The exchanges on *hispano/ibero-americanismo* evaluated in this chapter make clear that there was no consensus, either within Latin America or across the Atlantic in Spain on what the terms defined. Much like current debates surrounding Transatlantic and Iberian studies within Hispanism, views on *hispano/ibero-americanismo* included those who considered the signifier utopian and empty, while others saw it as a tool for transnational unification that could lead to productive action. Above all, however, a colonial legacy and hard-won national identities made reaching an understanding of *hispano/ibero-americanismo* that would be acceptable to a majority, impossible. Charting the discussions on *hispano/ibero-americanismo* across journals, however, offers a unique purview into a Latin American, and a transatlantic field of cultural production and its solid network of intellectual exchange.

At the turn of the century, the Spanish American War of 1898 signaled both the decline of the Spanish empire and the rise of the United States as an imperial power, marking a well-studied Western World order shift. Dating back to 1895, Spanish philosopher and writer Miguel de Unamuno published *En torno al casticismo*, a collection of essays that considers the state of Castilian culture as the political empire came to an end. Meanwhile, in Latin America, Uruguayan professor and scholar José Enrique Rodó wrote *Ariel* (1900), an essay directed at Latin America's youth, inciting them to be proud of and build their rich culture. Taking Rodó's message a step further two decades later, in *La raza cósmica* (1923), Mexican politician and philosopher José Vasconcelos professed the Latin American race to have the potential to be superior to all. Scholarship on each of these texts is significant, and my intent here is not to engage it. I only offer a schematic reflection on these texts, precisely because they are well-known and well-studied, in order to contextualize the topics debated in journals, magazines, and newspapers across Latin America and Spain in the wake of the Spanish American War. Race, culture, nationalism, and empire framed these writings and, as the debates taking place across print culture examined in this chapter demonstrate, would continue to instigate heated discussions decades after the war. This first section, therefore, briefly discusses *En torno al casticismo, Ariel,* and *La raza cósmica* in order to frame the 1920s print culture debates featured in the second half of this chapter.

Spain and *El desastre*: Miguel de Unamuno's *En torno al casticismo*

In Spain, the Spanish American War was referred to as *el desastre* [the disaster]. Except for its territories in Africa, Spain had been forced to relinquish its remaining colonial holdings, Cuba, Guam, and Puerto Rico, to the United States. As Gayle Rogers notes, "The war was contextualized as the endpoint of the long-festering *problema de España* [problem of Spain], the unsolvable question of why Spain's once-robust empire had declined" (*Incomparable* 21). One well-known attempt to understand this *problema* is Miguel de Unamuno's *En torno al casticismo* (1895), as noted earlier, a series of essays examining the state of Castilian culture at the turn of the century. Javier Krauel notes that "Despite being published before the Disaster of 1898, *En torno al casticismo* foreshadowed the painful, complex, and ambiguous adjustments that Spanish culture would later have to make as it strove to accept the loss of its last imperial remains" (*Imperial* 84). Thus, in this text, the Spanish novelist and philosopher takes the reader on his quest to comprehend why "Es un espectáculo deprimente el estado mental y moral de nuestra sociedad española" [[T]he current mental and moral state of our Spanish society is a depressing spectacle] (Unamuno *En torno* V n.p.). To do so, he closely scrutinizes the evolution of Castilian culture, exploring how and why it became the central and dominant culture in Spain and proposing it regenerate itself by employing the same strategies that made it great in the past.

Unamuno inscribes *casticismo* within nationalism and universalism.[3] For instance, he states that "Decir en España que un escritor es castizo, es dar a entender que le cree más español que otros" [To say in Spain, that one writer is *castizo,* is to imply that the writer is believed to be more Spanish than others] (Unamuno *En torno* I n.p.). Thus, to be Castilian is to be Spanish. At the same time, he suggests that achieving cultural dominance in Spain was the result of Castilian universalism. Unamuno explains that Castilian culture in Spain surpassed others on the peninsula because it grew from assimilating aspects of other cultures, "Castilla, en su exclusivismo, era menos exclusiva que los pueblos que, encerrados en sí, se dedicaban a su fomento interior; fue uno de los pueblos más *universales*" [Castille, in its exclusivity, was less exclusive than other peoples that, enclosed in themselves were dedicated to fostering their own interiority, it was one of the most *universal* peoples"] (Unamuno *En torno* I n.p.). As a result, Castille's language and religion surpassed all others, homogenizing a Spanish identity: "Castilla paralizó los centros reguladores de los demás pueblos españoles, inhibioles [*sic*] la conciencia histórica en gran parte, les echó en ella su idea, la idea del unitarismo conquistador, del a *catolización* del mundo, y esta idea se desarrolló y siguió su trayectoria, castellanizándolos" [Castille paralysed other Spanish cultural centres, largely inhibiting their historical consciousness, imposed its idea, of conquering unification, of the *catholization* of the world, and its trajectory developed from this idea, castilianizing them] (Unamuno *En torno* II n.p.).[4]

Drawing from Castilian cultural history, Unamuno proposes that, in order to overcome the "depressing spectacle" it had become, Castilian culture needed to both find its essence, *intrahistoria* [Unamunian term, loosely translates to inter-history] and, at the same time, be open to other influences and Europeanize.[5] For Unamuno, *intrahistoria* is at once tradition and present, "La tradición eterna española, que al ser eterna es más bien humana que española, es la que hemos de buscar los españoles en el presente vivo, y no en el pasado muerto [the eternal Spanish tradition, that, being eternal, is more precisely human than Spanish, it is the one Spaniards should look for in the present and not in the dead past] (Unamuno *En torno* I n.p.). *Intrahistoria* may draw from the past but is a living tradition in the present, the characteristics of Castilian culture found in everyday life that had always made it great. Unamuno attributes the present negative state of Castilian culture to a return to the Inquisition, a "dead past" that isolated the culture (Unamuno *En torno* I n.p.). As Gayle Rogers puts it, for Unamuno, "*Casticismo* had excluded popular history and daily life … and had ossified it into a tradition commensurate with the vision of the monarchic state" (Rogers *Incomparable* 144). In order to overcome this self-imposed isolation and cultural stagnation, Unamuno proposes that Spain must be open to other influences and Europeanize, "sólo abriendo las ventanas a vientos europeos, empapándonos en el ambiente continental, teniendo fe en que no perderemos nuestra personalidad al hacerlo, europeizándonos para hacer España y chapuzándonos en pueblo, regeneraremos esta etapa moral" [only by opening windows and allowing European winds to flow through them, soaking ourselves in a continental environment, trusting that we will not lose our personality in doing so, and Europeanizing ourselves to make Spain, and submerging ourselves in the folk, will we regenerate this moral stage] (Unamuno *En torno* II n.p.). Castilian culture must return to the universalist tendencies that made it great in the past. Therefore, as Krauel summarizes, Unamuno "calls for a breaking of ties with this traditional system of *casticista* norms and values by suspending and transforming them into a system of beliefs that combines particular identifications (which incorporate the *Volkgeist* of the Spanish people) and universal values (which represent an underlying common humanity that is open to European culture)" (*Imperial* 86).

Unamuno's proposal that Castile be open to other cultures and Europeanize sustains empire both within Spain and across the Atlantic. Krauel explains that

> In 1895 Unamuno succeeded in breaking emotional ties with the political, military, and religious dimensions of the early modern Spanish Empire, but in failing to address its cultural aspects, he did not successfully mourn this aspect of the Spanish Empire. This would have enormous consequences for Unamuno's later attitude toward the cultural production of the non-Castilian peoples that were part of the "first" Spanish empire. (*Imperial* 98)

Unamuno thus maintained that Castilian culture is Spanish culture and should therefore revitalize itself in order to maintain its strength and centrality. Across the Atlantic, Spain had lost political control over its colonies, but once regenerated, could re-assume its cultural authority as Rogers explains, "The losses in the Spanish American War could only be compensated by gains within Spain in order to exercise 'spiritual' authority over the cultures of the New World" (*Incomparable* 146). Unamuno's universalist view that cultures benefit and grow from interactions with others is thus Eurocentric. Only European cultures were worthy of re-invigorating Castilian cultures. Regional cultures within Spain, along with those of its former colonies, were to be part of one Castilian dominant culture. As Rogers puts it, Hispanic cultures across the Atlantic were to be dominated and not assimilated, "Unamuno saw a threat: the former colonies were not sites where *casticismo* was evolving and progressing; in fact, they were fragmenting Castilian and fusing it with the Indigenous, Black diasporic, or other elements that had no roots in Iberian soil or being" (*Incomparable* 146). This view, held by many Spanish thinkers at the beginning of the twentieth century, was consolidated as *hispanismo* in the mid-nineteenth century when Spanish colonies were gaining their independence, a phenomenon Alejandro

Mejías López notes in his contribution to *Empire's End*: "as the Spanish empire came to an end, hispanismo attempted to fill that void by positing the existence of a transnational Hispanic community that, nevertheless, assumed the 'natural' leadership of Spain, both as historical agent and as birthplace of the language over which it claimed ownership" (*Empire's End* Mejías López 207). Unsurprisingly, the debates discussed later in this chapter will show that not only was Spain's "natural leadership" polemical, but that *hispanismo* itself was understood in very different ways on both sides of the Atlantic.

Empire and Latin America: José Enrique Rodó's *Ariel*

Addressing the change in world order brought about by the Spanish American War from a Latin American perspective, José Enrique Rodó's "forward-looking" essay *Ariel* (1900) also took on the topic of empire (Franco 158). Yet, his focus was the emerging US empire. If Unamuno's *En torno al casticismo* sought to encourage Castilian culture to evolve from its current state of stagnation, *Ariel* professed pride in Latin American culture. Leaving Spain behind, Rodó's essay calls on Latin America's youth to bring new life to the region, developing its cultural richness. Citing the United States' futile and superficial materialism, he warns against becoming mesmerized by its progress, which Rodó deemed to be based on an unsustainable utilitarian ethic: "La civilización de un pueblo adquiere su carácter no de las manifestaciones de su prosperidad o de su grandeza material, sino de las superiores maneras de pensar y de sentir que dentro de ellas son posibles" [A people's civilization acquires its character not from manifestations of its prosperity or material greatness, but from the superior ways of thinking and feeling that are possible within it] (Rodó *Ariel* V n.p.). Rodó argues in favour of greater humanity for Latin American culture, one that transcends the United States' ephemeral and superficial prowess.

Just as Unamuno sought to incite Castilian culture to reconnect with its essence, Rodó similarly reminded Latin America's youth that its cultural independence was just as important as its political independence: "El cuidado de la independencia interior – la de la personalidad … es una principalísima forma del respeto propio" [Caring for interior independence – personality … is the most principle form of self-respect] (Rodó *Ariel* IV n.p.). Moreover, preemptively responding to those who would claim that Latin America had yet to have an independent "personality," Rodó emphasized that "en ausencia de esa índole perfectamente diferenciada y autonómica, tenemos – los americanos latinos – una herencia de raza, una gran tradición étinica que mantener, un vínculo sagrado que nos une a inmortales páginas de la historia, confiando a nuestro honor su continuación en lo futuro" [in the absence of that type of perfectly differentiated, autonomous character, we – American Latinos – have a racial heritage, a great ethnic tradition to maintain, a sacred bond that unites us to immortal pages in history, entrusting to our honour its continuation in the future] (Rodó *Ariel* IV n.p.).[6] Rodó stresses that the heritage and history shared by Latin American nations provides a strong foundation for "nuestro carácter colectivo" [our collective character] and the attraction to cosmopolitanism should not disqualify it (Rodó *Ariel* IV n.p.). His main purpose is thus to ensure that young Latin Americans value their own culture, one that brings them together across nations.

As Jean Franco has explained, Rodó's essay responded to a general consternation that permeated across Latin America in the aftermath of the Spanish American War: "As Latin Americans looked towards their own societies, many of them torn by civil war, others suffering under dictatorships, all of them economically backward, they inevitably compared their position with the United States. They could take little pride in national tradition" (Franco 158). Addressing this reality, Rodó concedes that there are positive aspects to US culture, such as its modern concept of liberty, its work ethic, and its efficiency. However, a culture that is "lejos de ser refinada ni espiritual" [far from refined or spiritual] could not provide an appropriate example for Latin America (Rodó *Ariel* VI n.p.). Latin America's youth needed to aspire to more than US culture. They needed to help build "la América que nosotros soñamos; hospitalaria para las cosas del espíritu … pensadora … serena y firme … resplandeciente en el encanto de una seriedad temprana y suave" [the America we dream of; hospitable to matters of the spirit … thinking … serene and firm … radiant in its soft and serious charm] (Rodó *Ariel* VII/ n.p.). And in order to do so, Latin Americans needed to see beyond the present.

Iberoamericanismo: José Vasconcelos's *La raza cósmica*

Two decades later, José Vasconcelos's *La raza cósmica* would expand upon Unamuno's *En torno al casticismo* and Rodó's *Ariel* by focusing on race, and *mestizaje* [miscegenation] in particular, in addition to culture, nationalism, and empire. Like Unamuno, Vasconcelos emphasizes that Spain and Latin America are bound by culture, *iberoamericanismo*. And, within the same line of thinking as *Ariel*, *La raza cósmica* proposes that Spanish America's Iberian American race (raza iberoamericana) would surpass the United States's Anglo-Saxon, white race. In *La raza cósmica*,

Vasconcelos proposes that the conquest and the subsequent Spanish imperial era were instrumental in creating a more evolved human race: "La colonización española creó mestizaje; esto señala su carácter, fija su responsabilidad y define su porvenir" [Spanish colonization created miscegenation; this points to its character, situates its responsibility, and defines its future] (Vasconcelos 58). According to Vasconcelos, brought about by the Spanish conquest, the blending of Spanish and Indigenous cultures, *mestizaje*, would become a more developed race, "la raza definitiva, la raza síntesis o raza integral, hecha con el genio y la sangre de todos los pueblos y, por lo mismo, más capaz de verdadera fraternidad y de vision realmente universal" [the definitive race, the synthesizing or integral race, made with the genius and blood of all peoples and, for this reason, more capable of true fraternity and of a truly universal vision] (Vasconcelos 60). In order for this race to come into being, however, Vasconcelos insists that Latin Americans would have embrace to their Spanish heritage, which is why he uses the term Iberian American (*iberoamericano*), given its affinity to Spain and the Iberian Peninsula, instead of Latin American (which comes from French imperial aspirations for the region), "nosotros no seremos grandes mientras el español de la América no se sienta tan español como los hijos de España" [we will not be great while Spanish Americans do not feel as Spanish as Spain's children] (Vasconcelos 51). In this sense, like Unamuno, Vasconcelos endorses one Spanish American culture. Although the Spanish intellectual focuses Castilian centrality and the Mexican thinker employs the term Spanish, both also coincide in their portended universalist view of culture, one that gets richer and stronger through interactions with other races and cultures. Just as Unamuno maintained that contact with other European cultures could help Castilian culture regenerate, Vasconcelos believed that "una estirpe mejor" [a better lineage] would emerge as races mixed in Spanish America.

Coinciding with Rodó, Vasconcelos also stressed that this new race developing in Spanish America would transcend US culture. First, Vasconcelos explains that while Spanish colonization created *mestizaje*, the foundation for this new, evolved race in formation, English colonization in the Americas had limited its racial development by exterminating Indigenous races. As a result, the US empire would become "el ultimo gran imperio de una sola raza: el imperio final del podería blanco" [the last great empire of only one race: the final white dominant empire] (Vasconcelos 60). Furthermore, Vasconcelos asserted that this uni-racial empire would actually need to turn to Spanish America: "Los mismos blancos, descontentos del materialismo y de la injusticia social en que ha caído su raza, vendrán a nosotros para ayudar en la conquista de la libertad" [Whites themselves, unhappy with materialism and the social injustice within which their race has fallen, will come to us for help in the conquest of liberty] (Vasconcelos 65). Thus, if Rodó urged Latin America's youth to value their own cultural heritage and not fall prey to the US ephemeral, utilitarian progress, Vasconcelos predicts that a Spanish American *mestizo* race could actually surpass the homogeneous white race.

Negotiating the frameworks of empire, *En torno al casticismo, Ariel,* and *La raza cósmica* share a push for racial/cultural unity in postcolonial Spain and Latin America. Rodó focuses on an independent Latin American culture that leaves a Spanish empire behind and distinguishes itself from the United States' looming empire while Unamuno and Vasconcelos seek cultural and racial solidarity across the Atlantic between Spain and its former colonies. Unamuno, however, endorses a transatlantic culture that simply revives Castilian dominance over Latin America, replicating a colonial paradigm, albeit cultural rather than political. More utopian than Unamuno, Vasconcelos overrides any nationalist tensions stemming from the conquest, a past colonial relationship with Spain, and wars of independence to propose unity with Spain that would evolve into a superior race. Despite these differences and limitations, read together, these essays point to the controversial topics surfacing in the debates and exchanges taking place across literary journals and magazines across Spain and Latin America during the 1920s. Ardent points of contention were how to define a transnational and/or transatlantic Latin American identity that transcended national borders, the nature of a postcolonial relationship between Spain and Latin America, and the United States as the incoming imperial power in the West. While Unamuno, Rodó, and Vasconcelos's texts describe these main topics, delving into the nuanced exchanges in 1920s print culture in this chapter's next section offers more multifaceted insight into the issues these writers highlight, thereby uniquely contextualizing them.

Conflict and Solidarity: Hispano, Ibero, and Latino americanismo(s)

As *En torno al casticismo, Ariel,* and *La raza cósmica* detail, in the aftermath of the Spanish American War, empire loomed as Spain came to terms with the loss of its political power, Latin America grappled with consolidating national identities in the midst of the United States' emerging dominance over the region. During the 1920s conflicting views on how racial and cultural identities fit into national imaginaries regularly appeared across journals, magazines, and newspapers throughout Latin America and across the Atlantic in Spain. Columns, articles, reviews, and essays addressed these topics in a plurality of contexts, from longstanding literary journals to newly minted youth publications. For example, the many debates and exchanges that ensued regarding varied perspectives on the terms *latino*, *ibero*, and *hispanoamericanismo* reflected the complex discussions taking place between Latin American nations as they tried to define 1) their own identities, 2) their relationship with each other, and 3) their approach to former and growing empires in the West. If *ibero* and *hispano* deemed *americanos* to be part of the Iberian/Hispanic culture, the term *latino*, coined by French statesman Michel Chevalier in the 1830s, implied an alliance with French culture. All of these terms were therefore controversial for their hegemonic implications, eliciting numerous national and transnational debates across Latin America. At the same time, just as they do today, definitions and understandings of these terms varied greatly and were often used interchangeably, leading to polemical encounters. Primarily employed for ideological, cultural, or political objectives, these terms were also subjected to a number of interpretations and were used for a variety of purposes. Moreover, objectives were not mutually exclusive. Illustrating a plurality of perspectives, the section that follows offers brief examples of commentary and debates surrounding understandings of *hispanoamericanismo* appearing in 1920s Argentine and Mexican journals.

Championing *hispanoamericanismo* as a means of achieving transnational cultural unity in Latin America, the Buenos Aires journal *Nosotros: Revista mensual de letras, arte, historia, filosofía y ciencias sociales* (Buenos Aires 1907–34), published "Hispanoamericanismo literario" [Literary Hispanic Americanism] by Federico García Godoy in August 1923. Referring to South American independence leader Simón Bolívar's dream of a politically united Latin America, the Cuban-born Dominican national acknowledged that such an ideal was becoming less likely with each passing day. A century after independence, Latin America remained divided into independent nations. Nevertheless, García Godoy affirmed that these separate nations remained bound by a shared *hispanoamericanismo*, a cultural identity that surpassed political borders. He optimistically proposed that transnational dialogues between Latin American intellectuals would help nurture and define this shared cultural identity: "Desde México, desde las Antillas, hasta las más lejanas tierras australes del Continente, échase de ver un movimiento intelectual … que demuestra cumplidamente … que el pensamiento y la sensibilidad hispanoamericanos, están saliendo ya, resuelta y triunfalmente, del período amorfo" [From Mexico, from the Antilles, to the most distant southern lands in the Continent, an intellectual movement is visible ... [one] that completely demonstrates ... that Hispanic American thought and sensibility, are finally arising, resolutely and triumphantly, from the amorphous period] (433). Therefore, even if Latin American nations could not come together as one political entity, Bolívar's vision could still be accomplished through *hispanoamericanismo*, which he described as "la vibración cultural armónica y coherente de pueblos identificados por la sangre, por el habla y por la Historia" [the harmonious and coherent cultural vibration of peoples that identify through blood, speech, and through History] (441). For García Godoy, language and a history of Spanish colonization constituted a shared cultural heritage, and he proposed that Latin Americans capitalize on these commonalities in order to strengthen transnational bonds. More than an idealistic vision, he maintained that his notion was also practical, a tool that could be used to stand against the United States' looming hegemonic aspirations. Thus, although more pragmatic than Rodó's ideological *Ariel*, García Godoy's support of Latin American cultural solidarity in light of the United States' increasing power recalls the Uruguayan writer's perspective. And while both stress unity across Latin America, as compared to Vasconcelos's racial understanding of *iberoamericanismo*, García Godoy's *hispanoamericanismo* can be seen as more broadly cultural, including language and history. Yet, García Godoy's utopian call for solidarity surrounding a colonial language and culture could be taken to undermine the violence of empire and the subsequent battles for independence.

Passionately opposing utopian views of *hispanoamericanismo* like García Godoy's, Argentine writer Pablo Rojas Paz indicted the term in the avant-garde publication *Martín Fierro* (Buenos Aires 1924–7). In a brief contribution entitled "Hispanoamericanismo" [Hispanic Americanism] (*Martín Fierro* 17 May 1925) Rojas Paz indicted *hispanoamericanismo* as an empty signifier because "no es ni un concepto geográfico ni político, ni étnico, ni idiomático" [it is neither a geographical, political, ethnic, nor an idiomatic concept] (112). For the Argentine, *Hispanoamericanismo* proposed unrealistic, borderless unity with Spain and other Latin American countries. Self-sufficient and culturally independent, Argentina was proud of its national borders and had no need for such affiliations. Admittedly, Rojas Paz noted, less developed countries like Bolivia might stand to benefit from such relationships, but not Argentina. Rojas Paz asserted that clearly defined national identities need not seek transnational support, "[e]n definitiva, la Argentina no tiene nada que ver con el hispanoamericanismo" [[d]efinitely, Argentina has nothing to do with Hispanicamericanism] (112). Furthermore, setting unattainable idealism aside, from a pragmatic perspective, the Argentine intellectual cited Spain's political oppression under Primo de Rivera's dictatorship as a deterrent to nurturing cultural reciprocity with the former empire. Even considering Spain's "formidable tradición artística" [formidable artistic tradition], he believed that Argentina would have nothing to gain from a relationship with a country in such political disarray (112). Interestingly, as we will see in chapter 2, the Spanish journal *El Estudiante* would champion *Iberoamericanismo* as a means of combating Primo de Rivera. But, going back to Rojas Paz, at most, he conceded that *hispanoamericanismo* could serve as a "tema literario para congresos y juegos florales" [a literary topic for conferences and floral games], although, he noted, such events were superficial and pointless (112). For Rojas Paz, a term that connected budding new nations to a defunct empire, was devoid of meaning.

Echoing many of Rojas Paz's reservations on the topic, Peruvian poet Alberto Hidalgo offered another dissenting view of *hispanoamericanismo* in his 1926 *Índice de la nueva poesía americana* [New American Poetry Index], which the Mexican avant-garde journal *Horizonte* (México 1926–7) would engage in its review of the volume. Co-edited with Chilean poet Vicente Huidobro and Argentine writer Jorge Luis Borges, this *Índice* is the first anthology of Latin American vanguard poetry, and in his introduction to the volume, Hidalgo boasted: "Dejo aquí asesinadas las distancias" [Here I obliterate distances], implying that this transnational poetic compilation annihilated the geographical separation between nations: "[s]e puede ir ahora en pocos minutos desde la esquina de Esmeralda y Corrientes en Buenos Aires, hasta la calle Magnolia, en México" [[o]ne can now go in a few minutes from the corner of Esmeralda and Corrientes in Buenos Aires to Magnolia street in Mexico] (5). Like journals, magazines, and newspapers, publishing transnational anthology quite literally "obliterates distances" and transcends geographical borders, thereby uniting Latin America. Yet, Hidalgo made clear that his effort to bring Latin American poetry together did not endorse *hispanoamericanismo* in any way. Like Rojas Paz, Hidalgo considered the term repugnant, "una cosa falsa, utópica y mendaz" [a false, utopian and misleading thing] (5). He argued that the "confraternidad" [fraternity] proclaimed by *hispanoamericanistas* was a fallacy because Latin American nations were too different to come together in utopian unity. Aligning with Rojas Paz's nationalist sentiments, Hidalgo stated that "Nada tiene que ver un peruano con un paraguayo. Entre un argentino y un colombiano el abismo que se columbra es inconmensurable" [A Peruvian has nothing to do with a

Paraguayan. The perceivable abyss between an Argentine and a Colombian is immense] (5). Surpassing borders to bring authors from multiple nationalities together in one volume did not deny the existence of unique national identities and boundaries. Moreover, disagreeing with García Godoy's view of *hispanoamericanismo*, Hidalgo affirmed that language did not constitute a premise for cultural affinity between Latin American countries. Representing empire, it was a tool for subjugation imposed by the Spanish, nothing more. He added that the Southern Cone's immigrant population (Russian, Italian) was rapidly increasing and erasing Spanish heritage in the region. Finally, with regard to US imperialism, Hidalgo believed that the emerging power would not threaten South America, although it could eventually overcome Mexico and Central America: "Nuestro continente, en cumplimiento de quién sabe qué secreto designio, está formado de tal modo, que toda una parte debe ser sajona; toda la otra latina" [Our continent, fulfilling who knows which secret design, is shaped in such a way, that one part must be Saxon and the other Latin] (6). While he clarified that he did not support *panamericanismo* [Panamericanism] either, he predicted the United States' appropriation of Mexico and Central America to be inevitable.

As noted above, Mexico's *Horizonte* reviewed the *Índice de la nueva poesía americana* in November 1926. Published by the avant-garde *estridentistas*, the journal applauded the co-edited anthology as the first compilation of "todos los poetas de América – en habla española – en un libro unido" [all the poets from Spanish-speaking America in one united book] (431). While *Horizonte* shared Hidalgo's views on *hispanoamericanismo*, unsurprisingly, the Mexican journal strongly opposed the Peruvian's forecast that the United States would soon overpower Mexico and Central America. The review conceded that the United States' influence on Latin America was undeniable, underscoring that even the poetry in the anthology "está fecundada por un ansia de vida nueva, que tiene su fábrica en ese gran país de los rascacielos y la industria gigantesca, que ha despertado la envidia y la maledicencia de una Europa mezquina y centavera" [is fructified by a yearning for new life that has its factory in that great country of skyscrapers and giant industry that has awakened miserly, penny pinching Europe's envy and slander] (431). However, sharing García Godoy's anti-imperialist views with regards to the United States, *Horizonte* postulated that Latin America had no obligation to welcome the United States' "aviesa intención imperialista" [malicious, imperialist intent] and reminded Hidalgo that despite the United States' influence, Latin Americans were a different race with their own "forma de desenvolverse" [way of being] that would remain intact (431). Although *Horizonte*'s point here would seem to resonate with Vasconcelos's views on a Latin American race in *La raza cósmica*, the journal does not elaborate on the topic and, as previously mentioned, did oppose *hispanoamericanismo* just like Hidalgo.

The views on *hispanoamericanismo* described so far, whether for or against, have primarily referred to the term as one that stands for surpassing national boundaries through cultural and/or linguistic affinities. Connecting *hispanoamericanismo* to race, however, the La Plata student-run activist journal *Valoraciones* (LaPlata 1923–8) published "Vasconcelos y el Uruguay" [Vasconcelos and Uruguay] (*Valoraciones* 9 March 1926). In this review of Vasconcelos's *La raza cósmica*, José Mora Galindo dismissed the Mexican philosopher's proposal as shallow and naïve, critiquing Vasconcelos's attempt to "crear una teoría hispanoamericanista" [create a Hispanic Americanist theory] and "hacer la unidad del continente Americano, por un nuevo procedimiento de aglutinación, como si ésta fuese una masa cómodamente moldeable" [create unity in the American continent by means of a new process of agglutination, as though it were an easily moldable mass] (290). Notably, although Vasconcelos consistently employs the term *iberoamericanismo* in *La raza cósmica*, Galindo uses "hispanoamericanista" to refer to the Mexican philosopher's theory, thus suggesting that he considered the terms to be interchangeable. Mora Galindo deemed Vasconcelos's theory inadequate because it relied on a non-existent racial homogeneity, thereby failing to acknowledge differences among Latin Americans. Additionally, Mora Galindo underscored that Vasconcelos failed to account for Indigenous cultures that were also Latin American but did not fall into the *mestizo* category he envisioned. And, coinciding with Rojas Paz and Hidalgo, Mora Galindo also insisted that despite racial similarities and a shared Spanish colonial legacy, Latin Americans were also part of distinct nations, each of which had struggled to define its identity.

National borders are thus a recurring theme in the above brief examples of commentary and debates surrounding understandings of *hispanoamericanismo*. Proponents like García Godoy see *hispanoamericanismo* as a positive attribute, shared cultural characteristics that transcend borders and bring nations together. Opponents, critical of such idealism, point to 1) a shared cultural heritage rooted in violence and colonialism, 2) racial and cultural differences that outweigh any commonalities, and 3) protecting hard-won national borders. Interestingly, these discussions on whether or not *hispanoamericanismo* could/should overcome national boundaries took place in a medium that simultaneously defines and surpasses borders. Journals, magazines, and newspapers are meant to be portable and physically cross over national bounds. At the same time, they include content from within and beyond national borders.

A longstanding journal like *Nosotros*, which means "us" and was very much rooted in Argentina, was also an open space where pieces from different disciplines, "letras, arte, historia, filosofía y ciencias sociales" [letters, art, history, philosophy, and social sciences] coexisted offering a variety of perspectives from within and beyond national confines. Owing in part to this expansive and pluralistic scope, it managed to stay alive for four decades. In contrast, *Martin Fierro* and *Horizonte* were avant-garde publications with very specific visions. Both were simultaneously nationalistic, Argentina and Mexico respectively, and deeply engaged in cosmopolitan dialogues centring on cutting-edge artistic tendencies. *Valoraciones*, based in La Plata, Argentina, was run by university students and, although inscribed in avant-garde circles, its main concern was educational reform. Bearing each journal's focus in mind, then, it makes sense that a journal with a broader scope like *Nosotros* would be more open to García Godoy's optimistic reading of *hispanoamericanismo*. More preoccupied with creating an aesthetic that represented a national identity and simultaneously engaged cutting-edge, avant-garde tendencies, journals like *Martín Fierro*, *Horizonte*, and *Valoraciones* would be less likely to ascribe to a unifying understanding of *hispanoamericanismo*.

Hispano-Ibero Americanismo(s) across the Atlantic

Simultaneously bordered and borderless, journals were also hospitable spaces that engaged transatlantic exchanges, enabling often contentious discussions surrounding Spain and Latin America's postcolonial relationship. As the previous section describes, many in Latin America rejected *hispanoamericanismo* for denoting a shared cultural heritage rooted in colonial oppression. Thus, unsurprisingly, empire and its legacy would feature prominently in transatlantic interactions taking place in journals, magazines, and newspapers between Spanish and Latin American intellectuals. Take Mexican avant-garde writer Xavier Villaurrutia's brief reflection in *Proa* (Buenos Aires 1924–6), a small, avant-garde literary journal founded by Jorge Luis Borges, Brandán Caraffa, Ricardo Güiraldes, and Pablo Rojas Paz. In May 1925 the member of the Mexican avant-garde group *Contemporáneos* observed that "Ningún americano de mediana cultura corre el riesgo de ser el Cristóbal Colón de tierras españolas" [No moderately cultured American runs the risk of being the Cristopher Columbus of Spanish lands], underscoring the uneven relationship between Spain and its former colonies ("Los caminos de Alfonso Reyes" [Alfonso Reyes's Paths] *Proa* 5). Villaurrutia was commenting on how, despite Mexican poet and critic Alfonso Reyes's literary success in Spain, the former empire's colonial attitude towards Latin America persisted. Yet, Villaurrutia conceded that Reyes's accomplishments did represent a positive step forward for the transatlantic relationship. In Spain, Reyes had gained respect as a poet and critic, particularly for his expertise on Spanish Golden Age poet Luis de Góngora. He thus noted that Reyes's most significant triumph had been forging strong relationships with Madrid's intelligentsia, including philosopher José Ortega y Gasset.[7] Unlike the violent Spanish conquest of the Americas, Reyes had gone to Spain as an emissary of solidarity and friendship: "Se trata del triunfo de la consideración, de la amistad y solidaridad conseguidas entre los hombres de letras de allá" [It is the triumph of consideration, friendship, and solidarity achieved among men of letters over there] ("Los caminos de Alfonso Reyes" [Alfonso Reyes's Paths] *Proa* 5).

This anecdote illustrates that even a century after independence, the relationship between Spain and Latin America remained tainted by a colonial legacy. Although many Latin American intellectuals were also interested in maintaining a relationship with Spain, as the example of Alfonso Reyes demonstrates, transatlantic reciprocity still faced many challenges. For the most part, Spain continued to view Latin America as an extension of Spain and, in turn, Latin Americans also harboured colonial resentments. Moreover, Latin Americans demanded a new relationship with the former empire, one that fully acknowledged their independence and distinct nationalisms. Supporting Akiko Tsuchiya and William G. Acree Jr.'s perspective that empire did not end in 1898 with the Spanish American War, the debates in 1920s print culture evaluated in what follows illustrate how: "Even within the borders of Spanish America, the "end of empire" is, in fact, a process that occurred over the course of the long nineteenth century and that continues to have real and symbolic ramifications beyond this period" (*Empire's End* 3). Journals, magazines, and newspapers offer a map of the oscillating push and pull between conflict and solidarity as intellectuals from both sides of the Atlantic negotiated a postcolonial relationship. Citing ignorance, the first selection from *Valoraciones*, "La Reconquista de América" (March 1926), critiques Spain's empty, superficial attempts to engage cultural reciprocity with Latin America. The second example features a letter from Spanish intellectual Guillermo de Torre published in *Martín Fierro* where the Spaniard's purported desire to create a new relationship across the Atlantic falls short in its inability to fully relinquish empire's values. Similarly, in his brief piece "Hispanidad," cited in this chapter's epigraph and published in the Argentine journal *Síntesis*, Unamuno attempts to define a Hispanic race that extends to

Latin America. Like de Torre, however, the thinker is unable to envision the concept without an imperial lens. Finally, tying into the previously described discussions on *hispanoamericanismo*, this chapter closes with an account of the riveting exchanges that surrounded Peruvian Edwin Elmore's proposal to create a "Congreso de intelectuales Hispano-Americanos" [Conference for Hispanic-American Intellectuals]. Taken individually, each of the following examples provides interesting insight into the postcolonial relationship landscape of the 1920s. Yet, read together across journal publications, they offer a more nuanced view of the ragged contours that shaped a turbulent path.

False Reciprocity: Spain's Vacuous Cultural Overtures

In March 1926, *Valoraciones* published "La reconquista de América" [The Reconquering of America], an editorial critiquing the Spanish journal *Hispania: revista de artes y letras de raza* (Madrid 1925–6) for its shallow attempts to establish a cultural relationship with Latin America. The Argentine journal criticized Spain's "americanismo para la exportación, irrisorio, con intenciones comerciales mal disimuladas y peor encaminadas" [ridiculous, exportable Americanism with thinly veiled and poorly conceived commercial intentions] evident in events like "días de la raza, viajes de príncipes y publicaciones palaciegas y gemebundas" [Columbus days, prince's trips and weepy palatial publications] (297–8). *Valoraciones*'s editorial explained that, while open to developing an intercultural relationship with Spain, Latin America could not accept Spain's misguided approach, which the journal editors attributed to "el confuso recuerdo de la colonia, convertida ahora en óptimo mercado de afrodisíacos literarios" [a confused memory of the colony, now converted into an optimal market for literary aphrodisiacs] (297).

For *Valoraciones*, Spain's uninformed gestures revealed the former empire's unwillingness to acknowledge Latin American independence. *Hispania*'s content, the editorial pronounced, displayed the directors' complete ignorance of Latin American reality. Calling the publication a "confraternidad de tarjeta postal" [post card fraternity], *Valoraciones* disparaged *Hispania*'s frivolous portrayal of Latin America (298). Rather than address real socio-economic and cultural developments in the region, *Hispania*, they opined, "Dedica abundantes páginas a describir trajes regionales, a publicar himnos, a darnos versitos de las esposas de gobernadores, a dilucidar con criterio de portero reumático la nacionalidad de Colón" [dedicates abundant pages to describing regional dress, publishing hymns, giving us little verses from governor's wives, elucidating Columbus's nationality with a rheumatic doorman's criteria] (298). While this fetishizing of their national identities enraged *Valoraciones*, the journal's editors found *Hispania*'s lack of cultural sensitivity towards Latin America to be even more disconcerting. The Spanish journal had published a picture of Venezuelan despot Juan Vicente Gómez next to an image of Latin America's acclaimed hero in the wars for independence from Spain, Simón Bolívar. Although both were Venezuelan, pairing them was a careless and "infame parangón" [infamous comparison] (298). Thus, according to *Valoraciones*, *Hispania*'s hasty effort suggests that the Spanish journal was less invested in strengthening cultural connections than in the economic gains transatlantic relationships could render. Such representations of Latin America might entice a Spanish readership, but overseas, their marketing ploy had fallen flat. In fact, *Hispania*'s actions prove Rojas Paz's estimation that *hispanoamericanismo* was no more than "a literary topic for conferences and floral games." Moreover, *Valoraciones*'s assumption that economic gains were the actual focus of *Hispania*'s cultural outreach was not far-fetched. As the examples in chapter 3 will show, *La Gaceta Literaria*'s mission to be "Ibérica, Americana e Internacional" [Iberian, American, and International] was also tied to financial aspirations.

Imperial Camaraderie: Guillermo de Torre in *Martín Fierro*

The previously mentioned avant-garde journal *Martín Fierro* (Buenos Aires 1924–7) sprung onto the Buenos Aires literary scene in 1924. At once cosmopolitan and nationalistic, the journal aimed to revitalize Argentine culture by breaking with tradition and welcoming diverse voices onto its pages. As part of this effort, in 1925 *Martín Fierro* invited Spanish poet and critic Guillermo de Torre to contribute to their publication. De Torre, whose often-divisive role in transatlantic debates between Spain and Latin America will also be evaluated in chapters 3 and 4, was one of the founders of the Spanish vanguard poetic movement *ultraísmo* in the early 1920s.[8] Active in the European vanguard aesthetics scene, de Torre published *Literaturas europeas de vanguardia* [European Vanguard Literatures] in 1925, an account of Futurism, Cubism, Dada, *creacionismo*, and *ultraísmo*. Effusively responding to *Martín Fierro*'s request, de Torre wrote an open letter to the journal's director, "Carta abierta a Évar Méndez" [Open Letter to Évar Méndez], which the journal published in two parts, the first on 26 June 1925 and the second on 18 July 1925. De Torre's letter begins enthusiastically welcoming the "pura y desinteresada aproximación intelectual américo-española que se inicia" [pure and selfless intellectual American-Spanish approximation that is beginning] and deems *Martín Fierro*'s gesture an important step in reconfiguring Spain and Latin America's postcolonial relationship (136). Setting aside "todos los equívocos y todos los recelos, fomentados por la estupidez de nuestros antecesores" [all the misunderstandings and all the misgivings, encouraged by our predecessors' stupidity], the younger generation of Spanish and Latin American intellectuals could create a new relationship of mutual reciprocity between equals, "como una ancha corriente unánime de claras simpatías recíprocas" [like a broad unanimous trend of clear reciprocal affection] (136). De Torre warned, however, that this new relationship's success was contingent upon both sides' willingness to abolish residual tensions from the colonial power structure, a suggestion that this very letter would contradict. At the same time, he advocated basing a renewed transatlantic relationship between Spain and Latin America on a shared Hispanic heritage. De Torre's emphasis on Hispanic heritage, however, did not take either Latin America's distinct national identities or its Indigenous cultures into account.

Maintaining a Eurocentric perspective tainted by empire, de Torre explained that one of his reasons for endorsing Hispanic camaraderie was to challenge French cultural dominance in the Western World: "Francia como un puente de conocimiento, está en vías de terminar" [France, as a bridge of knowledge, is on its way out] and, therefore, "lo más urgente y digno de conocimiento está en nosotros, en las propias fronteras del 'Dominio Español'" [what is most urgent and worthy of knowing lies in us, within the borders of Spanish Dominance] (136). Further articulating this point, de Torre quoted vanguard novelist Ramón Gómez de la Serna who had also encouraged Latin America's younger generation to turn to Spain: "La nota de renovación de las juventudes americanas no podía ser francesa: necesariamente tenían que volver a España" [America's youth's rejuvenating tone could not be French: they would necessarily need to turn to Spain] (136). Suggesting that Latin America needed to emulate Spain rather than France speaks to a nineteenth-century world order in which Paris was the "capital of the nineteenth century" (Walter Benjamin) and Spain was still a somewhat viable empire. In particular, de Torre's phrasing of "Dominio Español" intimated that, despite his rhetoric, he had not entirely shed his own colonial perspective, envisioning a world where one Spanish culture could rule others, thereby negating Latin American cultural independence. Moreover, his use of "Español" rather than "Hispano," which he had initially employed, implies supremacy of a Spanish nation and not a Hispanic culture. Yet, de Torre mitigated his use of such terminology by asserting that his words did not imply Spanish control over

Latin America. He assured *Martín Fierro*'s readership that "Dominio Español" referred to replacing French linguistic dominance in the West with the Spanish language. Moreover, returning to the *hispano* prefix, de Torre proposed using *Hispanoamérica* rather than *América Latina* to refer to the former colonies. After all, *Latina*, given its French origin, would be confusing if the goal were to promote Spanish as a dominant language. Closing his letter, de Torre assured *Martín Fierro*'s readership that he understood *hispanoamericanismo* as, "un fluir espontáneo de las simpatías y curiosidades intelectuales" [a spontaneous flow of intellectual curiosity and affection], a dialogue between Spain and Latin America free of imperialist aspirations (136). Empire, however, unmistakably framed his argument, contradicting his supposed intent. De Torre's inability to abandon empire would later resurface in the well-known contentious *polémica del meridiano intelectual* that he incited in 1927, which will be discussed in detail in chapter 3.

Miguel de Unamuno: From Casticismo to Hispanidad

Three decades after the end of the Spanish American War, Miguel de Unamuno revisited topics he addressed in *En torno al casticismo*. Expanding the understanding of race and culture he had outlined in his late nineteenth-century collection of essays, Unamuno published "Hispanidad" [Hispanicity], as noted above, in the Buenos Aires journal *Síntesis* (Buenos Aires 1927–30), founded by Galician emigrant Xavier Bóveda, in November 1927.[9] From the outset, this briefer essay is more inclusive than his earlier text. The Spanish thinker begins by providing three specific reasons for his use of "Hispanidad" instead of "Españolidad." He makes no mention of the term Casticismo in this article. First, he explains, *Hispanidad* refers to the "concepto histórico-geográfico de Hispania, que abarca toda la Península Ibérica, la Iberia occidental" [geo-historical concept of Hispania, that encompasses all of the Iberian Peninsula, Occidental Iberia] (305). Second, *Hispanidad* includes all lineages and spiritual races affiliated to the Hispania. And, finally, *Hispanidad* is a historical, and therefore spiritual, category that "ha hecho, en unidad, el alma de un territorio con sus contrastes y contradicciones interiores" [has made, in unity, the soul of a territory with its internal contrasts and contradictions] (305). Connecting culture to the land, as he does in *En torno al casticismo* when he examines the Castilian landscape's effect on the people's character, Unamuno asserts that Spain's rocky interior is Hispania's womb, its maternal soul. Coastal communities, however, were responsible for expanding Hispania across the Atlantic.

As the introduction to this chapter mentions, Unamuno does not offer a definitive definition of *Hispanidad*. However, the Spanish philosopher does point to elements that are part of it. For instance, language and race are integral to *Hispanidad*: "el catalán, y el aragonés, y el leonés, y el bable, y el castellano, y el gallego, y el portugués. De ellos salieron los idiomas literarios y oficiales. Y los lenguajes son las razas ... Pero más que raza de sangre, más que línea de sangre, raza de lenguaje" [Catalan, Aragonese, Leonese, Bable (Asturias), Castilian, Galician, Portuguese. Literary and official languages originated from them. And languages are races ... But more than blood races, more than a bloodline, race of language] (308). Language and race are therefore mutually exclusive and, more importantly, language, more than blood, determines race. This understanding thus allows for a much broader *raza Hispana* [Hispanic race]. In *En torno al casticismo* Unamuno focused solely on Castilian cultural dominance of a Spanish nation that included the Americas through the conquest. Here, however, in defining language as race, Unamuno seems to propose that *Hispanidad* encompasses a larger community than *Casticismo*, as it includes all who speak Castilian regardless of their lineage. Moreover, opposing his view in *En torno al casticismo* that Latin American diversity infringed upon *casticismo*, Unamuno sees America as the place where *hispanidad* was destined to find itself: "La hispanidad ansiosa de justicia absoluta, se vertió, allende el océano, en busca de su destino, buscándose a sí misma, y dio con otra alma de tierra, con otro cuerpo que era alma, con la americanidad" [Eager for absolute justice, hispanicity spilled overseas searching for its destiny, looking for itself, and came upon another earth soul, with another body that was soul, with americanism] (310). He further explains that although *americanidad* was integral to *hispanidad*'s destiny, *americanidad* also had its own distinct destiny. Thus diverging greatly from *En torno al casticismo* by admitting that Latin America had its own destiny, Unamuno also takes an important step in further developing a Spain–Latin America postcolonial relationship. Simply stating that *americanidad* "busca también su propio destino" [also searches for its own destiny], albeit subtly, acknowledges Latin American independence, which, despite his efforts, Guillermo de Torre had been unable to do in *Martín Fierro* (310). Of course, Unamuno's gesture does not compensate for the article's implied imperialist standpoint. *Hispanidad*, through language, dominates in no uncertain terms.

The brief examples described so far, *Valoriaciones*'s critique of *Hispania*, Guillermo de Torre's "Carta a Évar Méndez," and Unamuno's "Hispanidad," illustrate how empire's looming presence created borders that inhibited reconciling a postcolonial relationship between

Spain and the new nations that were once its colonies. *Hispania*, de Torre, and Unamuno indicate an intent to create pathways enabling transatlantic cultural unity and overcoming colonial resentments. Their approach, however, unwittingly reinforces an imperial paradigm and incites Latin American resistance to their proposals. *Hispania*'s superficial and inaccurate representation of Latin American figures reveals a disregard for the new nations' unique identities. Meanwhile, de Torre and Unamuno's view that Latin American cultures are part of a broader Hispanic culture, similarly illustrates an unwillingness to acknowledge individual national identities. Thus, *Hispania*, Unamuno, and de Torre's efforts to surpass borders fell short because they did not respect Latin American nations' boundaries. Moreover, within literary journals, although *Hispania*, de Torre, and Unamuno's articles physically transgress national borders, their content points to ideological boundaries that inhibit transcultural collaboration.

Edwin Elmore: Congreso de Intelectuales Hispano-Americanos

The ramifications of an inability to reach consensus on *hispanoamericanismo* become clear when the term needs to be applied for practical action as the following series of exchanges across Spanish and Latin American journals, magazines, and newspapers illustrates. Peruvian Edwin Elmore's 1923 initiative to organize a Congreso de Intelectuales Hispano-Americanos [Conference for Hispanic-American Intellectuals] led to a series of transnational and transatlantic intellectual exchanges over *hispano–iberoamericanismo* that extended through 1925. Writing in the journal *Mercurio Peruano* (Lima 1918–present) in March 1923, Elmore proposed convening a Congreso de Intelectuales Hispano-Americanos that was not affiliated with either official or diplomatic institutions. This event would 1) foster an open dialogue between Spanish and Latin American intellectuals on *hispanoamericanismo* in contrast to the *panamericanismo* proposed by the United States, and 2) strengthen cultural ties between Spain and Latin America. Elmore's optimistic idea garnered initial support from José Vasconcelos and from Colombian essayist and editor for Buenos Aires's *La Nación* (1870–present) Baldomero Sanín Cano, who wrote an open letter to Madrid's daily newspaper *El Sol* (1917–39) inviting Spanish intellectuals to participate. Elmore's "Congreso" then sparked a series of articles and correspondence (1923–5) that discussed the feasibility of such an event. For instance, Spanish politician and writer Luis Araquistáin's "Un congreso de escritores" [A Writers' Conference] (*El Sol* 21 November 1924, 1) was met with responses from Argentine poet Leopoldo Lugones and Peruvian essayist and critic José Carlos Mariátegui. In his article, Araquistáin supported Elmore's idea, but noted that the Peruvian had not defined how he would go about organizing such an event, suggesting that his plan was idealistic, "no un Congreso, sino la aspiración, casi el sueño, de un Congreso de intelectuales hispanoamericanos" [not a conference, but the hope, almost a dream, of a conference for Hispanic American intellectuals] (1). However, Araquistáin conceded that historically, great accomplishments often began as vague dreams. In addition, Araquistáin questioned how Elmore would define "intelectuales hispanoamericanos" in order to devise a guest list. Yet, he commended the Peruvian writer for his symbolic selection of Havana, Cuba as the first conference location. Holding a conference on Spanish and Latin American cultural relations at the place where Spain had lost its last colonies to the United States would set an ideal tone.

Peruvian writer José Carlos Mariátegui joined the discussion on Elmore's proposal in January 1925 with "Un congreso de escritores hispano-americanos" [A Hispanic American Writers' Conference] (*Mundial* 1 January 1925).[10] Coinciding with Araquistáin's position, Mariátegui believed that the topic should be debated and was in favour of the event, but he also felt that Elmore's project needed to be more clearly defined. First, he questioned whether a conference could provide the best forum to address *hispanoamericanismo* since this type of event often resulted in superficial discussions: "[c]asi inevitablemente, estos congresos degeneran en vacuas academias, esterilizadas por el íbero-americanismo formal y retórico de gente figurativa e histrionesca" [[a]lmost inevitably, these conferences degenerate into vacuous academies, sterilized by figurative and histrionic participants' formal and rhetorical Ibero-Americanism] (3).[11] Mariátegui noted the complexity of participant selection, fearing that a vague requirement like "escritor hispano-americano" [Hispanic-American writer] would bring a heterogeneous, and therefore unproductive, group together. While Mariátegui advocated *hispanoamericanismo,* he believed that the term implied profound spiritual unity among Latin Americans and needed to be addressed as such. Therefore, he urged Elmore to consider whether his conference could meet this goal. In order to organize a conference on *hispanoamericanismo,* a baseline understanding of the term would need to be set, and such a task could be infinitely controversial. Yet, despite his reservations, in closing, Mariátegui rebuked Argentine poet Leopoldo Lugones, for opposing Elmore's proposal. The only explanation for this posture, he surmised, were the Argentine poet's nationalist, reactionary, and fascist motivations, which he had proclaimed by revealing allegiance to Peruvian Augusto B. Leguía's autocratic rule during a celebration for the Battle of Ayacucho (a key battle in Peru's struggle for independence from Spain).[12]

Clarifying his opinion on Elmore's proposal, Lugones chimed into the discussion with "Un congreso libre de trabajadores intelectuales" [A Free Intellectual Workers' Conference] in *El Sol* (16 April 1925, 1). While it is likely he read Mariátegui's piece, Lugones did not address the Peruvian's criticism. Instead, he first deemed the conference impractical because participants would not be able to afford the costly journey. Most importantly, however, he dismissed Elmore's call for an "Organización del pensamiento hispanoamericano" [Organization of Hispanic American thought] deeming it an empty concept. Thus coinciding with Argentine Pablo Rojas Paz's view of *hispanoamericanismo*, Lugones noted that organizing so many nations, with varied geographies, distinct interests, and different races, was not feasible. *Hispanoamericanismo* could not unite such disparate entities. Moreover, defending *panamericanismo*, he insisted that the United States' political influence over Latin America was not only undeniable, but also necessary. Lugones firmly disagreed with Araquistáin's and Mariátegui's perspective that considered *hispanoamericanismo* a cultural and even spiritual bond based on a common heritage. For the Argentine *modernista* poet, "[l]a uniformidad de intereses hispanoamericanos es una ilusión engendrada por la comunidad del idioma" [uniformity in Hispanic American interests is an illusion engendered by the language commonality] (1). Advocating for the new empire, Lugones averred that the United States' profound impact on Argentina's economy, judicial system, and industry was greater than Spain's had been. Yet, immediately contradicting himself, the Argentine poet professed his nationalist pride, "los argentinos jamás subordinaremos la patria" [Argentines will never subordinate the homeland] (1). Like Rojas Paz, Lugones felt that independent and self-sufficient Argentina need not subscribe to any type of union.

Following Lugones's contribution to the discussion, Araquistáin countered in a series of articles published in *El Sol*: "Una carta desconsoladora" [A Distressing Letter] (17 April 1925) and "Lo explicable y lo inexplicable del Sr. Lugones" [The Explainable and the Inexplicable of Mr. Lugones] (18 April 1925), where he pointed to Lugones's incongruous affirmation of independence and simultaneous affiliation with the United States. He also denounced the poet's stance against disarmament. In a third article, "Organización de la cultura hispánica" [Organization of Hispanic Culture] (*El Sol* 20 April 1925), he firmly defended *hispanoamericanismo*, arguing, like Unamuno did in "Hispanidad," that Spain and Latin America shared a cultural affinity, an "entraña hispánica" [a Hispanic core], based on language (1). This common essence needed to be defended and maintained, especially in light of the United States' imposition of English on some Latin American countries.[13] More than a term to describe cultural commonalities, Araquistáin declared *hispanoamericanismo* a practical means of coming together in solidarity. Together, Hispanic countries could preserve their culture, oppose the United States' *panamericanismo,* and work to fight tyranny. The Spanish writer stressed, however, that *hispanoamericanismo* could not be attained while some Hispanic countries remained subjected to authoritarian governments because the term also implied peace and unity. As chapter 2's discussion on the university reform movement explains, such an understanding of *hispanoamericanismo* as a means of solidarity surrounding socio-political issues was broadly supported. Interestingly, Araquistáin's point that authoritarianism was a challenge to *hispanoamericanismo* seems to ignore the fact that Spain was under Primo de Rivera's dictatorial regime. Nevertheless, Araquistáin staunchly endorsed *hispanoamericanismo* and the conference meant to address it: "¿Pues quién mejor que los trabajadores de la inteligencia, reunidos en cualquier punto de América o de España, podría articular esos problemas de homogeneidad de lengua, cultura, formas de gobierno y política de paz hispanoamericana?" [Who better than intelligence workers, assembled in any location in America or Spain, to articulate problems of homogeneity, language, culture, forms of government, and politics for peace in Hispanic America?] (1). However, Araquistáin did have some practical suggestions: 1) that there be multiple conferences for intellectuals from different fields and 2) that more specific topics like book distribution between Spain and Latin America needed to be addressed. This concern over the literary market also points to *hispanoamericanismo*'s economic ramifications, a topic further studied in chapter 3's examination of the 1927 *polémica del meridiano intelectual* [Intellectual Meridian Polemic], which, as noted earlier, Guillermo de Torre spearheaded.

Mariátegui rejoined the discussion with "¿Existe un pensamiento hispano-americano?" [Does Hispanic American Thought Exist?] (*Mundial* 1 May 1925) adding one more important point to the conversation. Recalling *Valoraciones*'s José Mora Galindo's critique of Vasconcelos's *iberoamericanismo,* Mariátegui articulated his concern that deliberations on *hispanoamericanismo* ignored Indigenous populations and thus neglected to confront Latin America's racial diversity. Marginalized Indigenous populations, "el alma indígena, deprimida y huraña" [the Indigenous soul, depressed and hermit-like] needed to be taken into account. The violent conquest had subjugated these races and, in some "pueblos hispano-americanos" [Hispanic-American nations] their status had not changed (9). The Peruvian essayist could therefore sanction the idea of a "congreso de intelectuales ibero-americanos" [Iberian American Intellectuals' Conference] (Mariátegui employs hispano and ibero interchangeably) as long as it addressed all key issues pertaining to *hispanoamericanismo*, including racial diversity in Latin America (9).

Elmore's proposal thus generated a heated discussion on *hispanoamericanismo*, shedding light on controversies centring empire, nationalism, language, politics, and race in ideological and pragmatic terms. The conference itself, however, never came to be as the debate devolved into bloodshed. Ensuing tensions increased exponentially when Peruvian poet José Santos Chocano ascribed to Lugones's stance by endorsing Leguía's government. This action provoked Vasconcelos, who joined the debate with his article "Poetas y bufones" [Poets and Buffoons]. Calling Lugones and Santos Chocano "bufones," he condemned both for supporting tyranny in Latin America.[14] Moreover, he pointedly denounced Santos Chocano for his long legacy of sanctioning despotism in Latin America. Vasconcelos accused the Peruvian of supporting Pancho Villa during the Mexican Revolution and endorsing totalitarian regimes in Venezuela and Guatemala. For Vasconcelos, by legitimizing authoritarianism, Santos Chocano and Lugones had abdicated their title as poets and were nothing more than "retóricos en verso" [rhetorical in verse] (*Poetas y bufones* 11). Reacting to Vasconcelos, Santos Chocano retorted with "Apóstoles y farsantes: Vasconcelos sin mascara" [Apostles and Frauds: Unmasked Vasconcelos] in Mexico's daily newspaper *Excelsior* (México 1917–present), where he labelled the Mexican politician a fake.[15] Arguing that political views could not negate a poet's merits, Santos Chocano dismissed the connections that Vasconcelos drew between poetry and politics: "[e]l licenciado Vasconcelos tiene el candor de hacer creer que la Poesía debe quedar subordinada a la Política … es farsa" [graduate Vasconcelos has the candour to make believe that Poetry should be subordinated to Politics … it's a farse] (*Poetas y bufones* 27).[16] Furthermore, Santos Chocano called Vasconcelos a hypocrite for professing an all-inclusive *hispanoamericanismo*, when, in reality, he rejected those that did not share his political views.

Edwin Elmore intervened in this debate between Vasconcelos and Santos Chocano with "Un nuevo ibero-americanismo" [A New Iberian-Americanism] (*Horizonte* April 1926), the article that, according to Mexico's *Horizonte*, provoked Santos Chocano and led to Elmore's tragic fate.[17] Elmore lamented that, if views on *iberoamericanismo* as a means of uniting "la actividad espiritual de nuestros pueblos en un armonioso plan de cooperación internacional, en el que quepan las diversas tendencias y los variados elementos de nuestra cultura" [our peoples' spiritual activities in one harmonious plan of international cooperation, in which diverse tendencies and the varied elements of our culture have a place] had always varied, even among its proponents, the topic had become more divisive ("Un nuevo ibero-americanismo" [A New Iberian Americanism] 27). He explained that socio-political positions were infringing on *iberoamericanismo,* creating unnecessary friction and disputes over a term that had originally advocated cultural unity. In particular, Elmore supported Vasconcelos's claims and rebuked "La defección de los Poetas" [the Poets' defection] ("Un nuevo ibero-americanismo" 27), denouncing Santos Chocano and Lugones for their opposition to *iberoamericanismo* and support of violence: "Ayer, Lugones bajo la invocación de Ayacucho profetiza el culto de la Espada; después ... Chocano ... llama farsante a un apóstol respetado de nuestros sueños de confraternidad y justicia" [Yesterday, invoking Ayacucho, Lugones proclaimed the cult of the Sword; then ... Chocano ... calls a respected apostle of our dreams for fraternity and justice a fraud] ("Un nuevo ibero-americanismo" 28). Both poets had succumbed to fame and popularity, betraying a new generation of intellectuals ardently pursuing camaraderie.

In a surprising and tragic turn of events, this series of transatlantic and transnational exchanges over Elmore's proposed "Congreso de Intelectuales Hispano-Americanos" came to a shocking halt when Santos Chocano murdered Elmore. According to *El Sol*'s account at the time, enraged when Elmore took Vasconcelos's side, Santos Chocano confronted Elmore in front of the offices of the Peruvian newspaper *El Comercio.*[18] A physical altercation ensued and quickly ended when Santos Chocano shot and killed Elmore. Sparking transatlantic outrage, the event made headlines across Spanish journals and newspapers, such as Madrid's *El Estudiante,* which lamented the loss of "la figura de Edwin Elmore – hombre que laboró como nadie a favor del acercamiento de España y América" [the leading figure of Edwin Elmore – a man who worked like no other in favour of Spain and America's rapprochement)] ("Edwin Elmore" 5).

The transnational and transatlantic discussion surrounding *ibero/hispano-americanismo* that ensued surrounding Edwin Elmore's endeavour to create a "Congreso de Intelectuales Hispano-Americanos" was intriguing and dramatic. However, set within the broader context of contributions on the topic to journals, magazines, and newspapers at the time, as we have seen in this chapter, it is but one of many discussions on *ibero/hispano-americanismo.* Moreover, the perspectives supporting and countering Elmore's proposal are not unique to this particular series of exchanges. Views expressed regarding *ibero/hispano-americanismo* and the feasibility of Elmore's conference were similar to other contributions to print culture during the 1920s. Therefore, tracing these exchanges across journals, magazines, and newspapers offers insight into the scope of discussions of how race, national identity, politics, and empire factored into postcolonial Spanish and Latin American interactions that extends beyond the confines of published books like *En torno al casticismo*, *Ariel*, and *La raza cósmica*. Moreover, these dialogues across journals, magazines, and newspapers offer a concrete outline of interactions between a transnational and transatlantic network of intellectuals. As they deliberated over national borders and cultural unity that transcended nationalisms within a medium that both created and surpassed borders, Latin American and Spanish intellectuals built a network that ultimately overcame the boundaries they were debating.

This network made visible by debates and exchanges taking place in 1920s print culture broadens our understanding of the literary and socio-political developments at the turn of the twentieth century and the topics they engaged also speak to the present because they continue to be relevant. For instance, Hispanism in US academia today is still primarily divided across Latin Americanist/Peninsularist lines. Degrees within departments are structured according to this divide, offering courses on either Latin American or Peninsular literature. At the very least the debates and exchanges on *hispanoamericanismo* described in this chapter force us to consider a more nuanced understanding of this divide in general and of the idea of Latin American literature more specifically.[19] Alberto Hidalgo's rejection of *hispanoamericanismo* and the idea of a unified Latin America in his introduction to an anthology of Latin American poetry that brings poets from across the continent together, for example, could lead to very interesting discussions surrounding how literary production has been categorized and organized within Hispanism. More broadly, the exchanges surrounding *hispanoamericanismo*'s viability are not unlike the debates we continue to have regarding Transatlantic and Iberian Studies. Moreover, from these debates we can also derive lessons on bridging the disconnect between theoretical debates on *hispanoamericanismo* and their practical application, such as Edwin Elmore's attempt, could serve similar discussions in Hispanism today. Looking back on how print culture charted similar discussions can thus prove fruitful and perhaps help us eradicate false dichotomies that have structured Hispanism. While on one hand 1920s print culture reveals tensions and divisions, on the other hand, these exchanges created a network that surpassed the very controversies that built it. Print culture can thus serve as a blueprint for scholarship today. Revisiting debates surrounding Hispanism through print culture demands breaking with academic divisions and forces a reconsideration of current understandings of literary historiography. As Alejandro Mejías López suggests in his contribution to *Empire's End,* critics of Transatlantic Studies "have not meaningfully engaged its potential to find new ways to understand Spanish American and Spanish peninsular histories and production and to rearticulate a field still weighed down by two centuries of troublesome rejections and nostalgic unity" (*Empire's End* 213). Therefore, as this book sets out to demonstrate, as a medium, journals, magazines, and newspapers chart a path that enables Hispanism to delve into the interstices and fissures that actually shaped literary historiography in order to start leaving "troublesome rejections and nostalgic unity" behind.

Chapter Two

Transcultural Solidarity: Generational Shifts and Social Reform in Print Culture

> ha partido por el Pacífico y vía Nueva York en trascendente misión de confraternidad artística o intellectual de la juventud de América y Europa latina [has embarked on the Pacific and through New York on a transcendent mission of artistic or intellectual fraternity between America's and Latin Europe's youth].
>
> *Martín Fierro* 1.7 25 July 1924, 3

The above epigraph describes the beginning of a journey undertaken by Argentine avant-garde poet Oliverio Girondo and sponsored by Argentine journals *Martín Fierro* (Buenos Aires 1924–7), *Inicial* (Buenos Aires 1923–7), *Noticias Literarias* (Buenos Aires 1923–4), *Valoraciones* (La Plata 1923–8), along with Uruguayan journals *La Cruz del Sur* (Montevideo 1924–31) and *Teseo* (1923–4). According to the enthusiastic report entitled "Oliverio Girondo en misión intelectual" [Oliverio Girondo on an Intellectual Mission] published on 25 July 1924 in *Martín Fierro*, the poet's journey was meant to encourage cultural collaboration and promote Argentine and Uruguayan intellectuals (47). As "embajador de nuestra juventud intelectual" [ambassador for our intellectual youth] Girondo would also foster a transnational and transatlantic "intercambio de producciones, revistas y libros; ideas, poesía, arte" [exchange of production, journal, books; ideas, poetry, art] (47). This enterprise exemplifies print culture's efforts to simultaneously overcome borders and promote national identities. On the one hand, Girondo's journey endorsed transcultural solidarity throughout Latin America and across the Atlantic. But, on the other hand, the Argentine poet was very much a cultural ambassador for specific Argentine and Uruguayan journals. As we saw in chapter 1, hosting discussions centring on *hispano/ibero-americanismo* that both traversed borders and outlined boundaries, journals map a network of intellectual exchange within Latin America and across the Atlantic with Spain. However, owing to a lack of consensus on *hispanoamericanismo,* these exchanges were unable to translate theoretical dialogues into quantifiable action. In this chapter, as Girondo's endeavour illustrates, exchanges across print culture between Spanish and Latin American intellectuals manage to transcend animosity and develop relationships based on cross-cultural kinship by focusing on social reform.

This chapter offers two examples of how a younger generation in Spain and Latin America managed to create new transatlantic relationships based on solidarity surrounding social reform. Their focus on socio-political issues such as educational reform and amnesty enabled them to forge these relationships despite tensions between colonialism's legacy and hard-won national identities. Coming together as *hispano/ibero-americanos,* Latin American intellectuals spread a university reform movement from Argentina to Mexico, staunchly opposed tyrannical governments such as Augusto B. Leguía in Peru, and confronted US empirical overtures towards Latin America. First, this chapter evaluates a dialogue that ensued between Argentina's "Nueva Generación" [New Generation] (via two journals, *Inicial* and *Valoraciones*), and Spanish philosopher José Ortega y Gasset. Although the Spanish philosopher maintained an elitist perspective in which he imparted his wisdom upon younger Latin American counterparts, this telling series of interactions contributed to redefining a postcolonial relationship with Spain and strengthening a transatlantic network. The second part of this chapter considers an undertaking that actually inverted the postcolonial paradigm when the Spanish journal *El Estudiante* (Salamanca-Madrid 1924–6) sought support and camaraderie from Latin American counterparts to effect social change in Spain. Within Latin America, social reform movements promoting *Reforma Universitaria* (university reform) and opposing despotism spawned solidarity between Latin American intellectuals. These actions would encourage Salamanca students publishing *El Estudiante* who sought to overcome limitations imposed upon them by Miguel Primo de Rivera's oppressive rule. In their estimation, their country would be well served by paying attention to Latin America's fresh and innovative approaches.

Generational Shifts and the Postcolonial Paradigm: José Ortega y Gasset and Argentina's "Nueva Generación"[1]

Argentine poet and critic Alfredo Brandan Caraffa's "Voces de Castilla" [Voices from Castile] (*Proa* September 1924) reveals that, disenchanted with post–First World War Europe, many Spanish intellectuals saw

Latin America's younger generation as an audience ripe with promise. Reflecting upon a recent visit to Spain, in this article Caraffa narrates his interactions with Spanish intellectuals Ramón Gómez de la Serna, Rafael Cansinos Asséns, and José Ortega y Gasset. Ramón, who Caraffa described as having "algo de gnomo que gobierna con sus paradojas" [something of a gnome that governs through paradox], regretted the dialectical differences between Argentine and Castilian Spanish: "Me habla de Buenos Aires con cierto afectado decir de viajero antiguo. Se lamenta del lenguaje bastardo que empieza a tomar carta de ciudadanía en nuestro país" [He speaks to me of Buenos Aires with a certain affected tone of an ancient traveller. He laments the bastard language that is earning its citizenship in our country], one of the polarizing topics that would later be debated in the 1927 *polémica del meridiano intelectual* [Intellectual Meridian Polemic] (41). As Caraffa explains, Ramón attributed Argentina's "corrupt" Spanish to Italian immigration and to Spaniards' negligence: "no trabajan suficientemente para conservar el casticismo en *todas las Américas*" [They do not work hard enough to conserve purity in all of the Americas] (41). Meanwhile, Ortega, "[c]on su cabeza plástica de frente redonda y calva y un prestigio visible que baja como una túnica por su persona" [with his bald, round foreheaded plastic head and his visible prestige that embraces his person like a tunic], told Caraffa that despite difficulties adapting to Buenos Aires's climate during his visit (1916), the experience had reignited his confidence in the new generation (43). Although disappointed with Europe's young intellectuals, Ortega esteemed Argentina's younger generation's "sensibilidad comprensiva" [understanding sensibility] and "curiosidad universal" [universal curiosity] (44). In addition, Caraffa recounted that he was surprised to find that Ramón and Cansinos-Asséns shared Ortega's perspective: "Lo que más me sorprendió en estos tres hombres fue su interés coincidente por la juventud de América. Todos me declararon su expectativa por los nuevos valores que veían surgir inesperadamente" [What most astonished me about these three men was their condescending interest in Latin America's youth. They all declared their expectation for the new values that they were seeing emerge unexpectedly] (45). Moreover, Ramón, Ortega, and Cansinos-Asséns admitted to Caraffa that they wrote for a Latin American audience: "me dieron a entender que para quien escribían en realidad era para el público de ultramar" [they implied that they were actually writing for an overseas audience] (45). Disillusioned over their inability to reach Spain's young intellectuals, Latin America's enthusiastic readership provided them new opportunities for intellectual exchange. Ramón, Ortega, and Cansinos-Asséns's admission points to a genuine interest in fostering transatlantic ties, although their condescension suggests that they had all but dispensed with a colonial power dynamic. The following example of exchanges across journals, magazines, and newspapers between Ortega and Argentina's "Nueva Generación" [New Generation] demonstrates that hope for reform and cultural reciprocity could not overcome a Spanish desire to maintain cultural dominance over their country's former colonies.

During the 1920s, younger generations in Latin America were enthusiastic about Ortega's ideologies. In particular, they ascribed to the Spanish philosopher's theory on generations, which he detailed in *El tema de nuestro tiempo* [The Modern Theme] (1923).[2] For Ortega, while each generation was the product of the preceding generation, each also possessed its own entity, "un nuevo cuerpo social íntegro" [a new honest social body] imbued with its own "sensibilidad vital" [vital sensibility] (*OC* 563). Each generation's sensibility determined how it related to the previous generation. In some eras, generational sensibilities had much in common, and there was little friction between generations. Yet, when a new generation's sensibility differed greatly from that of the preceding generation, conflict would be inevitable. Latin America's intellectuals identified with the latter type of generation; they felt a great schism between their sensibility and that of the generation that preceded them. Ortega's theories provided a means of articulating this rift.

Although Ortega's ideas reached many countries in Latin America, he cultivated a particularly strong relationship with Argentina's young intellectuals. He first visited Argentina in 1916 and later became a frequent contributor to Buenos Aires's *La Nación* (1870–present). Argentina's young generation of intellectuals had adopted the banner "Nueva Generación" [New Generation] following a 1923 survey in the Buenos Aires journal *Nosotros* (1907–43) and came together around common aesthetic and socio-political pursuits that entailed severing ties with the preceding generation's ideologies. With regard to aesthetics, inspired by vanguard movements such as *ultraísmo* [Ultraism], this generation sought to break with previous literary and artistic traditions. At the same time they demanded social change, engaging activism such as the *Reforma Universitaria* [University Reform] movement that had begun in the Argentine city of Córdoba in 1918 and quickly spread throughout Latin America. Following Ortega's writings in *Revista de Occidente* (Madrid 1923–36) and in *La Nación*, this "Nueva Generación" related to the Spanish philosopher's perspective and frequently reviewed his works in their journals. Two publications that based much of their platform on his philosophies were *Valoraciones: Humanidades, crítica y polémica* (La Plata 1923–8) and *Inicial: Revista de la nueva generación* (Buenos Aires

1923–7). The section that follows first describes each journal and then details a series of exchanges they engaged in with Ortega y Gasset.

Students from the University of La Plata came together as "Grupo Renovación" [Renovation Group] and published the socio-politically engaged journal *Valoraciones*. Under Carlos Américo Amaya's direction, the journal professed a "rebeldía contra los valores gastados que perduran, y de afirmación de nuevos valores" [rebellion against worn-out values that endure and an affirmation of new values] ("Intenciones" 4). "Grupo Renovación" felt that Argentina needed to catch up with Europe "en material de cultura" [culturally] ("Intenciones" 4). Argentina's universities, for example, were ideologically stagnant: "atrofiadas bajo el grueso cascarón de la rutina, siguen siendo esas pesadas y desesperantes carretas del progreso, que llenaron de orgullo al espíritu resignado y elemental de nuestros abuelos" [atrophied under routine's thick shell, they continue to be heavy and exasperating wagons of progress that once filled our grandparents' resigned and elementary spirit with pride] ("Intenciones" [Intentions] 4). Nineteenth-century positivism may have been appropriate for their grandparents, but *Valoraciones* proclaimed that Argentine universities needed an influx of new ideas and philosophies. Moreover, universities could no longer be affiliated with either church or state.[3] Ascribing to Ortega's theory on generations, "Grupo Renovación" insisted that their generation had to break with the past because their era demanded new ways of thinking. A literary and politically engaged publication, *Valoraciones* would be key in bringing about this generational schism and advancing social change: "trataremos de hacer ... una labor constructiva, orientando a la juventud hacia rutas fundamentales de la alta cultura" [we will attempt a constructive endeavour, orienting youth towards high culture's fundamental paths] ("Intenciones" [Intentions] 5). To this end, although the *Reforma Universitaria* movement framed *Valoraciones*'s scope and content, the multifaceted journal also published articles on politics, history, philosophy, literature, and visual art.

Similarly representing this new Argentine generation, a month after *Valoraciones* emerged in La Plata (October 1923), Brandan Caraffa, Homero M. Guglielmini, Roberto Smith, and Roberto A. Ortelli published *Inicial: Revista de la nueva generación* in Buenos Aires. Their journal would be a platform for "esa juventud dispersa que vagabundea por las publicaciones y revistas más o menos desteñidas" [disperse youth that wanders across somewhat faded journals and magazines] where they could debate and express their positions on socio-political and aesthetic issues ("Inicial" 3). If *Valoraciones*'s "Grupo Renovación" sought reforms that embodied their generation's new sensibility, *Inicial* was the

"Revista de la nueva generación," [journal of the new generation] and would register "las palpitaciones de la juventud," [youth's pulse] calling on "todo lo que hay valiente, decidido y sano en las filas de la nueva generación" [all that is brave, determined, and healthy in the new generation's ranks] ("Inicial" 4). Like "Grupo Renovación," *Inicial*'s editors declared their commitment to their generation and to reform, "la juventud debe renovar constantemente sus horizontes y escalar siempre otros nuevos" [youth must constantly renew its horizons and always aspire to new ones] ("Inicial" 6). In contrast to *Valoraciones*, however, *Inicial*'s tone was much more aggressive, focusing on issues the editors opposed rather than on constructive goals: "Al fundar *Inicial* hemos pensado que en nuestro ambiente moral y artístico, hay hombres y cosas que es necesario combatir despiadadamente. Sentimos un profundo desprecio por todos aquellos que pontifican desde el pedestal de las artificiales consagraciones de cenáculo" [By founding *Inicial*, we have considered that in our moral and artistic environment there are men and things that we must mercilessly combat. We feel profound disdain for all those who pontificate from a pedestal artificially recognized by a limited group] ("Inicial" 3).[4]

Inicial would be more than "una simple revista" [a simple journal]; it would be "una antología pálida e inmóvil de los poetas y escritores jóvenes del país ... una cosa viva y dinámica, un registro sensible donde todas las palpitaciones de la juventud, hasta las más sútiles, dejen una huella que el porvenir puede descifrar" [a pale, immobile anthology of the country's young poets and writers ... alive and dynamic, a sensible register where all of youth's palpitations, even the most subtle, leave a trace that the future can decipher] ("Inicial" 4). Their journal was meant for "una juventud combativa y ardorosa, que odie y ame" [a combative, furtive youth that hates and loves] and opposed to a long list of views and groups such as, "snobs elegantes" [elegant snobs], "la crítica que todo lo niega y nada afirma"[criticism that denies everything and affirms nothing], "los grandes diarios malolientes del judaísmo" [Judaism's large and malodorous daily papers], "los que han hecho del comunismo y el obrerismo una mentira descarada" [those that have made communism and labour rights a shameless lie], and "los que explotan los ideales ingenuos de la juventud sana, postituyendo la Reforma de la Universidad a la caricia torpe de los advenedizos" [those that exploit a wholesome youth's naïve ideals, prostituting University Reform to latecomers' clumsy caresses] ("Inicial" 4–5).[5] Such pugnacious (not to mention chauvinist and anti-Semitic) rhetoric was met with resistance in Buenos Aires as *Inicial*'s second issue, November 1923, discloses. Opening with an article entitled "¿Reaccionarios?

¿Poco definidos?" [Reactionary? Poorly defined?], *Inicial* responded to criticism of its first issue's bellicose introduction. The journal defended its position explaining that its generation faced a different reality that demanded strong convictions: "Hoy todo ha cambiado. El mundo es un gigantesco laboratorio donde se liquida todo lo falso" [Today everything has changed. The world is a giant laboratory that liquidates all that is false] (3–4). Despite this militant rhetoric, however, *Inicial* did share some objectives with *Valoraciones*. Both journals displayed an awareness of their generation and of the new world it faced, and both aspired to effect change. Additionally, both journals drew on Ortega's theory of generations and regularly commented on the Spanish philosopher's publications, although *Inicial* more vehemently declared its allegiance to Ortega, describing him as "uno de los espíritus más cultos de Occidente" [one of the West's most cultured spirits] (6).

In 1923 and 1924, *Valoraciones* and *Inicial* reviewed Ortega's *España invertebrada* [Invertebrate Spain] (1921) and *El tema de nuestro tiempo* (1923) and the Spanish philosopher responded to both journals in a series of articles he published in *La Nación* in 1924, thereby establishing a transatlantic and transgenerational dialogue. Carlos Américo Amaya's review of *España invertebrada* for *Valoraciones* in September 1923 initiated the discussion by pointing to Ortega's value to the new generation. He emphasized that the philosopher's analysis took an important step back from detailed and superficial political problems in order to understand Spanish society from a broader perspective. Moreover, Amaya stressed that, while Ortega's book was about Spain, his discussion was also relevant to *Valoraciones*'s readership: "encierra problemas de tal magnitud que difícilmente no nos encontremos comprendidos en algunos, yo diría en todos los términos de sus proposiciones" [It encompasses problems of such magnitude that we would be hard pressed to not relate to at least some, I would say to all aspects of his proposals] (44). A few months later, in January 1924, *Valoraciones* also reviewed Ortega's important journal *Revista de Occidente* (Madrid 1923–36), underscoring the philosopher's publication as important for its effort to express "el pensar y sentir contemporáneo" [today's way of thinking and feeling], which further highlighted the Argentine journal's endorsement of the Spanish philosopher (158).

Although *Valoraciones*'s reviews exhibit the journal's alignment with Ortega and his assessment of the new era, *Inicial*, consistent with its aggressive tone, was much more forceful in championing the Spanish thinker. For example, *Inicial*'s December 1923 review of *El tema de nuestro tiempo* entitled "Un filósofo de la Nueva Generación" [A Philosopher for the New Generation], ardently promoted Orteguean thought as "la justificación filosófica de las nuevas inquietudes" [the philosophical justification of new inquisitiveness] (58). Like *Valoraciones, Inicial* appreciated Ortega's addressing of "la actual sensibilidad" [the current sensibility] but went further by bestowing him with the title "filósofo de la Nueva Generación" [philosopher of the new generation] because he articulated "los rumbos cardinales hacia los cuales se proyectan las maneras de pensar y de sentir contemporáneas" [the fundamental paths towards which contemporary thought and thinking is directed] (58). In particular, *Inicial* explained that Ortega's most original contribution was "el sentido que presta a la cultura ... Esa definición nos aclara todo el misticismo político e idealista de la pasada centuria, y nos abre el camino para la interpretación de las recientes aberraciones históricas" [the sense he lends culture ... That definition clarifies the last century's idealistic and political mysticism and opens a path towards interpreting recent historical abominations] (60). For *Inicial*, Ortega's theories confirmed their radical positions and justified their constant clashes with the previous generation.

Each issue of *Inicial* begins with an editorial that sets the tone for the entire volume. Unmistakably articulating their allegiance with Ortega, in *Inicial* 4 (January, February, March 1924), the opening editorial entitled "La nueva mentalidad de Occidente" [The West's New Mentality], which echoed the title of Ortega's journal *Revista de Occidente*, responded to accusations that the new generation lacked concrete ideals. Drawing from Orteguean postures, *Inicial* claimed that such assessments were rooted in the previous generation's inability to understand new generation approaches:

> Reclaman de la juventud intelectual del momento, la sensibilidad y la postura que caracterizaron a las generaciones del pasado, y del pasado más reciente. Y como no nos es posible servirles, a ellos, en bandeja de plata, el manjar a su sabor y gusto de un sistema bien ilustrado y sin resquicios ... enrostran al joven pensamiento su carencia de orientación concreta, de definiciones claras y de afirmaciones constructivas [They demand of the present intellectual youth, the sensibility and the posture that characterized generations of the past and of the recent past. And since it is not possible for us to indulge them, serving them delicacies that fit the palate of an enlightened, unscathed system on a silver platter ... they encroach their lack of concrete direction, of clear definitions, and of constructive affirmations upon youth's thinking]. (221)

Inicial further stressed that, as a new generation, they were responsible for maintaining an "afinidad filial" [fraternal affinity] with the older generation and, furthermore, that they could even become "la negación viviente de las que la precedieron" [the living denial of those that preceded them] (221). Explaining that their perspective was in line with the latest European currents, recalling Ortega, *Inicial* emphasized that contradictory sensibilities separated the new generation from the previous one. If the preceding generation employed dogmatic systems to address their reality, the new generation dismissed all systematic approaches as unfit for its new era. Moreover, *Inicial* declared that Oswald Spengler, Ortega, and Henri Bergson embodied the new sensibility because they created "el material intelectual de las nuevas generaciones, y están definiendo esa actitud de simpatía infinita, de relativismo tolerante, de amor a la vida concreta, de odio a la inteligencia abstracta, de escepticismo fecundo, de lucha al sistema, que son las notas de este momento culminante de la mentalidad occidental" [the new generations' intellectual material, and they are defining that attitude of infinite likeability, of tolerant relativism, of love for a concrete life, of hate towards abstract intelligence, of fecund scepticism, of resistance to the system, that are the notes of this culminating moment of the West's mentality] (221). Additionally, in this editorial, *Inicial* addressed complaints they received regarding their acceptance of Ortega's theories. Responding to claims that Ortega's thinking was pagan, *Inicial* argued that those rendering such an opinion had not understood Ortega. They conceded that Ortega's ideas had "algo de paganismo" [some paganism] since "eso de amor a la vida" [that [concept] of love of life] that the philosopher professed "es una frase de sabor pagano" [has a pagan hue to it] (226). However, *Inicial* defended Ortega explaining that "ese amor a la vida de las nuevas generaciones de Occidente no es el mismo del de los griegos, que era amor a la vida carnal ... La palabra vida, en concreto, ha adquirido otro sentido que el pagano" [that love of life that the new generations in the West [profess] is not the same as that of the Greeks, that was love for carnal life ... Concretely, the word life has acquired a sense other than the pagan] (226). Ortega promoted the ability to fully engage in and cultivate life, not carnal debauchery.

In the same *Inicial* issue, Uruguayan Ariosto D. González commented on Ortega's *España invertebrada*. Like Carlos Américo Amaya did in *Valoraciones*, González explained that although Ortega's book specifically evaluated the Spanish condition, it also applied to Latin America because, "Herederos del genio español, los países de la América nuestra reproducen las líneas esenciales de la vieja metrópoli" [Heirs of Spanish genius, countries in our America replicate the old metropolis's essential lines] (261). For example, according to González, Latin America was also guilty of "individualismo exagerado ... la ineptitud para crear firmes y vastas unidades internacionales; el carácter personalista y arbitrario de la política; la incapacidad administrativa; el amor a la existencia turbulenta" [excessive individualism ... an ineptitude to create firm and vast international units; an arbitrary and personalist political character; administrative incompetence; love for a turbulent existence] and "el concepto caballeresco y trágico del deber cívico" [a tragic and chivalrous understanding of civic duty] (261). While on the one hand, González points to deeply rooted connections between Spanish and Latin American cultures, the product of colonialism, his purview highlights negative traits that the newly independent countries must be aware of as they forge their future. As a result, González insisted that Latin Americans pay attention to Ortega's observations on Spain, not to strengthen transatlantic ties, but in order to avoid reaching "la actual depresión de la Madre Patria" [the Mother Country's current depression] (268). Breaking with the colonial paradigm, his support of Orteguean philosophy is thus a call to Latin Americans to learn from Spain's shortcomings in order to circumvent them, like a child determined to avoid replicating a parent's mistakes.

Inicial and *Valoraciones* thus ascribed to Orteguean ideas in as much as they served their particular platforms and goals for social reform. While they highly respected his intellect and publications, as Ariosto D. González's observations on *España Invertebrada* make clear, this new Argentine generation was open to philosophies that resonated with them and to learning from the past. However, their actions did not mean that they were replicating a colonial paradigm as they emulated the Spanish philosopher's teachings. Instead, they were taking what they needed and what they felt applied to them from Orteguean thought. As both *Inicial* and *Valoraciones* outlined with certainty, each journal had a clear goal towards social reform and was firmly Argentine. Reaching across the Atlantic to engage with the former empire did not threaten their hard-won national boundaries. For his part, however, as we will see, Ortega did not easily relinquish a colonial power structure in which he dictated lessons to his subjects from a pulpit.

José Ortega y Gasset Responds to the "Nueva Generación"

Ortega first visited Argentina from July 1916 to January 1917. Invited by the Institución Cultural Española [Spanish Culture Institution] to give a series of lectures, he primarily spoke in Buenos Aires, but also travelled to Argentine provinces Tucumán, Rosario, Mendoza, and Córdoba. In Buenos Aires, Ortega gave a ten-lecture series entitled "Introducción a los problemas generales de la filosofía" [Introduction to Philosophy's

General Problems] at the University of Buenos Aires and two public talks: one at the Teatro Odeón [Odeón Theatre] (15 November 1916) and the other at the Teatro de la Ópera [Opera Theatre] (22 November 1916). In particular, Ortega's lecture "La nueva sensibilidad" [The New Sensibility] at the Teatro Odeón articulated many of the ideas he would later publish in *El tema de nuestro tiempo* that profoundly influenced Argentina's "Nueva Generación." Ortega and his philosophies were well received in Buenos Aires, where many events were held in his honour, such as a banquet sponsored by the preceding generation's journal *Nosotros*. Moreover, the feeling was mutual as the Spanish philosopher recounted in his journal *El Espectador* [The Spectator] in 1917. He sensed that his ideas were better received in Argentina than in Spain: "*El Espectador* es y tal vez será mejor entendido – mejor sentido – en la Argentina que en España. Podrá herir nuestra nacional presunción, pero es el caso que ese pueblo, hijo de España, parece hoy más perspicaz más curioso, más capaz de emoción que el metropolitano" [*The Spectator* is and perhaps will be better understood – better felt – in Argentina than in Spain. It could hurt our national conceit, but the reality is that those peoples, children of Spain, seem today more perceptive, more curious, more capable of emotion, than the metropolis] (9). Although Ortega praises Latin America and critiques Spain, like a parent who always sees his offspring, even when they reach adulthood, as children, his comments are still deeply entrenched in a colonial paradigm. From this perspective, considering Argentina an extension of Spain, and its population part of the Spanish race, during this first visit, Ortega assumed the responsibility of guiding and educating the former colonies' zealous and motivated younger generation. As a result, following this trip, when Ortega became a frequent contributor to *La Nación*, where he published articles from 1923 to 1952, he engaged *Inicial* and *Valoraciones*. Gratified by the attention the journals had given him between September 1923 and March 1924, Ortega thus used this platform to acknowledge their enthusiasm for his teachings. He responded to *Valoraciones* and *Inicial* writing two articles in *La Nación*: "El deber de la nueva generación argentina" [Argentina's New Generation's Duty] (6 April 1924) and "Para dos revistas argentinas" [For Two Argentine Journals] (27 April 1924).[6]

In "El deber de la nueva generación argentina," Ortega first addressed Carlos Américo Amaya's review of *España invertebrada* in *Valoraciones*, calling it "la nota más exacta que se ha hecho sobre aquel libro mío" [The most precise note that has been written about that book of mine] (*Los escritos* 47).[7] He further appreciated the review because his book had received little attention in Spain. Ortega then offered his advice to *Valoraciones* and *Inicial* as representatives of Argentina's new generation. First, he explained that Spanish intellectual life was undergoing a period of what he termed "monolingüismo" [monolingualism] because, rather than participating in a productive discussion, Spanish intellectuals were aggressively disparaging each other (*Los escritos* 48). Fearing that the same could occur in Argentina and, by extension, in Latin America, Ortega urged Argentina's young intellectuals to seek a "férrea disciplina interior" [fierce interior discipline] because "[t]odas las labores valiosas que se han cumplido en la historia nacieron de esa disciplina dura, vibrante, que no sostiene el menor abandono o flojera" [all valuable acts that have been accomplished in history originated from that tough, vibrant discipline, that does not allow for the slightest abandon or weakness] (*Los escritos* 49). He thus encouraged them to employ disciplined reflection in order to effect constructive social change. According to Ortega, Argentina's new generation needed to become "Una juventud que aspire a ser no consecuencia, repercusión, eco del pretérito en decadencia, sino al contrario, iniciación de un proceso ascensional y constructor" [A youth that aspires to be, not a consequence or repercussion, echoing a preterite in decline, but to the contrary, the initiation of a rising and building process] (*Los escritos* 49). By taking on this role, however, the younger generation would bear the responsibility of leadership, which entails being open to outside influences, but also discerning in choosing models to follow. Discipline, reflection, and acumen would enable them to develop their own "repertorio de ideas claras y firmes" [repertoire of clear and firm ideas] (*Los escritos* 50). Therefore, most likely pointing to *Inicial*'s belligerence, Ortega expressed his concern that *Valoraciones* and *Inicial*'s approach was reactive, criticizing both journals for focusing "el ataque a lo que no se estima" [an attack on what is not esteemed] (*Los escritos* 50). Antagonistic cries for change were counterproductive because they did not promote lasting solutions.

Ortega's second article addressing *Inicial* and *Valoraciones*, "Para dos revistas argentinas," appeared in *La Nación* on 27 April 1924. First, he reiterated his appreciation for *Valoraciones*'s Carlos Américo Amaya, this time for his "certera nota" [accurate note] on *España invertebrada* (*Los escritos* 53). The focus of his article, however, was *Inicial*'s December 1923 review of *El tema de nuestro tiempo* entitled "Un filósofo de la nueva generación." While Ortega conceded that "[e]l autor ha penetrado bien en el sentido de mis pensamientos," [the author has accurately delved into the sense of my thoughts], he was disappointed that the article had linked his philosophies to pragmatism (*Los escritos* 53). For Ortega, such an association was the gravest offence that could be bestowed on a philosopher because "[e]l pragmatismo no ha sido nunca una filosofía de filósofos, sino, a lo sumo, una filosofía para los incapaces de tener ninguna" [pragmatism has never been a philosophy for philosophers, instead, at most, a philosophy for those incapable of having one] (*Los escritos* 54). In order to clarify *Inicial*'s misunderstanding of his philosophies, Ortega thus dedicated the remainder of the article to carefully articulating how his thinking was unrelated to pragmatism.

Ortega's response to *Inicial* proves surprising for two reasons. First, Ortega neglects to acknowledge the article's main focus, which details the value of his philosophies for the new generation. Second, although *Inicial* does consider pragmatism in its discussion of Ortega's philosophies, the review painstakingly details a nuanced perspective on the topic. *Inicial* mentions that it is true that Ortega's theories have some commonalities with pragmatism because they deal with "la verdad como un simple proceso biológico de adaptación a fines prácticos" [truth as a simple biological process to be adapted to practical ends] (59). However, the review makes clear that there is a huge difference between "el pragmatismo yanki" [Yankee pragmatism] and Ortega y Gasset's plain interpretation of the current moment (59). Unlike Ortega's views, pragmatism is speculative, "inventa un nuevo método flexible, cómodo, elástico, anchuroso, para darnos una explicación filosófica del relativismo científico y para adaptarlo a nuestros fines prácticos" [[it] invents a new flexible, comfortable, elastic, broad method that offers a philosophical explanation of scientific relativism in order to adapt it to practical matters] (60). For Ortega, on the other hand, according to *Inicial*, a new philosophical current lacking any systematic spirit is developing, one that affirms life's value through pure circumstantial spontaneity (60). *Inicial*'s discussion of pragmatism and Orteguean theory could thus be read as a defence of Ortega in opposition to pragmatism. Yet, in his assessment of *Inicial*'s review, Ortega does not consider the distinction the Argentine journal makes between pragmatism and his views.

Ortega's articles dedicated to *Valoraciones* and *Inicial* exhibit appreciation for the younger generation's attention to his work, but do not engage the intellectuals critiquing his work. Rather than participate in a dialogue, the Spanish writer takes the opportunity to "parent" *Valoraciones* and *Inicial*. His first article offers advice that, though useful especially in light of *Inicial*'s combativeness, does not lead to further discussion. Likewise, his second article is more concerned with ensuring his philosophies are accurately understood than in responding to *Inicial*'s commentary. As a result, although Ortega does theoretically respond to the Argentine journals, he misses the opportunity to develop a conversation regarding their distinct efforts to take his lessons and apply them to their present in order to effect social change. Nevertheless, *Inicial* and *Valoraciones* continued to address the philosopher.

Although not direct responses, following Ortega's articles in *La Nación*, *Inicial* and *Valoraciones* published two more articles on the Spanish philosopher in 1924. Homero M. Guglielmini's "Algo más sobre Ortega y Gasset" [Something Else about Ortega y Gasset] appeared in *Inicial* 5 (May 1924) and Carlos Américo Amaya reviewed *El tema de nuestro tiempo* for *Valoraciones* (July 1924). In "Algo más sobre Ortega y Gasset" Guglielmini noted that, unlike Argentina's "Nueva Generación," Europe's younger generation had not responded to Ortega, which is why, he claimed, Ortega had engaged in a dialogue with Argentina's new generation in *La Nación*. Guglielmini underscored that *Inicial* was proud to have played an important role in initiating a discussion with the Spanish philosopher. Offering yet another summary of Ortega's theories, Guglielmini emphasized that Ortega's greatest contribution as a philosopher was his ability to interpret his era (377). However, Guglielmini did not address Ortega's efforts to defend his philosophies against pragmatism. In fact, it would seem that Guglielmini either did not read, or did not pay close attention to Ortega's article in *La Nación* because he actually referred to Ortega's postures in *El tema de nuestro tiempo* as pragmatic. In closing, Guglielmini did note that Ortega had offered much advice to Argentina's younger generation, but that *Inicial* would respond to this topic at a later date.

Two months later, in a similar and brief account, Carlos Américo Amaya's review of *El tema de nuestro tiempo* (*Valoraciones* 4 July 1924) synthesized Ortega's theory on generations. Just as *Inicial* proposed in "Un filósofo de la Nueva Generación," Amaya accentuated the relevance of Ortega's ideas for Argentina's young intellectuals. Echoing Guglielmini's comment that Ortega's greatest achievement was his ability to assess the current era, Amaya affirmed that "Entre la nueva generación argentina, la influencia de Ortega es evidente; y no podía resultar de otro modo ya que este pensador al hacer la anatomía de nuestro tiempo, sugiere ideas, alude a hechos que constituyen algo así como la fisiología del momento histórico" [Among Argentina's new Generation, Ortega's influence is evident; and it could not be any other way since this thinker, in making the anatomy of our time, suggests ideas, alludes to facts that constitute something akin to the physiology of this moment in history] (78). Américo Amaya makes no mention of pragmatism.

Inicial did not respond to Ortega's advice in *La Nación* as Guglielmini had promised, but the journal did write Ortega a letter regarding

Revista de Occidente (Madrid 1923–36) in September 1924. If *Inicial* had advocated Ortega and his philosophies in almost every issue, this letter offered yet another expression of solidarity with the philosopher, his goals, and now, *Revista de Occidente*. First, *Inicial* underlined its kinship with *Revista de Occidente* because both journals were founded at about the same time (*Revista de Occidente* in July 1923 and *Inicial* in October 1923). Moreover, if *Revista de Occidente* embodied the "nueva sensibilidad" [new sensibility] in Spain, *Inicial* professed "esa manera de ver el actual momento histórico" [that way of seeing the present moment] on the other side of the Atlantic (489). According to *Inicial*, although *Revista de Occidente* could be considered "el fruto maduro de discreta y larga meditación" [the mature fruit of discreet and long meditation] while *Inicial* embodied "la expresión de un fervoroso entusiasmo juvenil" [the expression of youth's fervent enthusiasm], both journals shared "la misma ansiedad" [the same anxiety] (489). Therefore, *Inicial* and *Revista de Occidente* bridged the Atlantic by connecting Spain and Latin America in the united effort to reignite Hispanic culture: "La *Revista de Occidente* e INICIAL[*sic*] han surgido de una común inspiración, y realizan así, un acorde perfecto a través de la distancia, incorporándose a esa vaga armonía que en Europa y América entona el treno fúnebre de una cultura que muere y la música augural de una cultura que nace" [*Revista de Occidente* and *Inicial* have emerged from a common inspiration, and in this manner accomplish a perfect accord through the distance, joining that vague rhythm that in Europe and in America harmonizes the funeral chant of one culture that expires and the auspicious music of one that is born] (489). *Inicial*'s editors thus underscored that, not only did they ascribe to the Spanish philosopher's theoretical proposals, like *Revista de Occidente*, their journal also embodied them. Moreover, this review points to *Inicial*'s awareness that, as a medium, journals, magazines, and newspapers played a crucial role in traversing boundaries to shape a transatlantic postcolonial relationship between Spain and Latin America. In this particular case, print media not only crossed borders, but generations.

Ortega's "Generación contra generación" [Generation against Generation] (*La Nación* 28 July 1924), responded to a separate debate in *La Nación* on his theory of generations, but it is worth mentioning because he rearticulated his theory of generations from *El tema de nuestro tiempo* in order to defend the young Argentine intellectuals who were drawing fire for having assimilated his ideas.[8] "Carta a un joven argentino que estudia filosofía" [Letter to a Young Argentine Who Studies Philosophy] (*La Nación* 28 December 1924) concludes the series of articles that Ortega directed to *Inicial* and *Valoraciones*. In *Los escritos de Ortega y Gasset en* La

Nación *1923–1952* [Ortega y Gasset's Writings in *La Nación* 1923–1952], Natalio R. Botana speculates that this article most likely addressed *Inicial*'s Homero M.Guglielmini (65). Here Ortega summarized the main ideas he had been conveying to Argentina's young intellectuals. First, he stressed that while Argentina's new generation inspired much hope, he was not yet certain they would succeed in their endeavours:

> La nueva generación goza de una espléndida dosis de fuerza vital, condición primera de toda empresa histórica, por eso, espero en ella. Pero, a la vez, sospecho que carece por completo de disciplina interna – sin la cual la fuerza se desagrega y volatiliza –, por eso, desconfío de ella. No basta curiosidad para ir hacia las cosas: hace falta rigor mental para hacerse dueño de ellas [The new generation possesses a heaping dose of vital strength, the first condition necessary for all historical enterprises, which is why I trust it. But, at the same time, I suspect that it entirely lacks internal discipline – without which that strength disaggregates and becomes volatile – which is why I don't trust it. Curiosity is not enough to go towards things: mental rigour is necessary to own them]. (*Los escritos* 66)

Once again, Ortega accentuated the need for young intellectuals to be disciplined and constructive. Seeing "demasiado énfasis y poca precisión" [too much emphasis and too little precision] in the "Nueva Generación" journals, he observed that Argentina's young intellectuals, like all Latin Americans, were guilty of excessive narcissism (*Los escritos* 66). According to Ortega, narcissism led to superficial and reactionary evaluations of situations instead of more profound and productive analysis. Ortega insisted that Argentina's young generation overcome their limited perspective in order to effect real progress because "la ciencia y las letras no consisten en tomar posturas delante de las cosas, sino en irrumpir frenéticamente dentro de ellas" [Science and Letters do not consist of taking positions on things, but of frenetically bursting into them] (*Los escritos* 66). He also cautioned that, unless they became introspective and disciplined, they would not become self-sufficient and generate their own distinct ideas. Instead, they would depend "integralmente de Europa en el orden intelectual" [integrally on Europe in the intellectual realm] (*Los escritos* 66). Ortega concluded by reiterating that Argentina's "Nueva Generación" exhibited much promise, but would only earn his trust in their success when he noticed it "resuelta a cultivar muy en serio el gran deporte de la precisión mental" [resolved to very seriously cultivate the great sport of mental precision] (*Los escritos* 68). As the next part of this chapter explains, Spanish students from the University of Salamanca would see the "Nueva Generación" very differently. Moreover, by following Latin America's lead, they would "irrumpir frenéticamente" on the imperial paradigm framing Spain and Latin America's postcolonial relationship, reconfiguring it entirely.

In as much as journals and newspapers moved ideas across borders, the brief print exchanges between Argentina's new generation and José Ortega y Gasset were productive because it contributed to the development of a postcolonial transatlantic relationship between Spain and Latin America, effectively bridging the Atlantic. At the same time, however, these communications highlighted boundaries that were yet to be overcome. To an extent, all parties involved were unable to shed empire's longstanding demarcations. Although Ariosto D. González's contribution points out that Argentina's younger generation was applying Orteguean thought to their reality as a means of avoiding the backwardness Spain had succumbed to, the overall enthusiasm both *Inicial* and *Valoraciones* expressed for the Spanish thinker did, to an extent, replicate a colonial paradigm. At the same time, although Ortega encouraged the "Nueva Generación" to generate their own ideas and overcome their dependence on Europe, his paternalism reinforced the power structure that he preached against as he dictated behaviour from his pulpits at *La Nación* and the University of Buenos Aires.[9] Moreover, while the Spanish philosopher proclaimed that he wrote for Latin America's younger generation because he was disillusioned with young European intellectuals, Ortega also directed his writing to the "Nueva Generación" because he considered Argentina, at least culturally, an extension of Spain rather than an autonomous nation. Nevertheless, taking place across journals and newspapers, these interactions outline the new generation's distinct effort towards reconfiguring a postcolonial relationship. Both *Inicial* and *Valoraciones* would persist in their efforts to break with past practices and fuel a new, modern future through activism. Their work contributed to the university reform movement that began in Córdoba, Argentina, in 1918 and would spread throughout Latin America. And, as we will see, the university reform movement would play a pivotal role in inverting the colonial power structure between Spain and Latin America.

Inverting the Colonial Paradigm: Solidarity and University Reform

One of Argentina's New Generation's most significant contributions to breaking with the past and applying an Orteguean new sensibility to their reality was the university reform movement, which began in Córdoba in 1918 and quickly expanded across Latin America.[10] Most importantly, however, serving as a model for Spanish university students seeking to reconstruct their own archaic institutions, the *Reforma Universitaria* [University Reform] movement would significantly contribute to breaking with the colonial power structure that overwhelmingly characterized Spain and Latin America's transatlantic relationship. In order to explain how this consequential shift came to be, this section will first briefly contextualize the *Reforma Universitaria* movement within Latin America. It will then describe how, spurred by Latin American actions, the Spanish journal *El Estudiante* (Salamanca-Madrid 1924–6) would initiate an unprecedented transatlantic call for solidarity that completely redesigned a Spanish/Latin American cultural field.

In 1916, Hipólito Yrigoyen became president of Argentina, initiating a period of liberal governments that lasted until 1930 (including the presidency of Marcelo T. de Alvear from 1922 to 1928), with the *coup d'état* led by General José Félix Uriburu. Contrasting the conservative period that preceded his government, Yrigoyen supported freedom of the press and of expression. His liberal government enabled movements such as the 1918 *Reforma Universitaria*, which began when university students in Córdoba demanded the democratization of higher education. They called for academic freedom, free tuition, unrestricted access, and student participation in university governance. Journals, magazines, and newspapers would play a key part in disseminating this call for democratic change enabling the movement to quickly spread across national boundaries throughout Latin America and lead to events such as the 1925 Primer Congreso internacional de estudiantes [First International Student Conference] in Mexico City. As previously noted, in Argentina, *Valoraciones* appeared when students from the University of La Plata known as the "Grupo Renovación" came together in order to support *Reforma Universitaria*. Also from the University of La Plata, the journal *Sagitario* (La Plata 1924–7) promoted a similar agenda, and, in Mexico, José Vasconcelos's weekly *La Antorcha* (Mexico 1924–5) similarly endorsed student activism on educational reform. Efforts to promote University Reform in these publications were also connected to the contentious discussions surrounding *hispano/iberoamericanismo* discussed in chapter 1. Within the university reform context, however, the terms were used to promote transnational collaboration and effect change across Latin America, thereby circumventing the limitations that hard-won national identities and a colonial legacy of oppression posed to such unity. Solidarity regarding *hispano/iberoamericanismo* also hinged upon other social causes, such as political oppression, Augusto Leguía's government in Peru in particular, and US intervention in Latin

America. My focus here, however, is on university reform and the following examples from *Valoraciones* and *La Antorcha* illustrate how these journals endorsed this movement and used it to promote transnational solidarity across Latin America.

Valoraciones, as noted above, primarily reported on issues pertaining to *Reforma Universitaria* in Argentine universities such as the Universidad de La Plata and the Universidad de Buenos Aires. However, traversing national bounds, the journal also paid attention to the movement's broader scope throughout Latin America. For instance, the second issue (January 1924) honoured recently deceased Argentine poet and activist Héctor Ripa Alberdi precisely for his efforts in advancing university reform across national borders. Dedicating the entire tome to Alberdi, *Valoraciones* published his poetry along with his speeches to university students in Mexico and in Peru. For instance, at the previously mentioned Primer Congreso internacional de estudiantes [First International Student Conference] in Mexico, Alberdi had pronounced the speech, "Por la unión moral de América" [For America's Moral Unification], where he called on all Latin American university students to participate in "el renacer vigoroso de la filosofía idealista y la sana rebeldía de la juventud" [a vigorous rebirth of idealist philosophy and youth's healthy rebellion] (115). From Alberdi's perspective, *Reforma Universitaria* needed to be a transnational effort in Latin America if it expected to effect systemic change: "Contribuyamos todos a este nuevo despertar del espíritu ... es menester arrojar a los mercaderes de la enseñanza, derrumbar la universidad profesionalista y levantar sobre sus escombros la academia ideal de los hombres" [Let us all contribute to this new spiritual awakening ... it is imperative that education merchants be tossed, that the professionalism-focused university be demolished, and that its wreckage becomes the ideal academy for humanity] (115).

Sharing Héctor Ripa Alberdi's perspective, in Mexico, José Vasconcelos's *La Antorcha* (Mexico 1924–5), as we will see, endorsed a cooperative, transnational vision of *Reforma Universitaria*. As Secretary of Education (1921–4), Vasconcelos had revolutionized his country's educational system. He reorganized the department of education into three branches (schools, arts and libraries, and archives) and promoted education by founding schools in provincial communities, making literature available to the masses by publishing inexpensive editions, creating libraries, and inaugurating the first national book fair in Mexico, an event that takes place to this day. The Mexican thinker was also responsible for commissioning murals by now well-known Mexican artists Diego Rivera, José Clemente Orozco, Diego Alfaro Siqueiros, Roberto

Montenegro, and Jean Charlot on government buildings. Moreover, his journals *El Maestro* (Mexico 1921–3) and *La Antorcha* played a significant role in publicizing his vision of reform for Mexico and for Latin America. Although Vasconcelos claimed that *La Antorcha* would have "una entonación general y elevada que esté por encima de las ambiciones mezquinas y de las pasiones personales" [a general and elevated tone that surpasses miserly ambitions and personal passions], the journal primarily focused on his interest in education: "Educar al pueblo para que el progreso adquirido se conserve. Educarlo para que, como una consecuencia natural, desaparezca el caudillo. Convencerlo de que no es posible que un solo hombre encarne el talento o encarne la fuerza o encarne el éxito" [Educate the people so that acquired progress may be preserved. Educate it so that a natural consequence is the eradication of autocratic leaders. Convince the people that it is not possible for only one man to embody talent, strength, and success] ("Programa" [Program] 1). For Vasconcelos, education was the only means of achieving peace and solidarity. He wanted to educate people to understand that change could only be attained through collaboration. And, affirming egalitarian views that opposed racial and cultural hegemonies, Vasconcelos's journal was also meant to "demostrarle [al pueblo] que el talento, la fuerza o el éxito, no son monopolio de nadie en los pueblos que han sobrepasado el régimen de tribu" [prove [to the people] that no individual can monopolize talent, strength, and success in peoples that have surpassed tribal regimes]; for him, reform was a collective endeavour ("Programa" [Program] 1).

Going back to *La Antorcha*'s support of a *Reforma Universitaria* as the transnational movement Héctor Ripa Alberdi had envisioned, the journal consistently reported on actions taking place throughout the continent. For example, it featured multiple articles by Argentine political thinker Alfredo Palacios, such as his address "A la juventud universitaria de Iberoamérica" [To Ibero America's University Youth], in which he incited Latin America's young generation to abandon European models in their quest for educational reform. Palacios argued that, currently in a state of decadence, Europe could no longer provide a suitable example for Latin America. Thus, coinciding with Ortega y Gasset's advice to Argentina's "Nueva Generación," Palacios encouraged Latin Americans to focus on themselves by coming together in solidarity to effect change. Endorsing Palacios's ideology, *La Antorcha* helped promote the university reform movement throughout Latin America. For instance, in "Las tres claridades" [The Three Clarities] (*La Antorcha* 4 1924) Vasconcelos responded to a request for support from the "Asociación de Estudiantes Universitarios e Intelectuales de Costa Rica" [Costa Rican

Association of University Students and Intellectuals]. These Costa Rican intellectuals pledged their solidarity with Vasconcelos's vision as "Una legión de jóvenes, vinculados por una misma sangre, ungidos por una misma lengua, quemados por un mismo ideal … [c]reemos en la raza que palpita en todos los pechos de las generaciones vivientes de Nuestra América" [A legion of young men and women, bound by one blood, anointed by one language, inflamed by the same ideal … [w]e believe in the race that beats in all living generations in Our America], and asked for Vasconcelos's guidance ("Proclama de los Estudiantes e Intelectuales de Costa Rica al Lic. Jose Vasconcelos" [Costa Rican Students and Intellectuals Proclamation to Lic. Jose Vasconcelos] 18). Humbled that they had addressed him as "maestro" [teacher/master], and inspired by their conviction, Vasconcelos pledged that, even from a distance, he would work with them ("Las tres claridades" [The Three Clarities]1–2). Finally, consistent with his vision of a united Hispanic race detailed in *La raza cósmica* [The Cosmic Race] (1923) discussed in chapter 1, Vasconcelos also endorsed transatlantic ventures promoting *Reforma Universitaria*. For example, *La Antorcha* published a "Mensaje de la Federación universitaria americana a las juventudes de América y España" [Message from the American University Federation to youth in America and Spain] (10 January 1925), which called for collaboration between Spanish and Latin American students.

Inverting the Paradigm: *El Estudiante* Shifts the Cultural Field[11]

Vasconcelos's *La Antorcha*, and La Plata's *Valoraciones* exemplify how journals that were notably committed to specific nations, were also transgressing national confines across Latin America to promote transnational solidarity surrounding university reform during the 1920s. Social reform was thus able to accomplish the cultural unity that proponents of *hispanoamericanismo* like Federico García Godoy, described in chapter 1, envisioned. Whereas ascribing to *hispano/iberoamericanismo*, for many, implied relinquishing national cultural identities in favour of a transnational one that emerged from the violence and oppression of colonization, social reform allowed nations to champion a common goal without this sacrifice. As a medium able to simultaneously endorse strong national identities while welcoming voices from across the continent (and the Atlantic for that matter), journals, magazines, and newspapers were an ideal conduit to make it possible. Not only could each volume take readers across borders from one page to the next, as Girondo's previously described journey illustrates, journals could also physically travel as national emissaries. The next example illustrates how, landing across the Atlantic into the hands of enthusiastic students at the University of Salamanca, Latin American journals would bring the spirit of university reform to the former empire and inspire its new generation.

Contradicting Ortega y Gasset's claim that young European intellectuals were demoralized, in May 1925 a group of students from the University of Salamanca intent on transforming Spain's educational stagnation and overall cultural decay founded *El Estudiante: Semanario de la juventud escolar española* (Salamanca and Madrid 1925–6). The new Latin American generation that demanded university reform and was committed to divesting itself from antiquated ideals energized Spanish students in *El Estudiante* who similarly wanted to free Spain from "sombras engañosas de otro siglo" [deceiving shadows from another century] ("Nuestra Misión" 1). Their very institution, the University of Salamanca founded in 1134, stood as an indisputable symbol for Spain's past, which they felt still weighted down the present. This generation of Salamanca students thus wanted to remove the cobwebs that prevented their country from entering modernity and viewed higher education reform as an important first step. Cultural and political transformation in Spain implied resistance to Miguel Primo de Rivera's dictatorship and *El Estudiante* daringly touted an anti-oppression political agenda despite the regime's censorship (visible in every issue of the magazine). Reaching far beyond their institution's walls, *El Estudiante* provided a democratic space in which university students from all across Spain could express their views on education, such as the role of women in the classroom, incompetent professors, and the misguided use of testing. In so doing, *El Estudiante*'s editors hoped to inform, unite, and enlist other Spanish students in their cause.

While Ortega y Gasset's theories fuelled *Valoraciones*'s and *Inicial*'s objectives, in turn, *El Estudiante* sought to emulate "La acción removedora de las juventudes universitarias de América" [America's university youth's agitating action], thereby inverting the colonial paradigm ("Nuestra Misión" [Our Mission] 1). Just as *Reforma Universitaria* across Latin America had contributed "como nadie a crear la Universidad nueva, hoy próspera y fecunda, liquidando la triste herencia escolástica de la época colonial" [like no one to create the new University, prosperous and fecund today, liquidating the colonial era's sad scholastic legacy], *El Estudiante* wanted the Old World to shed colonial-era ideologies through educational reform ("Nuestra Misión" [Our Mission] 1). Thus, seeking guidance from their Latin American counterparts, *El*

Estudiante's first issue initiated a transatlantic dialogue when it introduced the recurring section "América":

> Enviamos desde aquí un saludo reverente a los grandes maestros de tierras americanas y un mensaje de cordial solidaridad a aquellas juventudes estudiosas, que representan acaso lo mejor de la savia espiritual vitalizadora de nuestra vieja España. Y les pedimos el calor de su simpatía, un aliento fraternal, para nuestra empresa apasionada de lucha por ideales que nos son comunes [From here we send a reverent greeting to America's great teachers and a message of cordial solidarity to its studious youth that, perhaps, represents the best of ancient Spain's spiritual vitality. And we request the warmth of their friendship, fraternal support for our passionate enterprise that fights for ideals we share]. (8)

Focusing on reform and appealing to a shared cultural heritage, the Salamanca students sought solidarity with Latin America and wanted to establish a new transatlantic relationship that could overcome a history of colonization and violent struggles for independence: "La nueva generación ... nuestra juventud universitaria victoriosa, es la llamada a abrir a nuestra nación la ruta espiritual de América, y esta vez no en son de conquista, sino en empresa de hermandad" [The new generation ... our young victorious university students, are called upon to open for our nation, a spiritual route towards America, and, this time, not to conquer, but as an enterprise of fellowship] ("Otra vez la voz de América" [Again, America's Voice] July 1925, 10). Thus, if print exchanges between *Valoraciones* and *Inicial* and Ortega y Gasset had largely replicated colonial power structures, *El Estudiante* more faithfully promoted the values of the "Nueva Generación." Albeit briefly, the Spanish journal daringly established an entirely new transatlantic relationship initiating dialogues with *Valoraciones*, *Sagitario*, Argentine politician Alfredo L. Palacios, and Mexican philosopher José Vasconcelos.

Endorsing to *El Estudiante*'s proposed shift in a transatlantic Spanish American field, *Valoraciones* and "Grupo Renovación" responded to the Spanish journal's call for solidarity, reviewing it in June 1925. In "De la España joven" [From Young Spain], *Valoraciones* applauded the Salamanca students' audacious undertaking by declaring them "bravos amigos del quijotesco Unamuno" [fierce friends of quixotic Unamuno] (315). First, Spanish novelist Miguel de Unamuno and Salamanca go hand in hand, as he was dean of the university and famously removed from his two university chairs in 1924 by Miguel Primo de Rivera. In fact, *El Estudiante* dedicated its first issue to the one Spanish intellectual they sought to emulate. Second, the adjective quijotesco alludes to the fact that just like Miguel de Cervantes Saavedra's well-known protagonist, Don Quijote, in his efforts to uphold his ideals, Unamuno was valiant. Therefore, in underscoring the students' connection to Unamuno in this manner, the Argentine journal implied that *El Estudiante*'s action was also heroic. In particular, the Argentine journal commended *El Estudiante*'s brave stance against Primo de Rivera's dictatorship and wondered why more Spanish intellectuals did not join their cause: "[s]i en Salamanca, donde todo lo vetusto tiene su origen y asiento, pueden decirse verdades tan rotundas, ¿cómo el resto de la masa liberal española permanece callada?" [If in Salamanca, birthplace of everything ancient, such bold truths can be told, how is it that the rest of Spain's liberal population remains silent?] (315). According to *Valoraciones, El Estudiante* proved that reform movements were possible in Spain, even during a dictatorship, because their effort emerged from one of Spain's most conservative institutions.

Concurrent with its exchange with *Valoraciones, El Estudiante* engaged a brief dialogue with another journal from the University of La Plata also directed by Carlos Américo Amaya, *Sagitario* (La Plata, 1925–8). Praising the journal's position that educational reform played a crucial role in achieving broader social progress, *El Estudiante* reviewed *Sagitario* in "Una nueva revista" [A New Magazine] in July 1925. *Sagitario* responded enthusiastically in March 1926 and, like *Valoraciones*, lauded *El Estudiante*'s dauntless stance against Spain's political oppression. The Argentine journal expressed its solidarity with the Spanish students' struggle: "Los representantes de la España digna, para América y para los hombres libres, no están en los ministerios, están en *El Estudiante* … Con el nuevo espíritu, toda nuestra solidaridad" [Representatives of a dignified Spain, for America and for free peoples, are not in governmental departments, they are in *El Estudiante* … With this new spirit, all of our solidarity] ("Una nueva revista" [A New Magazine] 10).

In addition to its interactions with Argentine journals, *El Estudiante* sought guidance from Latin American intellectuals Alfredo L. Palacios in Argentina and José Vasconcelos in Mexico. In doing so, the journal not only inverted the colonial power structure but also wrested authority from Ortega y Gasset, a prominent figure in their field of cultural production. The Spanish publication thus made its position clear: Latin American, not Spanish, models would be instrumental in seeking progress and reform in Spain. *El Estudiante* commented on Palacios's speech "A la juventud universitaria de Iberoamérica" [To Spanish America's University Youth] in its second issue (25 May 1925), a gesture that the Argentine politician would respond to in "A los estudiantes españoles"

[To Spanish Students] (6 December 1925). In "A la juventud universitaria de Iberoamérica," Palacios advocated educational reform and a federation of Spanish American countries. The Argentine politician incited Latin America's young generation to abandon European models in their quest for educational reform, arguing that, currently in a state of decline, Europe could no longer provide a suitable example for Latin America. And, coinciding with Ortega y Gasset's advice to Argentina's "Nueva Generación," Palacios encouraged Latin Americans to focus on themselves by coming together in solidarity to effect change (*La Antorcha* 15, 9) His views and support of students across Latin America earned him the title "Maestro de la Juventud" [Teacher of Youth], granted by the 1925 Primer Congreso internacional de estudiantes [First International Student Conference]held in Mexico. Seeing Palacios as their "maestro" as well, *El Estudiante* praised the Argentine's efforts to bridge "nuestro pueblo con la joven y vigorosa nación argentina" [our people with Argentina's young and vigorous nation] ("América" 9). The journal also championed Palacios's call for a "confederación de los pueblos ibero-americanos" [Confederation of Spanish American Nations] as a means of strengthening Hispanic culture against the United States' expanding hegemony ("América" 9). In his response to *El Estudiante* entitled "A los estudiantes españoles," Palacios enthusiastically offered his solidarity with the Spanish cause and commended the journal's views on *iberoamericanismo,* a topic this chapter will address in the following section. He believed that Spain and Latin America needed to capitalize on their shared racial heritage to bring about change: "nuestra raza deberá decir al mundo su palabra, portadora de un mensaje de justicia y de fraternidad" [our race should voice its message of justice and fellowship to the world] ("A los estudiantes españoles 2). *El Estudiante* shared Palacios's view on *iberoamericanismo* and would similarly coincide with José Vasconcelos's position on this debate, discussed earlier in chapter 1.

El Estudiante dedicated its eighth issue to José Vasconcelos (June 1925), opening with a "Saludo a Vasconcelos" [Greeting to Vasconcelos] that highlighted its admiration for the Mexican leader in educational reform. The Spanish students pointed to his "voz de maestro, de campeón de empresas ideales ... tal vez, en el presente, la más potente y sonora de toda América latina" [voice of a teacher, champion of idealist enterprises ... perhaps, at present, the most powerful and resounding one in Latin America] as an alternative to Spain's "casta de 'intelectuales' dormilones" [cast of sluggish intellectuals] ("Saludo a Vasconcelos" [Greeting to Vasconcelos] 1). The same issue contains Vasconcelos's response to *El Estudiante* in "Vasconcelos los estudiantes españoles"

[Vasconcelos to Spanish Students]. Since the Mexican intellectual firmly advocated *iberoamericanismo,* he supported *El Estudiante*'s appeal for solidarity between Spain and Latin America based on a shared heritage: "Jóvenes españoles, sois europeos y está bien que viváis con Europa, pero recordad ... que esa misma sangre que en vosotros hierve es la sangre que, renovada en la América, se enciende en el afán de un mundo espiritual nuevo" [Young Spaniards, you are European and it is well and good that you live in Europe, but remember ... that the same blood that boils in you, rejuvenated in America, lights up in a desire for a new spiritual world] ("Vasconcelos a los estudiantes españoles" [Vasconcelos to Spanish Students] 2). Vasconcelos emphasized that, although Spain and Latin America were bound by the same race, in a role reversal, Latin America, progressive and innovative, had become a model for the former empire's decaying society. However, the Mexican philosopher insisted that Spain's younger generation bore a responsibility imposed upon them by the conquest. He called on Spanish youth to recognize that they also shared a cultural affinity with Indigenous races. Moreover, Vasconcelos affirmed that although they were European, they were also Spanish and "principalmente, por ser españoles, sois también iberoamericanos" [precisely because you are Spanish, you are also Spanish American] ("Vasconcelos a los estudiantes españoles" [Vasconcelos to Spanish Students] 2). Furthermore, sharing *El Estudiante*'s vision of creating a new relationship with Latin America that could transcend colonial resentments, the Mexican politician acknowledged that the time had arrived to move forward: "La América española no guarda rencor al pueblo español, porque junto con nosotros ha sufrido, porque nuestras penas y nuestros yerros han sido comunes. Haced vosotros, los jóvenes de hoy, que también sea común el esfuerzo ardiente de la libertad y el amor al progreso." [Spanish America harbours no rancour towards the Spanish people, because along with us, Spain has suffered; we share sorrows and errors. You, today's youth, come together in a joint ardent effort towards liberty and love of progress] ("Vasconcelos a los estudiantes españoles" [Vasconcelos to Spanish Students] 2). For Vasconcelos, cultural solidarity outweighed resentments about a past that could not be changed. But, more importantly, as *iberoamericanos,* Latin Americans and Spaniards were one race and, as such, equally responsible for their violent history.

Returning to ongoing debates on *hispano/iberoamericanismo* discussed earlier, *El Estudiante*'s exchanges with Palacios and Vasconcelos reveal its stance on the controversial topic. As chapter 1 illustrates, in Latin America, positions on *hispano/iberoamericanismo* ranged from 1) those who fully endorsed the term as a means of promoting cultural unity across the continent, 2) those who questioned endorsing cultural unity that stemmed from a legacy of colonization, 3) those who saw the term as a superficial attempt to tie the former colonies to Spain, and 4) those who simply saw the term as inadequate for Latin America, either because it failed to acknowledge hard-won national identities or an Indigenous population. Above all, however, these terms surfaced tensions concerning empire, not only the aforementioned Spanish colonial legacy, but also the United States' emergence as a superpower. *El Estudiante*'s position-taking on *iberoamericanismo* proved bold in its head on approach to empire's looming presence. For one, as noted above, the Spanish journal endorsed a new type of relationship between Spain and Latin America, one that not only acknowledged the former colonies' independent national identities, but that also saw them as innovative models to follow. In "Otra vez la voz de América" [Again, America's Voice] (July 1925), for instance, *El Estudiante* took an unequivocal position on the issue surrounding *hispano/iberoamericanismo*. The Spanish journal firmly opposed Spanish imperialism towards Latin America and also stood against similar incursions from the United States. In order to make its anti–United States stance more explicit, *El Estudiante* endorsed Argentina's "Grupo Renovación" and its progress towards organizing a "Unión Latino-Americana," which was part of "[e]l clamoroso hervor del espíritu de la América Latina que, acuciado y encendido … se levanta viril contra el materialismo opresor de Norteamérica" [the resounding fervour of Latin America's spirit that, driven and lit … stands up with virility against the North American materialist oppressor] ("Otra vez" [Again] 10). *El Estudiante* further proclaimed an unwavering opposition to *panamericanismo* and to a "Unión Panamericana" [Panamerican Union], which it viewed as "el órgano embrionario de un supergobierno que el imperialismo del Norte pretende establecer en el Nuevo Mundo" [the embryonic instrument of a super government that the North's imperialism expects to establish in the New World] ("Otra vez" [Again] 10). Thus the Spanish journal professed its commitment to *iberoamericanismo* as a means of forging Hispanic solidarity in opposition to the United States: "He aquí la legítima lid del verdadero hispano-americanismo, que, para ser algo, algo vivo y fecundo y digno de ser, ha de ser comunidad de lucha ideal, unidad de alientos para una gesta histórica común" [Here lies Spanish Americanism's legitimate battle, which, in order to become alive, fecund, and worthy of existing, must be a community of ideal struggle, uniting towards a common historic effort] ("Otra vez" [Again]10).

Finally, *El Estudiante*'s rhetoric surrounding its solidarity with activism in Latin America was also intended to indirectly address political oppression in Spain under Miguel Primo de Rivera. For example, in the article cited above, supporting *iberoamericanismo, El Estudiante* professed its desire to "luchar al lado de América por la libertad de la propia civilización, que es también la nuestra, y por los altos ideales de pueblo que son patrimonio conjunto de nuestra raza" [[to] fight alongside America for our civilization's freedom, and for the high ideals of our peoples that stem from our shared racial heritage] but emphasized that in order to do so, Spain would first face the "enemigo ... dentro de nosotros" [[the] enemy among us] and overthrow the regime ("Otra vez" [Again] 10). Similarly, its final installment of "América," entitled "Significación social de la Argentina" [Argentina's Social Significance] (*El Estudiante* 13 July 1925), examined Argentina's progress in the *Reforma Universitaria* movement and simultaneously offered a critique of dictatorship in Spain. While a cursory glance reveals effusive praise for Argentina's *Reforma Universitaria*, closer inspection betrays *El Estudiante*'s underlying message. For instance, the article expressed admiration for how Argentina's movements had employed "la repudiación revolucionaria de los dogmas de orden y de autoridad, proclamada dentro de la Academia [que] trasciende ahora a postulado del pueblo todo y a grito de combate contra oligarquías y despotismos" [the revolutionary repudiation of the Academy's proclaimed tenets of order and authority now becomes the people's postulate, a battle call against oligarchy and despotism] ("Significación social de la Argentina" [Argentina's Social Significance] 11). In context, "repudiación revolucionaria" [revolutionary repudiation] and "grito de combate contra oligarquías y despotismos" [battle call against oligarchy and despotisms] do apply to *Reforma Universitaria* in Argentina; this wording also discloses *El Estudiante*'s call to action against their own country's tyrannical government. Crossing borders in transatlantic solidarity thus enabled *El Estudiante* to address political oppression at home, taking a step towards reform within national boundaries.

Subscribing to the Latin American *Reforma Universitaria* movement, *El Estudiante* managed to redefine Spain and Latin America's postcolonial relationship when it acknowledged that Spain had something to learn from the new, modern nations. Rather than focus its appeal on a shared cultural heritage that was tainted by a legacy of colonization, *El Estudiante* chose social reform as a conduit to establishing a new transatlantic relationship between Spain and Latin America. This focus on social reform thus enabled the journal to, much like Girondo's "Misión Intelctual" [Intellectual Mission] described at the beginning of this chapter, simultaneously transcend borders while respecting national boundaries. As a result, the Spanish journal was able to overcome the obstacles that hindered consensus in discussions on *hispano/iberoamericanismo*, such as those described in chapter 1. Furthermore, *El Estudiante*'s blatant rejection of empire's oppressive legacy in addition to an overt effort to surpass it offered a radical alternative to the status quo that Ortega had maintained in his interactions with *Inicial* and *Valoraciones*. When he chose to pontificate on appropriate behaviour, Ortega missed the opportunity to engage in a discussion on how Argentina's "Nueva Generación" could practically apply his ideas in order to make meaningful change. Comparatively, in their responses to *El Estudiante*, Palacios and Vasconcelos did participate in a dialogue with the Spanish younger generation, proving that more fruitful exchanges were possible.

Chapter Three

La Gaceta Literaria (1927–31): Postcolonial Networks, Cultural Capital, and the Literary Market

Todo parte de una confusión y es que el que estampó lo de "Madrid meridiano intelectual" quiso decir meridiano "editorial" y que no se trataba de nada de arte sino de economía [All stems from confusion, and it is that the one who purported the notion of "Madrid Intellectual Meridian," meant "Editorial" and that it was not about art, but about economics].

"Opinión autorizada" (Authorized Opinion)
Miguel de Unamuno, *Martín Fierro*, Alemany Bay 128

In his brief, yet poignant, participation in the 1927 *Polémica del meridiano intelectual* [Intellectual Meridian Polemic], cited above, the Spanish novelist and essayist Miguel de Unamuno argued that the heated dispute initiated by *La Gaceta Literaria* (1927–31), over whether Madrid could be the intellectual meridian for Spain and Latin America was centred on the literary market and not aesthetics. This chapter will argue that, not only was Unamuno correct but that an interest in securing a strong foothold in the literary market drove *La Gaceta* throughout its years of publication. In the 15 July 1928 issue of *La Gaceta Literaria*, the journal's founder and director Ernesto Giménez Caballero, also known as Gecé, boasted that only one year and a half after his journal's first appearance, *La Gaceta Literaria* had met the ambitious goals it had set for itself: to be Iberian, American, and international.[1] Framed around these ambitious objectives, *La Gaceta Literaria* is a unique example of a journal that, in crossing borders while defining boundaries, created vast transnational and transatlantic networks.[2] Centring on its efforts to be Iberian and American, this chapter will illustrate how *La Gaceta Literaria*'s success in accomplishing its lofty goals was tied to an intentional focus on the literary market. This chapter opens with a general overview of *La Gaceta Literaria* and its efforts to be American and Iberian. Paying particular attention to the previously noted, well-known *polémica del meridiano intelectual* and its connection to the journal's larger goal of promoting transatlantic book distribution between Spain and Latin America, this chapter then evaluates how *La Gaceta Literaria* goes about being "American." The next section delves into *La Gaceta Literaria*'s attempts to be Iberian and closes with a discussion of the journal's book fairs: the Exposición del libro catalán [Catalan Book Expo], the Exposición del libro portugués [Portuguese Book Expo], and the Exposición del libro Argentino y Uruguayo en Madrid [Argentine and Uruguayan Book Expo in Madrid]. Investing in book fairs aimed at promoting transnational and transatlantic book distribution, *La Gaceta Literaria* created networks across the Iberian Peninsula and the Atlantic. Yet, an inability to relinquish empire, as the polemics it incited reveal, marred this accomplishment.[3] Although *La Gaceta Literaria*'s rhetoric and structure promoted cultural reciprocity and equanimity both within Spain and the Iberian Peninsula as well as across Europe and the Atlantic, a Castilian-centred perspective dominated its pages.[4] In spite of these shortcomings, *La Gaceta Literaria*'s practical approach towards shaping networks of exchange throughout the Iberian Peninsula and with Latin America offers a unique example of how Iberian Studies and Transatlantic Studies can be successful in transcending borders to generate cultural production. Moreover, it illustrates why scholarship today can benefit from adopting an Iberian/Transatlantic purview when evaluating early twentieth-century literary, cultural, and intellectual production.

La Gaceta Literaria (Madrid 1927–31): Ibérica, Americana, e Internacional

When Ernesto Giménez Caballero's *La Gaceta Literaria* sprang onto Madrid's literary scene on 1 January 1927, the journal framed itself to be "ibérica, americana e internacional" [Iberian, American, and international][5] and outlined two main goals: 1) to "cuajar ese hueco ibérico" [fill that Iberian gap] and to "incorporarse a la tipicidad mundial europea" [join global European typicality] ("Salutación" [Salutation] 1). The Madrid-based vanguard journal thus envisioned strengthening ties across the Iberian Peninsula while simultaneously activating Spain's participation in a European cultural field. Both objectives suggest an intent to transcend national and transnational bounds, and a literary journal like *La Gaceta Literaria* would be precisely the vehicle Spain needed to make them a reality. According to *La Gaceta Literaria*, Spain lacked this type of "periódico de letras" [literary newspaper], an already developing medium in post-war France, Germany, Italy, and England, and *La Gaceta Literaria* would meet this need for "nuestra área hispánica" [our Hispanic area], outlining its Iberian and American geographical scope ("Salutación" [Salutation] 1).[6] For *La Gaceta Literaria*, "our Hispanic area" extended across national and cultural borders, "donde los límites, alcancen de América al Pirineo, pasando hasta por ese rincón histórico de los sefardíes" [where limits extend from America to the Pyrenees, extending to the Sephardic historic region (southern Spain)] (Salutación 1). On the one hand, *La Gaceta Literaria*'s transnational aspirations seem to promote cross-regional inclusion. But, on the other hand, the notion of "our Hispanic area" inevitably recalls empire, as the areas were either within Spain's national boundaries or had at some point been under its control. Transgressing borders, *La Gaceta Literaria*'s vast geographical enterprise was therefore meant primarily as a gateway for more Spanish participation in Western modernity.

Establishing itself as a journal of the avant-garde, throughout its years of publication from 1927 to 1931, *La Gaceta Literaria*'s content also clearly illustrated the journal's Iberian, American, and international objectives.[7] Regularly publishing, reviewing, and commenting upon Iberian, international (Eastern European, Western European, and Russian), and Latin American literary affairs, each journal issue transcended national boundaries. A literary journal aligned with the avant-garde that focused on "Letras-Artes-Ciencia" [Letters, Arts, Science], *La Gaceta Literaria* was also cross-disciplinary, including sections on art criticism, theatre, poetry, books, cinema, and sports, enabling it to create transcultural dialogues across many areas of interest. The journal thus created a vibrant and engaging intellectual forum in every issue. Recurring columns, such as "Postales" [Post Cards], that were "Ibéricas, Americanas, and Internacionales" [Iberian, American, and international] are evidence of the journal's commitment to its objectives. While "Postales Americanas" [American Postcards] featured news from across Latin American countries, "Postales Ibéricas" [Iberian Postcards] reported on regions throughout Spain, and "Postales Internacionales" [International Postcards] offered headlines on the latest literary/artistic happenings from around the globe, although primarily in Europe. The "Escaparate de Libros" [Books Showcase] column, often subdivided into "Libros" [Books] sections, such as Libros españoles [Spanish Books], americanos [American Books], portugueses [Portuguese Books], rusos [Russian Books], alemanes [German Books], franceses [French Books], and italianos [Italian Books], also illustrates *La Gaceta Literaria*'s effort to fulfil its promise to be Iberian, American, and international. While the journal's international scope in "Libros" is clearly Western European dominant, it often did publish "Libros Yanquis" [Yankee Books].

The Iberian Post Cards and Books Showcase were fairly consistent columns throughout the journal's publication period and subsections within these columns would often grow and begin to appear independently, such as "Libros catalanes" [Catalan Books] and "Postais de Lisboa" [Postcards from Lisbon], often published in Portuguese. The "Poemas en Mapa" [Poems in a Map] section highlighted poetry from areas such as Galicia, Castilla, Canarias, Valencia, Portugal, Cataluña, Argentina, Cuba, and Chile. Sometimes the journal published brief columns such as "Poemas andaluces" [Andalusian Poems].[8] A "Mapa de Revistas" [Journal Map] also appeared occasionally. For example, "Mapa Hispanoamericano de Revistas" [Spanish American Journal Map] charted leading literary journals published across Spain and Latin America, while a "Mapa Ibérico de Revistas" [Iberian Journal Map] featured primarily Spanish publications (Burgos, Cádiz, Málaga, and Bayona). This survey of periodicals would later be published as "Itinerario de Revistas" [Journal Itinerary]. Finally, similar to "Poemas en Mapa," the "Cuentos" [Short Stories] column published one story at a time from a specific place, such as "Cuento portugués" [Portuguese Short Story], "Cuentos americanos" [American Short Stories], and "Cuentos españoles" [Spanish Short Stories].

In addition to recurring sections and columns, *La Gaceta Literaria* also regularly included a variety of articles that addressed the goals set forth in its first issue. It reported on different areas of Spain and the Iberian Peninsula, as well as on European and Latin American countries. In an apparent effort to respect national identities and cultural boundaries, *La Gaceta Literaria* took the bold step of publishing many of these articles in the country or region's native language, such as Catalan, Italian, French, and Portuguese.[9] Additionally, *La Gaceta Literaria* would also regularly devote issues to literary and artistic developments from either specific Spanish regions or European and Latin American countries.[10] Finally, as *La Gaceta Literaria* grew, the journal created smaller "gacetas" [gazettes] dedicated both to its interdisciplinary and transnational scope. These smaller gazettes included a Gaceta Americana [American Gazette], a Gaceta Científica [Scientific Gazette], a Gaceta Política y Diplomática [Political and Diplomatic Gazette], a Gaceta Catalana [Catalonian Gazette], a Gaceta Bibliográfica [Bibliographic Gazette], a Gaceta del Arte [Art Gazette], and a Gaceta Portuguesa [Portuguese Gazette].

Americanismo and the *Polémica del meridiano intelectual*

Only four months into its first year of publication, *La Gaceta Literaria*'s intent to engage a dialogue between Spain and Latin America had a rocky, yet exciting, beginning when the journal published the 15 April 1927 editorial entitled "Madrid, Meridiano intelectual de Hispanoamérica" [Madrid, Hispanic America's Intellectual Meridian]. Appearing anonymously, although the author is known to be Guillermo de Torre, front and centre, on the issue's cover page, the article proposed that Madrid act as an intellectual meridian for Spanish and Latin American literature. The ideas presented in this brief op ed echo those de Torre published in his "Carta abierta a Évar Méndez" [Open Letter to Évar Méndez] in *Martin Fierro*, discussed in chapter 1. De Torre similarly proposed kinship and camaraderie between Spain and Latin America on the one hand, but, on the other hand, failed to respect the fact that the former colonies now had distinct national boundaries and identities. The bold and controversial notion of Madrid as a meridian predictably provoked heated responses from Latin American intellectuals in Argentina, Uruguay, Peru, Cuba, and Mexico, igniting a fascinating debate that spanned multiple journals and countries across Europe and Latin America and extended well into 1929.[11] In kindling controversy, *La Gaceta Literaria* thus generated a large network of exchange that surpassed borders as it engaged discussions on defining and defending national boundaries, effectively meeting its goal to be "Ibérica, Americana, Internacional."

Scholarship on the *polémica del meridiano intelectual* has primarily focused on the intriguing rhetorical debates that stemmed from de Torre's provocative editorial and, more recently, noted the polemic's economic aspirations rooted in book distribution.[12] Adding to this dialogue, this next section first evaluates the polemic as a riveting example of how, as noted above, a literary journal, within and beyond its pages, managed to overcome borders and create a broad transnational, transcontinental, and transatlantic network of intellectual exchange. Employing controversy to propel a discussion on cultural, geographical, and national boundaries was, ironically, a remarkably effective strategy that forged relationships through contentious deliberations. This section will then consider how this extensive debate offers keen insight into *La Gaceta Literaria*'s "Americanismo" [Americanism], adding to the much larger discussion on topics such as *hispano/iberoamericanismo* taking place across journals, magazines, and newspapers regarding Spain and Latin America's postcolonial relationship. Charting competitions over cultural capital, this section then considers how the *polémica del meridiano intelectual* also sparked peripheral disputes among Spanish provinces, across Latin American nations, and between other European countries and Latin America. The *polémica del meridiano intelectual* thus enabled *La Gaceta Literiaria* to prominently situate itself within a broad cultural field, imbuing it with prestige that would, in turn, facilitate its intent to gain a foothold in an Iberian and Transatlantic literary market.

Polémica del meridiano intelectual: A Match, a Field Brawl, and a World Cup of Letters

The *polémica del meridiano intelectual* has much in common with debates and exchanges taking place in journals, magazines, and newspapers discussed in this book. Yet, it stands out due to its structure, breadth, and scope. Similarities between the *polémica del meridiano intelectual* and other debates considered in this book include the arbitrations surrounding *hispano/iberoamericanismo*. Additionally, just like the exchanges surrounding Edwin Elmore's proposal of a "Congreso de intelectuales Hispano-Americanos" discussed in chapter 1, it involved a variety of voices from across Latin America and Spain and included multifaceted perspectives. However, this particular polemic's structure is both more organized and more complex. One overarching debate between *La Gaceta Literaria* and the Buenos Aires avant-garde journal *Martín Fierro* (Buenos Aires 1924–7) frames the *polémica*, complicated by miscellaneous contributions from other groups, journals, and individuals across Europe and Latin America. At the same time, spinoff dialogues that ranged from regional disputes within Spain, to transnational tensions across Latin America, and between Latin American nations and other European countries, took place on the sidelines. As a result, engaging more than forty intellectuals and over ten periodical publications, the *polémica del meridiano intelectual* generated a comprehensive and nuanced series of deliberations on cultural relationships, borders, and national identities. This next section first outlines the polemic's basic structure and then summarizes its points of contention.

The main exchange in the *polémica del meridiano intelectual*, as noted earlier, was set off by Guillermo de Torre's initial op ed in *La Gaceta Literaria* when a group of *martinfierristas* published scathing retorts in their journal.[13] *Martín Fierro*, also discussed in chapter 1, published by Évar Méndez and Samuel Glusberg, first appeared in February 1924. In form and content, the Argentine journal shared some commonalities with *La Gaceta Literaria*. Like its Spanish counterpart, it was a bi-weekly publication formatted like a newspaper that championed national and international vanguard aesthetics. On 10 July 1927, taking up two entire large pages under the provocative heading "Un llamado a la realidad" [A Reality Check], *Martín Fierro* featured articles with inflammatory titles such as "Imperialismo baldío" [Vain Imperialism] and "A un meridiano encontrao en una fiambrera" [To a Meridian Found in a Lunchbox]. Among the authors that penned this series of fiery replies were Pablo Rojas Paz, Raúl Scalabrini Ortiz, Jorge Luis Borges, Carlos Mastronardi, Santiago Ganduglia, Nicolás Olivari, and Ricardo Molinari. Taking this act as the shove that initiated a field brawl in a soccer match, *La Gaceta Literaria* wrote back using a similar format and playing with soccer jargon. Just as *Martín Fierro* had done, *La Gaceta Literaria* published a series of responses under one heading, "Un debate apasionado. Campeonato para un meridiano intelectual" [A Passionate Debate: Championship for an Intellectual Meridian] on 1 September 1927.

Attempting to have the last word, *Martín Fierro* chimed in again with the article "Asunto fundamental" [Fundamental Issue] in its 31 August–15 November 1927 issue, which included an introduction from journal editor Évar Méndez as well as contributions from other *martinfierristas*. But *La Gaceta Literaria* once again intercepted with "La verbena del meridiano" [The Meridian's Verbena], an anonymous editorial, on its front page on 15 September 1927. Just as *Martín Fierro* and *Gaceta Literaria* confronted each other on the main field, however, interjections on the matter appeared in other publications, such as Uruguayan *La Pluma* (Montevideo 1927–31) and *La Cruz del Sur* (Montevideo 1924–31), Cuban *Revista de Avance* (La Habana 1927–30), *Ulises* (1927–8) in Mexico, *Repertorio Americano* (1919–59) in Costa Rica, Madrid's *El Sol* (1917–39), Italy's *La feria letteraria* (Milano 1925–36), and Buenos Aires's *Nosotros* (1907–34) and *Síntesis* (1927–30). Spin-off matches showcased 1) regional tensions within Spain centring on Castilian hegemony, 2) that Buenos Aires and Mexico City were vying for cultural capital within Latin America, and 3) unresolved enmity between Italy and Argentina regarding the European country's influence on its Latin American counterpart's language.

The debate outlined above centred on deliberations over Castilian hegemonic aspirations kindled by de Torre's op ed. Reading the editorial as an attempt to gain control over cultural capital, most Latin Americans, and primarily Argentine *martinfierristas*, proclaimed that the proposal showed a lack of respect for hard-won national boundaries and threatened the former colonies' cultural independence from Spain. Alluding to empire, the editorial argued that, in light of French and Italian cultural dominance in the West (and, as we shall see, it was referring to the literary market), Spain and Latin America needed to capitalize on their cultural and linguistic commonalities and strengthen their ties in order to form a unified front.[14] De Torre thus proposed that a consolidated transatlantic Spanish American culture needed a centre, and Madrid would be the ideal intellectual meridian: "señalemos en nuestra geografía espiritual a Madrid como el más certero punto meridiano, como la más auténtica línea de intersección entre América y España. Madrid: punto convergente del hispanoamericanismo equilibrado" [in our spiritual geography, lets point towards Madrid as the most accurate meridian point, as the most authentic intersection between America and Spain. Madrid: [the] convergence point for well-balanced *hispanoamericanismo*] (Alemany Bay 66).[15] De Torre's argument in favour of transatlantic cultural solidarity would thus seem to have much in common with *El Estudiante*'s views described in chapter 2, and even with Edwin Elmore's ideation for a convening of minds coming together in cultural unity as detailed in chapter 1. However, unlike *El Estudiante*, which sought solidarity surrounding social reform, and Edwin Elmore, who genuinely wanted to create a space for intellectual discussion, de Torre's proposal betrayed a desire for hegemonic control over cultural capital. Creating a network of transatlantic book distribution, as we will see, was a key motivation behind proposing Madrid as a cultural meridian.

The front-page editorial spoke of camaraderie, a "fraternidad desinteresada" [disinterested fraternity], and insisted that *La Gaceta Literaria*'s endorsement of *hispanoamericanismo* did not imply "hegemonía política o intelectual de ninguna clase" [any sort of political hegemony] (AB 66). Unlike French and Italian *latinismo* and US *panamericanismo*, Spanish *hispanoamericanismo* was not tainted by any aspiration for control over Latin America. Instead, de Torre's editorial emphasized that *La Gaceta Literaria* considered Latin America an extension of Spain, which was not to be interpreted as entailing "un propósito anexionista reprobable" [a reprehensible annexationist purpose] (AB 66). *La Gaceta Literaria* merely hoped to erase boundaries and bring Latin American and Spanish intellectuals together, "anular diferencias valoradoras, juzgando con el mismo espíritu personas y obras de aquende y allende el Atlántico" [annul valuing differences, judging people and works from either side of the Atlantic] (AB 67). *La Gaceta Literaria*'s overture, according to the editorial, was friendly, altruistic, and uninterested in attaining cultural or political gains over Latin America. However, as examples in chapter 1 and chapter 2 have illustrated, from a Latin American perspective, describing Latin America as an extension of Spain and suggesting that boundaries be erased, fails to respect national identities and cultural independence. The editorial further maintained that *La Gaceta Literaria*'s understanding of *hispanoamericanismo* was radically different from other Spanish interpretations of the term and more profound than cursory celebrations. *La Gaceta Literaria* was therefore opposed to "torpes excesos del hispanoamericanismo infausto" [clumsy excesses of ill-fated Hispanic Americanism] characterized by perfunctory displays of Hispanic camaraderie, such as "[b]anquetes y cachupinadas, tremolar de banderas, fuegos de artificio retórico" [banquets and celebrations, flag waving, and rhetorical fireworks], and instead sought to establish a deeper and more authentic intellectual exchange with Latin Americans (AB 67). Thus, in contrast to previous vacuous interpretations of the term, *La Gaceta Literaria*'s amicable and true overture towards Latin America wanted to solidify "la instauración de un nuevo espíritu amistoso entre dos mundos fraternos" [the establishment of a new friendly spirit between two fraternal worlds] (AB 67). As we will see, this "amicable and true overture" also intended to help Spain gain a stronger foothold in the transatlantic literary market.

Unsurprisingly, intellectuals across the Atlantic were sceptical of this "benevolent" position and responded in kind. Arguing that empire was at the core of de Torre's proposal, Argentine *Martinfierristas* vehemently defended Latin America's, and more specifically Argentina's, cultural independence from Spain, questioned the term *hispanoamericanismo*, and disparaged Spain. As chapter 2's account of Oliverio Girondo's "misión intellectual" [intellectual mission] illustrates, *Martín Fierro* promoted collaboration that transcended national boundaries. However, *Martín Fierro* also unabashedly defended Argentine nationalism. Its very name, *Martín Fierro*, was taken from José Hernández's late nineteenth-century epic poem about a gaucho, a figure regarded as a national symbol. Therefore, although *Martín Fierro* created a space for transnational and transatlantic expression and welcomed a plurality of voices on its pages, for *martinfierristas*, crossing borders did not mean erasing nationalisms. Summing up their responses, Évar Méndez stated, "Todas las respuestas del MARTÍN FIERRO pueden condensarse así: 'No necesitamos ni meridianos ni tutelajes intelectuales de España; América es América y debe buscarse en sí misma; hemos roto todo cordón umbilical con España; nuestro idioma no es ya el mismo ni lo será; España, intelectual, es de valor relativo'" [All of *Martín Fierro*'s responses can be condensed like this: We don't need either meridians or intellectual tutelage from Spain; America is America and should find itself within itself; we have cut the umbilical cord <with/from> Spain; our language is no longer the same nor will it be; intellectual Spain has a relative value] (AB 75). *Martín Fierro* thus advocated full Argentine participation in a World Cup of letters as its own team. A vital, new, forward-thinking nation, Argentina had earned both its national identity and its ability to fully engage in a Western field of cultural production. As Uruguayan Idelfonso Pereda Valdés, who wrote in support of *martinfierristas*, put it, "El meridiano intelectual de América no es Madrid, es Buenos Aires" [America's intellectual meridian is not Madrid, it is Buenos Aires] (AB 70).

De Torre's argument that Castilian (Spanish) created an irrevocable cultural bond between Spain and Latin America also provoked boisterous responses from *martinfierristas* because national identity in Argentina was tightly connected to dialectical variances. Argentine Spanish deviated from Castilian's "pure" form as it employed the distinctive *voseo*, a conjugation that replaced the Castilian *tú* [you] form with *vos* [you].[16] In addition, immigrant populations from Italy, Romania, and other European countries that converged in Buenos Aires spoke *lunfardo*, a distinct dialect that had little in common with Castilian Spanish. Proud of their unique linguistic identity, Raúl Scalabrini Ortiz and Pablo Rojas Paz vigorously refuted the notion that a homogeneous language linked Spain and Latin America. And, stressing the same point, Jorge Luis Borges and Carlos Mastronardi mocked de Torre's editorial in their previously mentioned article "A un meridiano encontrao en una fiambrera," which they wrote in *lunfardo*.

Addressing the very provincialism that *La Gaceta Literaria* had set out to overcome, a recurring argument across *martinfierrista* responses asserted that Spain's backwardness could not compete with Latin America's youth and vitality. *Martinfierristas* also insisted that the former empire had lost its lustre and was unfit to act as a meridian. Spain was entrenched in its old ways and, more importantly, controlled by a dictator. The defunct empire thus remained stagnant.[17] Meanwhile, comprising multiple younger nations, Latin America was still in the process of self-discovery as it modernized and developed. As Nicolás Olivari declared, for instance, Spain had much more to gain from Latin America: "No tenemos interés ni por Madrid, ni por España. No hay allí ascensores, ni calefacción, ni tangos porteños. No hay interés. Si ellos quieren ... no tenemos inconveniente en reconocer que nosotros somos los conquistadores y ellos los conquistados" [We have no interest either in Madrid or in Spain. They lack elevators, heating, and Porteño tangos. There is no interest. If they want ... we have no problem conceding that we are the conquerors and they are the conquered] (AB 71). Latin American nations were engaging modernity on their own terms, prospering economically and participating in cutting-edge social and artistic movements, as they defined distinct national identities. Spain had much to learn from them and not the other way around. Further underscoring this point, Ricardo Molinari ridiculed Spain's political situation under feeble dictator Miguel Primo de Rivera and his botched attempts to maintain Spanish territories in Morocco calling the capital "Madrid: 'meridiano' de trastornos marroquíes y las payasadas de Primo de 'la costanera'" [Madrid: "Meridian" of Moroccan Upsets and Coastal Primo's Buffoonery] (AB 69). Moreover, *martinfierristas* stressed Spain's ignorance when it came to Latin America and its unique national identities. As Borges stated, "Madrid no nos entiende. Una ciudad cuyas orquestas no pueden intentar un tango sin desalmarlo ... una ciudad cuyo Irigoyen es Primo de Rivera; una ciudad cuyos actores no distinguen a un mejicano de un oriental" [Madrid doesn't understand us. A city whose orchestras can't attempt a tango without dismantling it ... a city where Irigoyen is Primo de Rivera; a city whose actors cannot distinguish between a Mexican and a person of Asian descent] (AB 71). Argentine *martinfierristas* thus pointed out what Salamanca students in *El Estudiante* (Salamanca-Madrid 1924–6) knew to be true about their country; that it was stuck in the past and stagnant under a dictatorship. And, emphatically defending their national autonomy against Madrid's proposal, *martinfierristas* also proclaimed Buenos Aires a more reasonable choice for a meridian.

While the pugnacious exchanges between *Martín Fierro* and *La Gaceta Literaria* framed the *polémica del meridiano intelectual*, intellectuals from other Latin American countries, including Uruguay, Peru, Cuba, and Mexico also participated in this tournament, offering diverse perspectives and making it a World Cup of Letters. Uruguayans, writing in *La Pluma* and *Cruz del Sur*, fully supported the *martinfierrista* position in defence of Latin America's national borders. Upholding these views, Peruvian writers Angélica Palma ("Literaturas de América," published in *El Sol* on 7 December 1927) and José Carlos Mariátegui ("Batalla de *Martín Fierro*," published in Lima's *Variedades* on 24 September 1927[18]) endorsed *Martín Fierro*'s stance. Mariátegui, in particular, called on Latin America's new generation to come together in opposing "la tardía reinvidicación española" [Spain's belated vindication] (AB 113).

Cuban intellectuals similarly spoke out against the idea that Madrid should be an intellectual meridian for Spain and Latin America. Although they otherwise broadly sided with *martinfierristas*, some Cuban voices, such as Alejo Carpentier in *El diario de la marina*, and journals *Revista de Avance* and *Orto*, noted that *martinfierrista* language was uncalled for and inappropriate.[19] *Revista de Avance* added that taking Madrid as meridian would actually be a step backwards for modern Latin American nations. In *Revista de Avance*'s estimation, Darío's *modernismo* had been a counter-conquest that had earned Latin America the right to be treated as equals by Spain (AB 99). Finally, *Orto* critiqued both *martinfierristas* and *La Gaceta Literaria* for even engaging in such a superficial and unproductive skirmish (AB 114).

Contrasting Uruguayan, Peruvian, and Cuban overarching support of *martinfierristas'* views, Mexican *Contemporáneos* came out against their Argentine counterparts in their journal *Ulises* and in Costa Rica's *Repertorio Americano* (1919–58). *Ulises*, directed by Salvador Novo and Xavier Villaurrutia, published "Madrid, Meridiano intelectual de Hispanoamérica" [Madrid, Hispanic America's Intellectual Meridian], in October 1927, which was most likely written by Villaurrutia. In addition, Jaime Torres Bodet penned "La geografía intelectual de América, Un meridiano de modestia" [America's Intellectual Geography, a Modest Meridian], which appeared in Costa Rica's *Repertorio Americano* on 3 December 1927.[20] As Rosa García Gutiérrez notes, the *Contemporáneos*'s antagonism towards *martinfierristas* was connected to their position on national aesthetic debates taking place in Mexico at the time, which will be further discussed in chapter 4. However, these articles also reveal an underlying rivallry between Mexico and Argentina in which both countries seemed to be positioning themselves as competing meridians. *Contemporáneos* were less concerned with opposing Spain than with staking their claim on cultural capital across Latin America.

Other Competitions: *El Sol* and *La Fiera Letteraria*

The *polémica del meridiano intelectual* also propelled three secondary disputes. The first two altercations featured Catalonian and Galician writers who contested the editorial's pronouncement of Castilian hegemony within Spain, thereby calling *La Gaceta Literaria*'s purported Iberianism into question. A third clash extended the debate beyond Iberia into Europe when an unexpected Italian intervention generated a third contest centring on Italy's influence over Argentine culture. The first controversial exchange took place in Madrid's *El Sol* between two of the journal's contributors, Ricardo Baeza and Catalan journalist Gaziel (Agustí Calvet Pascual). On 31 August 1927, Gaziel opened the discussion with "Los meridianos de Hispanoamérica" [Spanish America's Meridians]. Baeza responded with "¿Con *Martín Fierro* o con *Don Quijote*?" [With *Martín Fierro* or *Don Quijote*?] on 3 September 1927 and Gaziel had the last word with "¿Imperio o Confederación?" [Empire or Confederation?] on 13 September 1927. Offering a nuanced perspective on the polemic, Gaziel first acknowledged that he did not think *La Gaceta Literaria* had in any way intended to "empequeñecer y localizar el hispanoamericanismo" [belittle and localize *hispanoamericanismo*] (AB 80) and that *martinfierrista* language was blasphemous in their responses. Yet Gaziel pointed out that he could also see why *martinfierristas* would interpret the editorial as they did. In his estimation, even provinces in Spain, such as Galicia and Cataluña, might have a similar reaction to the idea of designating Madrid an intellectual meridian. The Castilian-centred suggestion implied hegemonic aspirations that failed to acknowledge distinct national and cultural identities.

Baeza, in turn, sided with *La Gaceta Literaria* and echoed the original editorial's voice positing that all regions in Spain and Latin American countries that spoke Castilian Spanish comprised a "comunidad del lenguaje" [language community], which also implied that Spain and Latin America "forman una unidad cultural" [formed a cultural unity] (AB 93). Provinces across Spain and Latin American countries were, thereby, culturally, an extension of Castile. Baeza's perspective here then fuelled another exchange with Galician Villar Ponte, who wrote in *El Pueblo Gallego*.[21] Baeza narrated the controversy in "La escuela de Don Quijote" [Don Quijote's School] which he published in *El Sol* on 24 September 1927. Villar Ponte, as a Galician with a distinct regional identity within Spain, supported *martinfierristas'* opposition to a Madrid meridian. Baeza countered Villar Ponte taking issue with what he called uncompromising regionalism. He contended that "toda interpretación del regionalismo que signifique exclusión y restricción del espíritu, acotamiento y delimitación infelxibles" [any interpretation of regionalism that implies exclusion and restriction of spirit, restriction, and inflexible delimitations] was "viciosa" [depraved] and "nociva" [harmful] (AB 110). Baeza maintained that he did not intend to discredit Villar Ponte but insisted that disputes of this nature were pointless. Of course, his own view that there was one inclusive Spanish culture to which Latin American countries and all regions in Spain belonged was actually exclusive and restrictive in its inability to embrace the plurality of cultures, races, and languages that comprised Iberia and America.

Extending the *polémica del meridiano intelectual* beyond the Iberian Peninsula and into Europe, Italy's *La Fiera Letteraria* (1925–36, Milan and Rome) chimed in with A.R. Ferrarin's article "Buenos Aires contro Madrid" [Buenos Aires Against Madrid] (18 September 1927). Ferrarin supported the *martinfierrista* position, pointed out that Italy's migrant population in Argentina had influenced the Latin American country's culture, and taunted Spanish intellectuals, proclaiming that if Argentines were to follow a European model, it would be Rome, not Madrid (AB 105). His article thus elicited a response from Spanish avant-garde writer Francisco Ayala who published "En torno al 'meridiano'. El minutero de Italia" [Surrounding the "Meridian," Italy's Minute Hand] (1 October 1927) in *La Gaceta Literaria*. Predictably, Ayala asserted that the notion that Italy had any stake in "la espiritualidad argentina" [Argentine spirituality] as unfounded (AB 117). This exchange, however, led the Buenos Aires journal *Nosotros* to take on the topic by publishing a survey on Italian influence in Argentina.

Responding to the *Nosotros* survey, and ultimately claiming the last word in the *polémica del meridiano intelectual, La Gaceta Literaria* published "No quiere pasar por Roma el meridiano" [The Meridian Does Not Want to Go through Rome] on 15 May 1928. This anonymous article, likely penned by Giménez Caballero, first dismissed Ferrarin's view that Italian culture was influential in Argentina and then turned to concluding the *polémica del meridiano intelectual.* Reflecting on the reactions that their use of the word *meridiano* had instigated, as it had previously stated in "La verbena del meridiano" [The Meridian's Verbena] in September 1927, *La Gaceta Literaria* proclaimed that the original article,"Madrid, Meridiano intelectual de Hispanoamérica," had achieved the intended effect. The incendiary topic had stimulated communication that was long overdue: "El *Meridiano* ha sido una malla que ha logrado a todos los ánimos – trasatlánticos y aquendeatlánticos – reunirnos seriamente, desde hace ya muchos años que no nos reuníamos" [The *Meridian* has been a net that has managed to bring all spirits – transatlantic and nearatlantic – together seriously, after so many years of not having done so] (AB 168). Even if many of the exchanges had been aggressive, passionate altercations were preferable to "los comportamientos aislados, las ausencias abismales" [isolated performances, vast absences] (AB 168). And, returning to the soccer championship metaphor it had previously employed, *La Gaceta Literaria* declared the match tied: "Ha resultado higiénico y enérgico. Nos encontramos hoy con ese foco alegre de los equipos que han empatado, bebiendo juntos las gaseosas, sin acordarse ya de las porterías" [The result has been healthy and energizing. We find ourselves with that bright torch of teams that have tied, drinking sodas together, no longer remembering goals] (AB 168). And he was right. The outlandish proposal that Madrid act as a cultural meridian for Spain and Latin America had, in fact, brought intellectuals from across Spain, Europe, and Latin America together in what could be considered an Iberian, American, and international discussion. A controversy over geographical borders and national boundaries had transgressed the former and strengthened the latter, bringing all parties involved closer together. As we will see, however, opening these channels of communication was also intended to help *La Gaceta Literaria* gain a strong foothold in the literary market on both sides of the Atlantic.

Polémica del meridiano and the Literary Market

Overriding "Madrid: meridiano intelectual de Hispanoamérica's" provocative rhetoric, the article's closing lines display an underlying intent to promote a network for transatlantic book distribution in which Spain had a prominent role in the Latin American book market:

> ¿Además, de qué ha servido tamaño estruendo verbalista, cuál ha sido, en el orden práctico, su utilidad inmediata, si nuestra exportación de libros y revistas a América es muy escasa, en proporción con las cifras que debiera alcanzar, si el libro español, en la mayor parte de Suramérica, no puede competir en precios con el libro francés e italiano; y si, por otra parte, la reciprocidad no existe? [Besides, what has been the point of such boisterous, verbal uproar, in practical terms, what has its immediate utility been if, in proportion to the figures we ought to reach, we scarcely export books and magazines to America, if the Spanish book, in most of South America, can't compete with French and Italian book pricing; and if, on the other hand, there is no reciprocity?] (AB 67)

Here de Torre claims to deplore empty bombastic proclamations promoting an abstract transatlantic relationship. Understood from this perspective, his op ed's objective was therefore to turn conceptual rhetoric into practical, economic partnerships through transatlantic book distribution. If Latin American books were insufficiently sold in Spain, however, de Torre was primarily concerned with limited sales of Spanish books in Latin America. He maintained that Spain only exported small amounts of books and journals to Latin America because they could not compete with cheaper French and Italian books for sale in the Latin American market.[22] Therefore, if throughout the editorial the Spanish intellectual spoke of French and Italian cultural dominance in abstract terms, this conclusion clarifies that he was referring to economic hegemony and the literary market. Developing a strong Spanish–Latin American network within the publishing industry could effectively challenge French and Italian power within the field.

Martinfierristas and other polemic contributors did not miss de Torre's point regarding the literary market in the editorial. For instance, Santiago Ganduglia, Eduardo González Lanuza, and Raúl Scalabrini Ortiz commented that de Torre's so-called desire for cultural camaraderie covered aspirations to gain control over the Latin American literary market. Also writing in *Martin Fierro,* Spanish writer Miguel de Unamuno, cited in this chapter's opening epigraph, deemed the core issue at stake a "meridiano editorial" [editorial meridian] (AB 128).

Additionally, further emphasizing this perspective, the Buenos Aires journal *Síntesis*, founded by Galician emigrant Xavier Bóveda, published a series of articles between July and November 1927 addressing the *polémica del meridiano intelectual* and affirming that transatlantic book distribution was at the heart of the controversy.[23]

Xavier Bóveda's elegant journal appeared in Buenos Aires in June 1927. Akin to Spanish philosopher José Ortega y Gasset's *Revista de Occidente* (Madrid 1923–36) in form and issue length (over one hundred pages each), *Síntesis* laid out simple goals: "Aspiramos a resumir a través de nuestras columnas, y en forma sintética, toda manifestación artística, intelectual y científica, [*sic*] de los pueblos de habla castellana" [We aspire to summarize in our columns, succinctly, all artistic, intellectual, and scientific production pertaining to Castilian-speaking peoples] (5). Affirming its support of a *hispanoamericanismo* based on cultural commonalities, *Síntesis* also set out to promote "una cultura hispano-americana" [a Spanish American culture], and to "[u]nificar la curiosidad científica e intelectual, de los pueblos de progenie hispánica" [unite scientific and intellectual curiosity of peoples of Hispanic progeny] (5).[24] Staying true to these initial goals, *Síntesis*, whose board included notable *Martín Fierro* contributor Jorge Luis Borges, would later welcome and prominently feature de Torre himself upon his arrival in Buenos Aires in 1928.

Contributing to the *polémica del meridiano intelectual*, in July 1927 *Síntesis* published "La prodigiosa y díscola ciudad del idioma común" [The Prodigious and Unruly City of a Common Language] by Argentine poet Arturo Capdevila, a piece that had appeared two months earlier in Buenos Aires's *La Prensa* (1869–present). In a brief introduction to Capdevila's article, Bóveda explained that *Síntesis* deemed the points the poet made particularly relevant at a time when "se habla de señalar a Madrid como meridiano intelectual de América" [there is talk of identifying Madrid as America's intellectual meridian], implying that the article in question was meant as *Síntesis* position-taking in this polemic (118). Capdevila's article centred unequal reciprocity in book distribution between Spain and Argentina. He noted that Argentine publications were highly esteemed in France, England, Germany, and every other European country except Spain. Although there were exceptions, such as poet Rafael Cansinos Assens, "hay cien que moran en lo inaccesible de la indiferencia, del desprecio y del orgullo" [there are a hundred that dwell in the inaccessible realm of indifference, disdain, and pride] (118). In addition, on a visit to a library in Madrid, he observed that a book by an important Argentine author was conspicuously untouched. Capdevila therefore concluded that sending books to Spain was pointless because Spaniards were uninterested in Argentina's literary production. To further support his argument, Capdevila cited a 1923 debate between Argentine Eduardo Schiaffino and Spanish journalist Andrenio. While Andrenio claimed that Latin Americans were at fault for Argentine literature's scant presence on Spanish bookshelves, Schiaffino argued that Spanish booksellers rarely carried Latin American books because they feared that it would hinder their national literature sales. Thus, in the wake of the *polémica del meridiano intelectual,* Capdevila noted that in five years little had changed since the 1923 altercation.

Echoing *Síntesis*'s take on the debate, on 1 September 1927, five months after the initial editorial that set the debate in motion, *La Gaceta Literaria* itself published an anonymous article entitled "El verdadero meridiano de Hispanoamérica: La traducción" [Hispanic America's True Meridian: Translation].[25] Again adopting soccer terminology, the front-page article deemed the ensuing debate a "torneo de mutuas vanidades" [tournament of mutual vanity] and proposed that both teams refocus their attention on Madrid and Buenos Aires bookstores (99). Close inspection of book distribution, the article claimed, revealed deficiencies on both sides of the Atlantic. First, Latin American books were hard to find in Spanish bookstores: "No hay un escaparate español de librería donde el libro americano luche con los demás. Se diría que no existe" [There is no Spanish bookstore display case in which an American book competes with others. It could be said that it does not exist] (99). While the article acknowledges that Argentine booksellers lacked the necessary financial means to export their merchandise and compete in an international market, it also blamed Argentines for their weak attempts to enter the Spanish literary market. At the same time, the article pointed to Spain's lack of initiative in establishing reciprocal book distribution with Latin America. And it further underscored that a larger problem within Spain was that national books were not promoted either. Instead of marketing Spanish books, publishing houses in Spain featured German, French, and Anglophone literature, often in translation. Furthermore, Spanish publishing houses distributed these foreign texts to Latin America, which undermined Spanish cultural influence across the Atlantic. In broad strokes, then, the article argued that the Spanish book industry was promoting other cultures instead of their own both at home and abroad. As a result, the article thus concluded that Spain had no right to call for an intellectual meridian in Madrid: "Por tanto, queridos españoles: ¿por qué chillar tanto sobre el Meridiano de Madrid? El auténtico y triste Meridiano actual de Hispanoamérica es el servil de la traducción" [Therefore, dear Spaniards: why squeal so much about a Madrid

Meridian? Hispanic America's authentic and sad current Meridian is the servile one of translation] (99). This piece thus discredited the ember fuelling the *polémica del meridiano intelectual*'s fire. There was no point in even considering a meridian when both sides were equally culpable in failing to establish economically practical cultural ties across the Atlantic. Yet, even as this article was prominently featured on the front page, the same issue included the previously described "Campeonato para un meridiano intelectual" [Championship for an Intellectual Meridian], boisterous Spanish responses to *Martín Fierro*'s initial response to the debate. As a result, this perspective on the literary market would get lost in the shuffle. But, as this chapter will address later, it would eventually reemerge when *La Gaceta Literaria* hosted the "Exposición del libro argentino-uruguayo en Madrid" in 1928. This event, and the journal's publications surrounding it, evidenced once and for all that the Spanish journal's "americanismo" was propelled by gaining a foothold in the Latin American literary market. The same endgame spurred *La Gaceta Literaria*'s "iberismo" as the next sections substantiate.

Iberismo

Iberismo in *La Gaceta Literaria* appeared much like *americanismo*. It occupied recurring sections, incited debates, although none were comparable to the *polémica del meridiano intelectual*, and was clearly linked to the Madrid journal's interest in gaining traction in the literary market. *La Gaceta Literiaria*'s *iberismo* appears in several recurring sections: "Postales Ibéricas" [Iberian Postcards], "Escaparate de libros" [Books Schowcase], "Poemas en Mapa" [Poems in a Map], and "Cuentos" [Short Stories]. Another less frequent column, "Itinerario de Revistas" [Magazine Itinerary] is also Iberian in scope. In some cases, these brief sections would evolve into distinct "Gacetas," [Gazettes] such as *Gaceta Portuguesa* [Portuguese Gazette], and *Gaceta Catalana* [Catalan Gazette], becoming journals within a journal. "Postales Ibéricas" reported on the latest events occurring across Iberia. Cataluña (usually appearing first) Levante (primarily detailing events in Valencia), Galicia, Andalucía, and Portugal appeared most frequently. Other areas that received attention include Castilla, Asturias, Vasconia, Canarias, and Baleares. Notably, although *La Gaceta Literaria* was published in Madrid and the majority of its content was therefore Castilian-centred, the journal still included Castilla in its Postales Ibéricas, as though the area needed additional attention. Topics covered in Postales Ibéricas included recent art exhibits, book publications, the appearance of new literary journals, and editorials.

Three recurring topics shape *La Gaceta Literaria*'s Iberian purview: language, regionalism, and empire. First, the journal made a clear attempt to be more linguistically inclusive. *La Gaceta Literaria* published articles in languages other than Castilian, notably Portuguese and Catalan, although there were also instances in which texts appeared in Galician or Valencian. In the 1 July 1927 issue, for example, a "Cuento portugués" [Portuguese Short Story] in Portuguese, a report on "Libros catalanes" [Catalan Books], in Castilian, and an article in Catalan, "Les doctrines politiques en la Catalunya medieval" [Medieval Catalonia's Political Doctrines] border a "Poemas en Mapa" on Galicia, which is published in Galician (3). Publishing texts in regional and national languages showcased Iberian cultural diversity and respected identities. Nevertheless, the move sparked controversy akin to the one engaged in the *polémica del meridiano intelectual*, such as the brief debate "El diálogo de las lenguas" [The Dialogue on Languages]. Writing in the journal *Diari de Sabadell* (Sabadell 1910–36), Catalan Francesc Trabal criticized *La Gaceta Literaria* for publishing articles in Catalan. He claimed that publishing in Catalan discredited Catalonian culture because readers that could not read the language would not be able to understand and, therefore, appreciate it. Ironically, from Trabal's perspective, the journal had insufficiently crossed borders because it did not account for linguistic boundaries. *La Gaceta Literaria* expressed dismay at the complaint, especially because it came from Cataluña, an area with which, as compared to others in Iberia (Burgos or Valladolid, for example) the journal felt it had a strong kinship. Moreover, *La Gaceta Literaria* explained that its effort was meant precisely to endorse Catalonian culture and support its language's legitimacy.[26] In this sense, the journal recognized national boundaries, a consideration that *martinfierristas* felt that the Madrid journal had not had with Latin American nations. Yet, *La Gaceta Literaria* would also contradict its own action in a subsequent [1 March 1927] publication of "Postales Ibéricas." In a report on Levante, the journal praises the wonderful news that a new train will connect Valencia and Madrid. Proximity to Madrid, it claimed, would help Valencia's "drama de su bilinguidad" [bilingualism drama] since neither Valencian nor Castilian were, from the article's perspective, spoken well in Valencia. Rather than endorse Valencian, or bilingualism for that matter, the journal optimistically touted that Valencians' newfound proximity to the Castilian centre would enable them to perfect the dominant language.

A second topic that often surfaced within *La Gaceta Literaria*'s *iberismo* is one I have labelled "regionalism/provincialism," which the journal looked down upon. *Iberismo*, for *La Gaceta Literaria*, meant letting go of regionalist tendencies that hindered transcultural appreciation. For instance, a brief piece by José María Salaverría, "Estilo de Extremadura" [Extremadura's Style] in *La Gaceta Literaria*'s second issue from 1 February 1927, exalts Extremadura's ability to surpass regionalist/provincialist tendencies. Salaverría describes Extremadura's character in contrast to other areas in Iberia: "Extremadura es el no hallar la manifestación española más pronunciada … [l]a jactancia une al catalán y al andaluz, al vasco y al aragonés, al gallego y al castellano. En Extremadura falta ese dejo unificador. Se evade del acervo nacional" [Extremadura is to not find the most pronounced manifestation of "Spanishness" … haughtiness unites the Catalonian, the Andalusian, the Basque, the Aragonese, the Galician, and the Castilian. That unifying arrogance is absent in Extremadura. National heritage is evaded] (2). Thus, according to Salaverría, Extremadura is above regionalisms and nationalisms that characterize other Iberian areas, which, as the next examples demonstrate, were very much present across Iberia.

In two more examples, *La Gaceta Literaria* dismisses Galician and Andalusian journals for their narrow regional and provincial perspectives. First, in the 15 May 1927 edition of Postales Ibéricas, *La Gaceta Literaria* reported that the journal *El País Gallego* complained that Galicia was insufficiently present in *La Gaceta Literaria*. While *La Gaceta Literaria* rebuked the accusation by listing the many times it had already published Galicia, it also revealed a disparaging attitude towards the area, "Es lamentable que regiones que se dicen henchidas de vida espiritual como Galicia, no nos envíen su colaboración y noticiario, como lo hacen auténticas comarcas literarias de la Península" [It is a shame that regions that claim to have a brimming spiritual life like Galicia don't send us their collaborations and news, as the authentic literary areas of the Peninsula do] (2). Moreover, *La Gaceta Literaria* accused Galicia of regionalism: "Laborar. No gritar. Ese es el problema de todo regionalismo" [Working. Not screaming. That is the issue with every regionalism] (2). Two months later, *La Gaceta Literaria* assumed a similar view regarding provincialism with the Andalusian journal *Revista Popular* (1925) published in Córdoba. In the 1 July 1927 edition of Postales Ibéricas, *La Gaceta Literaria* first expressed gratitude to the journal for supporting its views in the *polémica del meridiano intelectual*. However, *La Gaceta Literaria* then admonished *Revista Popular* for its provincial and reactionary content.

Bias against such regionalism/provincialism in *La Gaceta Literaria* speaks to the limits of the journal's Iberian scope and betrays a Castilian/Madrid-centred purview. Given its purported inclusive stance with regard to Iberia, *La Gaceta Literaria*'s critique of narrow-minded regionalism and provincialism could be understandable. However, the journal's harsh and, often belittling, language also seems to discredit the cultural pluralism it claims to embrace. Moreover, there is a clear hierarchy to *La Gaceta Literaria*'s Iberian vision. Cataluña and Portugal occupy a much more prominent space in the journal with Galicia and Levante/Valencia coming in at a somewhat distant second and scattered accounts of all other areas such as Canarias, Baleares, and País Vasco. And, despite its objective Castile remains dominant throughout *La Gaceta Literaria*'s Iberianism. Illustrating this point, two drawings by journal director Ernesto Giménez Caballero himself unequivocally situate Madrid and Castile as the central and dominant Iberian area: "Universo de la literatura española contemporánea" [Contemporary Spanish Literature Universe] (15 July 1927) and "Cartel de la Nueva literatura" [New Literature's Poster] (15 April 1928).

In "Universo de la literatura española contemporánea," briefly described in this book's introduction, planets, stars, and comets represent prominent literary figures and artists (primarily from Madrid, although Mexican Alfonso Reyes and Catalans Eugeni D'Ors and Joan Miró make the cut) alongside journals. The most prominent journals are Madrid-based *Revista de Occidente* (1923–36), *Revista de las Españas* (1926–36), and, of course, *La Gaceta Literaria*, which are near Ramón Gómez de La Serna's Madrid tertulia [gathering] "Pombo." Avant-garde journals from other areas such as Murcia's *Verso y Prosa* (1927–8), Huevla's *Papel de Aleluyas* (1927–8), and Sevilla's *Mediodía* (1926–9) are smaller and relegated to periphery of the "universe." The second image, "Cartel de la nueva literatura," is a pentagon "tres triángulos netos y uno en preforma" [three net triangles and one in pre-form] with coordinates (alpha, omega, beta, each representing an area) that hierarchically depict literary networks, including those built by print culture (primarily avant-garde journals), in Spain. Aránzazu Ascunce Arenas and Eric Bulson have carefully evaluated this image. Ascunce Arenas explains that "the new literary movement in Madrid is greater than in Barcelona, which is greater than in Andalucía, which is greater than Galicia and Portugal" (20), and Bulson underscores that "[t]his theorem was his attempt to justify why Madrid was at the centre" (44). Gecé's visual representations of Iberia's field of cultural production therefore illustrate an Iberianism and Americanism for that matter, that revolves around Madrid and Castile. As the next section in this chapter articulates, *La Gaceta Literaria*'s *iberismo* and *americanismo* were not only Madrid-centred but also connected to the journal's interest in having a stake in Luso-Hispanic book distribution.

Exposicones de libro: Iberismo and Americanismo

La Gaceta Literaria's *iberismo* and *americanismo* extended into the literary market itself. The Madrid journal invested greatly in organizing and funding book fairs that included banquets, speaker series, and featured major publishers. The first was the "Exposición del libro catalán" (1927) [Catalan Book Expo] followed by an "Exposición del libro portugués" [Portuguese Book Expo] (1928), and the "Exposición del libro argentino y uruguayo en Madrid" [Argentine and Uruguayan Book Expo in Madrid] (1928). *La Gaceta Literaria* promoted these events months before they took place. Even the "Exposición del libro portugués," which received remarkably less coverage overall than the other two, was regularly mentioned in almost every issue leading up to it. Moreover, marketing and event promotion for all three events occurred concurrently, regularly assuring readers that *La Gaceta Literaria* was staying true to its Iberian and American objectives by actively seeking to develop reciprocal relationships across the Iberian Peninsula and the Atlantic. For example, in the 15 January 1928 issue, *La Gaceta Literaria* reported on the "Exposición del libro catalán," published an article on Spain's relationship with Portugal (presumably setting readership up for the next Expo), and an account of a lecture Guillermo de Torre, who was instrumental in the "Exposición del libro argentino-uruguayo en Madrid," gave in Buenos Aires. While on one hand, these Book Expos are an example of how *La Gaceta Literaria* practised the rhetoric it preached in terms of supporting cultural reciprocity, on the other hand, the journal's significant investment in these endeavours suggests that gaining terrain in both the Iberian and the American literary market was at the heart of the Madrid-centred journal's *iberismo* and *americanismo*.

Exposición del libro catalán

Just as *La Gaceta Literaria* began to announce its first Book Expo, the "Exposición del libro catalán," the journal also created a new section it called *La Gaceta del Bibliófilo* [Bibliophile's Gazette] in its twenty-first issue, 1 November 1927: "Inauguramos en este número una sección constante que creemos responde a una necesidad sentida desde hace tiempo en nuestras letras: encauzar el movimiento bibliófilo de nuestro país y orientar a los amigos del libro antiguo, sobre su mercado y cotización" [We inaugurate in this issue a consistent section that we believe responds to a need our letters have had for some time: to channel our country's bibliophile movement and guide those interested in ancient books about their market value] (6). Articles in this section are primarily dedicated to promoting booksellers. For instance, the first instalment featured an interview between Barcelona avant-garde scene Uruguayan artist Rafael Barradas and López Llásuas, a Catalonian bookseller. It describes López Lláusas bookstore, Librería Catalonia, and emphasizes that they sell books in Castilian (as opposed to Catalan) that would be of interest to a Spanish American readership. Similarly, the second instalment of *La Gaceta del Bibliófilo* promotes a Madrid bookseller, Francisco Beltrán. Appearing in the issue dedicated to the "Exposición del libro catalán," the third instalment is a two-page section with large adds for booksellers in Madrid and in Barcelona, such as La Casa del Libro (Madrid), Montaner y Simón (Barcelona), and Espasa Calpe (Madrid). In addition to showcasing booksellers, *La Gaceta del Bibliófilo* also published descriptions of manuscript collections, such as the Marqués de Laurencin's collection (15 December 1927) and articles of interest related to the literary market. In a particularly intriguing piece entitled "El precio de los libros de ocasión" [The price of second-hand books] (15 January 1928), Jenaro Artiles Rodríguez evaluates how book prices have historically been determined. He describes the Brunet barometer for pricing, which he deems outdated, as well as the Salvá and the Heredia. Interestingly, he notes that Latin America, the nouveau riche, and the First World War have re-shaped the literary market. Setting the stage for the "Exposiciones" to come, the topics addressed in this section thus emphasize *La Gaceta Literaria*'s clear interest in participating in the literary market. Moreover, its first appearance only two issues prior to the inauguration of the "Exposición del libro catalán" further underscores the importance the journal placed on book distribution.

The *Exposición del libro catalán* opened on 5 December 1927 in the Biblioteca Nacional de Madrid [Madrid National Library] and closed on the 21st. *La Gaceta Literaria* reported on the event in four issues, from 1 December 1927 through 15 January 1928. The first three issues (1 December, 15 December, and 1 January) feature the book fair in Madrid as Castilians welcomed Catalans, and the last issue (15 January) narrates Catalans hosting Castilians in Barcelona. Additionally, *La Gaceta Literaria* deemed the event so successful that it published an account in the book *Cataluña ante España* [Catalonia Facing Spain] (Madrid 1930) as part of its series "Los cuadernos de *La Gaceta Literaria*" [*La Gaceta Literaria*'s Notebooks]. Together, journal issues and the book offer a comprehensive perspective of the event. *La Gaceta Literaria* reported on the schedule of events, highlighted happenings, such as banquets, published selected talks and articles, either on the event or on related topics (such as features on Catalan intellectuals), and dedicated significant print space to a catalogue of books for sale along with numerous ads for booksellers.

Offering a more comprehensive account than the journal's pages, *Cataluña ante España* details "toda una etapa histórica de relaciones culturales entre Castilla y Cataluña a partir de 1927 hasta ahora, 1930" (7) [an entire period of historic cultural relations between Castile and Catalonia from 1927 to the present, 1930]. Documentation on this "period of historic cultural relations" included all articles that *La Gaceta Literaria* published concerning the *Exposición del libro catalán* from 1 December 1927 through 1 February 1928, as well as print versions of lectures given during the book fair. Catalans such as Tomás Garcés, Miguel Ferra, Carles Soldevila, and Juan Esterlich covered topics including theatre, history, archeology, poetry, language, and, notably, editorial practices. These lectures were meant to contextualize Catalan cultural production for a Castilian audience.[27] *Cataluña ante España* also published accounts on the book fair from other newspapers, including *La Voz* (1920–39), *El Sol* (1917–39), and *ABC* (1903–present) in Madrid and Barcelona's *La Publicitat* (1922–39) and *La veu de Catalunya* (1899–1937). Notably, *La Gaceta Literaria* organized the "Exposición del libro catalán" as a reciprocal project. Madrid would host Barcelona and Catalonia would replicate the gesture shortly thereafter. Although this exchange is duly noted on journal pages, *Cataluña ante España*'s division into two parts, "El libro catalán en Madrid" [The Catalan Book in Madrid] and "Los intelectuales castellanos en Cataluña" [Castilian Intellectuals in Catalonia], seems to more firmly emphasize the importance of this event's reciprocity.

The first issue of *La Gaceta Literaria* dedicated to the "Exposición del libro catalán," 1 December 1927 includes a guide to the book fair, articles (in Castilian and in Catalan) about Catalan culture and artistic production, and many adds for Catalan bookstores and recent publications from Cataluña. Its opening article, "Saludo a Cataluña" [Greetings Catalonia], located front and centre on the first page, employed lofty rhetoric that was, presumably, meant to celebrate a new spirit of collaboration between Castile and Cataluña. However, a self-congratulatory tone throughout primarily touted *La Gaceta Literaria*'s admirable accomplishment, "A penas cumplido un año de su fundación, "*La Gaceta Literaria*" ve iniciarse el cumplimiento de uno de sus más tenaces ideales (por el que campó desde su número inaugural): la comprensión intelectual con Cataluña" [Just under a year since its founding, "*La Gaceta Literaria*" begins to accomplish one of its most ambitious ideals (for which it stood out since its inaugural issue): intellectual understanding with Cataluña] (1). Despite being relatively unknown in Madrid, *La Gaceta Literaria* states that Catalan letters possessed "auge y esplendor" [growth and splendour]. Cataluña had every right to be resentful of Castile's lack of attention to its cultural production and instead turn to France and Italy for intellectual exchange. Making amends, *La Gaceta Literaria* employed "modestísimas fuerzas" [modest forces] and "intentó corregir esa desviación vital de nuestra atención castellana" [attempted to correct that vital deviation of Castilian attention] (1). However, the journal makes the case that its aim was not "por pura política" [for pure politics] (1). Instead, their efforts were magnanimous and rooted in "un ideal ancho, liberalísimo y de dimensiones históricas" [a broad, very liberal ideal with historic dimensions] (1). Thus, in this opening article, *La Gaceta Literaria* portrays itself as a broad-minded entity that "humbly" corrected a grave, centuries-old wrongdoing. Despite portraying itself as selfless in its endeavour to establish cultural reciprocity with Catalonia, there is much telling evidence in *La Gaceta Literaria*'s promotion of the Catalan book fair that points to an underlying interest in the literary market. While an entire page dedicated to publishing companies, another detailing the exhibit catalogue of books, and large ads for editions and booksellers on seven of the issue's eight pages offer insight into who helped fund the *La Gaceta Literaria*'s event, these cursory examples also point to the Madrid journal's interest in the industry.

Two talks that opened the book fair (published in *Cataluña ante España*) illustrate the tension between a theoretical desire for cultural exchange and a Castilian inability to relinquish its historical role as empire's centre. In the first talk, conservative journalist and literary critic Andrenio (Eduardo López Barquero) spoke on behalf of Castile. He celebrated Catalan cultural accomplishments and acknowledged the importance of healthy Castilian–Catalan relations. Yet, his speech was nevertheless Castile-centred:

> no reniego de mi castellano, no me aparto del amor ni del orgullo de mi lengua. El castellano ha creado una de las cuatro principales literaturas modernas de Europa … Hoy mismo tiene figuras que pueden codearse con las primeras de Europa … Al castellano le cupo el más alto destino que puede corresponder a un idioma: ser lengua de naciones, sembrar un verbo por el Mundo [I don't deny my Castilian(ness), I don't set aside either my love or my pride for my language. Castilian has created one of Europe's four main, modern literatures … It presently has figures that can hold their own with the best in Europe … Castilian was bestowed with the most prestigious purpose that a language can have: to be a language for nations, to plant its verb throughout the World]. (*Cataluña ante España* 26)

Andrenio's praise for Castile thus directly contradicts the spirit of intellectual exchange among equals that was supposed to frame the event and instead recalls the power dynamic that the book fair was meant to help overcome.

Interestingly, at least according to the account available in *Cataluña ante España,* turning a blind eye to these remarks in his rejoinder to Andrenio's speech, Catalan Juan Esterlich "Elogió al maestro 'Andrenio', espíritu juvenil y generoso, que con ese gesto acogedor señala la grandeza y cordialidad de los intelectuales castellanos" [Praised master "Andrenio," [a] young and generous spirit whose inviting gesture points to the greatness and cordiality of Castilian intellectuals] (*Cataluña ante España* 27). Contrasting the Castilian's opening remarks, Esterlich's comments were fully in keeping with the proposed objectives for the book fair. Esterlich affirmed that Catalans were not interested in "localismos ni particularismo, que son injusticia y angostura mental. Nuestro resurgir significa la restauración de la vida interna de Cataluña. No discutimos ni nos defendemos. Sencillamente, trabajamos, afirmamos" [localisms or particularism, which are injustice and narrow-mindedness. Our resurgence implies the restoration of Cataluña's internal life. We neither quarrel nor defend ourselves. We simply work and affirm] (*Cataluña ante España* 27). Esterlich's views therefore more closely reflect those set forth by *La Gaceta Literaria* as values shaping its *iberismo,* one that promotes cultural inclusion but rejects petty regionalisms.

Putting Esterlich's rhetoric into action, Catalans hosted Castilians shortly after the Madrid book fair. The main purpose for this Castilian visit to Cataluña was an exhibition featuring Giménez Caballero's previously mentioned *Carteles* [Posters]. Just as Madrid had welcomed Cataluña with pomp and circumstance, Catalans responded in kind holding banquets in honour of their Castilian guests that also included a series of lectures. While the 15 January 1928 issue of *La Gaceta Literaria* printed a feature article on the first page, "Un Raid de '*La Gaceta Literaria*'" [A *La Gaceta Literaria* Raid] and a review by Antonio Espina entitled "Los carteles de Gecé" [Gecé's Posters], the journal paid considerably less attention to the Catalan events than it did to previous happenings in Madrid. *Cataluña ante España,* however, provides a more thorough account. It includes a schedule of events, talks given at the banquet, and articles by Catalan and Castilian intellectuals rendering their appraisal of the events. Since *Cataluña ante España* is a *La Gaceta Literaria* publication, true to form, its version of these events highlights the journal's very important role in making them happen: "*La Gaceta Literaria,* tenazmente, durante cuatro años de difícil censura, fué [*sic*] abriendo camino y haciendo posible el acto inolvidable que va reseñado a continuación" [*La Gaceta Literaria*, tenaciously, during four years of challenging censorship, was forging a path and making possible the unforgettable act that is being reviewed in what follows] (249).

Cataluña ante España also includes Gecé's commentary on the visit, which, in light of the Madrid-centred *Carteles* he was exhibiting in the Dalmau Gallery in Barcelona, proves ironic. For instance, he remarked that "Mis mejores amigos peninsulares no están en Madrid, sino en nuestra Barcelona. No están en una capital abstracta, sino en este concreto pueblo" [My best Peninsular friends are not in Madrid; they are in Barcelona. They are not in an abstract capital; they are in this concrete town] (264). Contradicting these statements, however, his "Universo the la literarura española contemporánea," described earlier, openly depicts Madrid as the centre of a Spanish literary field. At the same time, Gecé does not miss an opportunity to take credit for the cultural collaboration taking place: "fui el primero en inicar con entusiasmo lo que ahora comprobamos en la realidad" [I was the first to enthusiastically initiate what we now confirm in reality], which is perhaps why his journal occupies highest value space in his "Cartel de la nueva literatura" (274). As Ascunce Arenas explains, in these *Carteles*, journals, magazines, and newspapers set the coordinates for Gecé's pentagon with five triangles. And, unsurprisingly, Madrid and its print publications have the highest value. From Ascunce Arenas's perspective, this calculation could, in fact, have been owing to *La Gaceta Literaria*'s *iberismo*, "No other periodical involved in the new literary movement in Spain worked so diligently toward creating a more unified Spain through the arts. The value he placed on this 'higher' mission may be one of the reasons why the beta triangle, the one corresponding to Madrid, is greater than the alpha or the one corresponding to Barcelona" (20–1). Of course, Gecé's giving his own Madrid-based journal more value because of its work towards cultural inclusion seems to undermine the very *iberismo* it purported to endorse, one that seeks to equally embrace and promote the unique identities that shape the peninsula.

Exposición del libro Portugués

As the Castilian visit to Cataluña concluded, *La Gaceta Literaria* began announcing its next Iberian venture, the "Exposición del libro portugués" on 15 February 1928: "Como ya anunciamos desde nuestros primeros números *La Gaceta Literaria* prosigue en su programa ancho peninsular de inteligencias y comprensiones a base de intelectual pureza" [Just as we announced in our first issues, *La Gaceta Literaria* continues its broad Peninsular program supporting intelligences and understandings based on intellectual purity] (1). The journal underscored that, like the Exposición del libro Catalán, this upcoming event was proof that it was meeting the goals set forth in its first issue to "cuajar ese hueco ibérico" [fill that Iberian gap] ("Salutación" [Salutation] 1). Further noting their hope for a book fair in Buenos Aires, *La Gaceta Literaria* reminded its readers that, more than Iberian it was also American. Subsequent issues of *La Gaceta Literaria* would therefore update readers on the progress they were making towards organizing the "Exposicion del libro Portugués." For example, on 1 April 1928 *La Gaceta Literaria* mentioned that a Spanish organizing committee met with the Portuguese embassy and on 1 May 1928 it gave a detailed account of how Giménez Caballero was selected to lead a trip to Lisbon to start working with a Portuguese organizing committee. It describes how well the Portuguese received the founder of *La Gaceta Literaria,* noting that his visit was widely reported across the nation's periodicals. Additionally, the Madrid journal announced the eventual publication of a *Gaceta Portuguesa* [Portuguese Gazette]. While articles on developing the Portuguese book fair primarily appeared in the Iberian Postcards section, building up to the event, issues also included more articles related to Portugal, some in Portuguese. For instance, the 1 April 1928 issue dedicated to Catholicism and literature featured an article on Catholicism in Portugal published in Portuguese. A "Postal Portuguesa" [Portuguese Postcard] would also appear on 1 August 1928 with an article entitled "España y la Saudade" [Spain and Longing] by Aparicio that, in an effort towards cultural translation, explains how to apply the Portuguese concept of saudade [to yearn for] to Spain. Finally, the Iberian Postcards section frequently included notes on Portuguese periodicals, paying particular attention to *Presença* (Coimbra 1927–40).

Just like the "Exposición del libro catalán" before it, the "Exposición del libro portugués" took place at Madrid's National Library in October 1928. Dedicated entirely to Spanish–Portuguese relations *La Gaceta Literaria*'s 1 November 1928 issue offers a detailed account of the event. Again, akin to the "Exposición del libro catalán," this book fair also included a series of lectures and banquets. Likewise, a long list of editors and publishers representing a vast array of topics, including history, science, medicine, law, and pedagogy, made the event interdisciplinary as well as transcultural. Articles in this issue promote Portuguese culture and address Spanish–Portuguese relations. First, a series of articles offer detailed accounts of events surrounding the book fair. Again, these are similar to the account the journal gave of the "Exposición del libro catalán." This issue also promotes Portuguese culture with articles written in Portuguese on figures such as Oliveria Martins, Camillo Castelo Branco, and Latino Coelho. Other articles in Portuguese include Norberto de Araujo's "Duas obras notaveis" [Two notable works] and an anonymous article on editor Ventura Abrantes. *La Gaceta Literaria* also created space for Brazil. An article on Brazilian "Carlos Maul" is in Spanish, but a section entitled "Crónica brasileira" [Brazilian Chronicle] by Clodoaldo M. Marcondes is in Portuguese and offers an account of Brazil's recent literary historiography (since the nineteenth century). Disappointingly, however, empire's lens shapes his account that emphasizes Brazil's provincialism and fails to include the former colony's bustling avant-garde scene and its well-known 1922 Semana de Arte Moderna [Modern Art Week]. Instead, Marcondes argues that, in his estimation, Brazilian literature imitated European trends.

Opening with Ernesto Giménez Caballero's article "Saludo a Portugal" [Greetings Portugal], reciprocity between Spain and Portugal framed this 1 November 1928 issue of *La Gaceta Literaria*. Gecé enthusiastically thanks Portugal's intellectuals, editors, and press for acknowledging *La Gaceta Literaria*'s efforts to make the event possible. He then expresses dismay with Spain's lack of enthusiasm for this event: "Contrasta mucho esa nobleza desinteresada de Portugal con el silencio, que sería inexplicable si no fuese muy explicable, de los intelectuales editores y la prensa central de la Península frente al mismo hecho" [Portugal's selfless nobility stands in stark contrast to the silence, which would be unexplainable were it not so explainable, of intellectual editors and the Peninsula's central press on the same event] (1). However, he makes it a point to exclude Cataluña from critique, "Cataluña no. Cataluña, siempre alerta y vital, nos interpeló generosamente en seguida solicitándonos trasladar allí esta misma Exposición" [Not Catalonia. Catalonia, always alert and vital, generously asked us if we wanted to hold the exhibition there] (1). *La Gaceta Literaria*'s efforts to unify Iberia were thus met with support from the periphery (Portugal and Cataluña) but were largely ignored by the centre, Madrid, despite being the journal's place of publication and the site for these events intended to promote cultural reciprocity. Nevertheless, Gecé professes a steadfast commitment to include Iberian languages and cultures set forth in his journal's first issue:

> Pero al saludar ahora a Portugal, nosotros, que desde nuestro primer número hemos abierto nuestras columnas a la lengua fraterna; nosotros, que hemos procurado seguir en todo lo posible el movimiento literario luso; nosotros, que hemos iniciado las Exposiciones de libros en España con carácter de comprensión peninsular, podemos alzar la voz y decir:

> ¡La Exposición del Libro Portugués en Madrid no significará nada si no se respeta y subraya por todos el espíritu que la informó! [But, as we greet Portugal, we, who from our first issue opened our columns to the fraternal language; we, who have procured to follow Luso literary movements to the extent that it is possible; we, who have initiated Book Fairs in Spain that seek to promote Peninsular understanding, can raise our voice and say: The Portuguese Book Fair in Madrid will not mean anything if the spirit that informed it is not respected and underscored by all!] (1)

Moreover, he further maintains that cultural exchange should be the event's most important outcome, "que, obras de lengua y cultura hermanas, convivan y conferencien con las nuestras" [that works of sibling languages and cultures live and confer with ours] (1). Neglecting to mention the obvious economic framework that drives this type of commercial event, Gecé underscores the book fair's importance as a means of creating "Peninsular understanding."

Interestingly, Giménez Caballero's wording in "Saludo a Portugal" has much in common with Guillermo de Torre's discourse in the editorial that instigated the *polémica del meridiano intelectual*. Like de Torre, Gecé speaks in idealistic terms of language and culture as unifying agents that supersede borders. Further echoing de Torre's "Madrid, meridiano intelectual," Gecé's "Saludo a Portugal" proposes "un intercambio de amistad que hace iluminar estampas de viejos siglos" [a friendship exchange that makes prints from past centuries light up] (1), that would strengthen Luso-Hispanism and make it a cultural meridian. Again, his rhetoric is quite similar to de Torre's proposal for a Madrid meridian between Spain and Latin America: "mientras el meridiano de la cultura de la Península siga pasando por París, Londres, Berlín, Roma, será una insensatez en que pase un día por Barcelona, Madrid, Lisboa, Buenos Aires, Río de Janeiro" [while the Peninsula's cultural meridian continues to go through Paris, London, Berlin, Rome, it will be foolish for it to one day go through Barcelona, Madrid, Lisbon, Buenos Aires, Río de Janeiro] (1). Both de Torre and Gecé present similar arguments in favour of capitalizing on cultural commonalities and linguistic affinities in order to shift "meridians" and gain prestige within the field.

Gecé claims that the book fair's objective is to "educar a todos los nuestros a mirar insistentemente todo lo nuestro" [to educate all of ours to insistently look upon what is ours] and this issue of *La Gaceta Literaria* does make it a point to inform its readers of a history of literary reciprocity between Spain and Portugal with articles such as "Enlaces literarios de Galicia y Portugal" [Galician and Portuguese Literary Liaisons] by Correa Calderón. Detailing a history of ethnic affinity between

Galicia and Portugal, separated politically by Castilian dominance of Spain and geographically by the Miño [Minho] River, Correa Calderón's article offers an example of why a cultural and literary alliance between Spain and Portugal is natural and organic. He notes that Castilian dominance of Spain inhibited the Galician language's evolution and that, as a result, it is currently closest to an archaic form of Portuguese. Nevertheless, for Correa Calderón, the deep-seated connections between Galicia and Portugal are a strength that can help enable Iberian cultural reciprocity.

Moving beyond rhetorical discussions surrounding Iberian cultural reciprocity, this *La Gaceta Literaria* issue does acknowledge the tangible exchange of books in the market as a key reason for the event. A clear intent to highlight, publishers, booksellers, and recent publications underscore the industry's importance in this event. The issue's "Guía de la Exposición" [Expo Guide], for instance, lists the many editors and publishing houses present at the "Exposición del libro portugués." Additionally, much like the issue detailing the "Exposición del libro catalán," ads for editors, bookstores, and publishing houses pepper the lengthy eight-page tome. And, as might be expected, the "Escaparate de libros" [Books Showcase] column features "Libros portugueses"[Portuguese Books], highlighting recent Portuguese publications and the import editors responsible for their distribution. This section also includes a list of ten Portuguese publications with either a short summary or a quote along with its publication information. Norberto de Araujo's earlier-mentioned article in Portuguese, "Duas obras notaveis" [Two Notable Works] promotes *O Guia de Portugal* [The Portugal Guide] and the national edition of *Os Lusiadas* [The Lusiads], published by the Portuguese National Library. Alongside it, a piece on Norberto de Araujo himself makes it a point to state that his novel *Novela do Amor Humilde* (1927) [Humble Love Novel] was published by Aillaud e Bertrand, "la más importante librería editora de Portugal" [the most important publishing house in Portugal] also shape this section (3). Finally, a large ad for Espasa-Calpe separates the "Escaparate de libros" on "Libros portugueses" from an article on Portuguese journalist and writer Antonio Ferro and a piece on Portuguese bookseller and publisher Ventura Abrantes.

Various articles in this issue further corroborate *La Gaceta Literaria*'s interest in making its way into the Portuguese literary market. For example, in their contributions to the issue, M. García Blanco and Vitorino Nemesio point to the literary market when they speak of cultural exchange between Portugal and Spain. In "Coimbra en alta voz" [Coimbra Out Loud], M. García Blanco exalts the "Exposición del libro portugués" for achieving mutual understanding (6). Promoting healing and camaraderie, García Blanco says that the university city of Coimbra in Portugal is eager to engage Castilian cultural movements. Notably he describes Madrid as a geographic centre and "meridiano de Iberia" [Iberian Meridian], but argues that Coimbra, and not Lisbon, will be the most receptive to literary exchange: "Los universitarios españoles tendrán excelente acogida en Coimbra; sus libros lograrán pléyade de lectores, y sus conferencias, oyentes capacitados" [Spanish university students will be warmly welcomed in Coimbra; their books will earn distinguished readers, and their conferences will have well-trained participants] (6). Further calling attention to Coimbra as a key node for Iberian book distribution, in "Coimbra e o livro Portugués" [Coimbra and the Portuguese Book], Vitorino Nemesio echoes García Blanco's point that, as a college town, Coimbra pays a significant role in the literary market. Nemesio traces Coimbra's participation in the literary industry back to the thirteenth century and underscores that "Hoje, o libro é um dos produtos mais ricos de Coimbra, que conta seis grandes livrarias e três casas editoras de vulto" [Today, the book is one of Coimbra's richest products, with six great bookstores and three notable publishing houses] (6). While both articles promote inter-Iberian exchange and introduce *La Gaceta Literaria*'s readers to Portuguese culture, their distinct focus on the literary market also supports the Madrid journal's objective to procure solid footing in the publishing industry.

Perhaps the most conspicuous indication of *La Gaceta Literaria*'s interest in gaining access to the Portuguese literary market is an interview with Portuguese bookseller Alejo Correa, "El libro español en Portugal" [The Spanish Book in Portugal]. This anonymous article explains that Correa is a key figure in the literary market for peninsular and foreign books as well as print culture in Portugal (7). His Sociedad Comercial Portuguesa de Publicaciones y Telegrafía [Portuguese Commercial Society of Publications and Telegraphy], is "la institución que necesitaban los editores portugueses y de la que no pueden prescindir tampoco los editores españoles que deseen introducir el libro español en Portugal" [the institution that Portuguese editors needed and that Spanish editors interested in bringing the Spanish book to Portugal cannot do without] (7). Correa tells the interviewer that his Sociedad Comercial Portuguesa de Publicaciones made possible twenty-three bookstores at train stations with more than three hundred agents throughout the country. He further specifies that foreign tomes, including Spanish publications, sell most in Portugal and, among books sold, French books come in only second to Portuguese books. When asked to explain why French books sell so much better than Spanish books in Portugal, Correa explained that it had much to do with French editors' process and organization. They regularly send books in bulk, which enables selling them at cheaper prices than Spanish books that arrive in small and often damaged shipments. Pressing Correa, the interviewer asks him to speculate on what successful book distribution in Portugal could look like. Correa acknowledges that there is a market for Spanish books in Portugal, but stresses that much would need to be done in order to establish this relationship. On the one hand, acceptable conventions would need to be negotiated and Spain would have to create an efficient export organization. On the other hand, the relationship would need to be reciprocal and Spanish editors would have to agree to publish Portuguese books.

Exposición del libro Argentino Uruguayo

Just as the "Exposición del libro catalán" and the "Exposición del libro portugués" suggest that *La Gaceta Literaria*'s *iberismo* was tied to the journal's aspirations of monetizing cultural reciprocity through book distribution, the journal's sponsorship of an "Exposición del libro argentino-uruguayo en Madrid" in 1929 signals the reason for its investment in *americanismo*. Moreover, the timely occurrence of the "Exposición del libro argentino-uruguayo en Madrid" in the wake of the *polémica del meridiano intelectual* supports the notion that *La Gaceta Literaria*'s underlying goal in publishing the editorial was to establish a network for transatlantic book distribution. Notably, in the first of a series of articles that de Torre would publish leading up to the event entitled "Ante la exposición del libro argentino y uruguayo en Madrid" [In light of the Argentine and Uruguayan Book Expo in Madrid] (*La Gaceta Literaria* 1 August 1928), he clarified that the debate's core issue was transatlantic book distribution: "todo este pleito inevitable y salutífero entraña más bien un problema editorial y librero" [this entire inevitable and healthy feud more precisely entails more of an editorial and bookseller problem] (243). He further proclaimed that the upcoming event was an important step towards resolving the *polémica del meridiano intelectual*'s central conflict and asserted that, despite their animosity, the heated disputes over cultural hegemony in the polemic actually concealed a desire for transatlantic collaboration.

"Ante la exposición del libro argentino y uruguayo en Madrid" can be read as a revision to de Torre's controversial 1927 editorial, one that underscores how the practical application of cultural reciprocity could be beneficial to all parties involved. The Spanish author and editor detailed how a Madrid meridian was simply a concrete solution to book distribution obstacles faced by both Spanish and Latin American publishers. First, he noted that transatlantic travel was easier than travelling within Latin America. He explained that Spanish intellectuals had come into contact with Latin Americans from different nationalities because they more regularly ventured across the Atlantic than throughout their own continent. Spaniards had therefore met Latin Americans from more nationalities than Latin Americans had themselves. He thus argued that Spaniards, paradoxically, had a more continental vision of Latin America than most Latin Americans. As a result, de Torre reasoned that, given its geographical advantages, Madrid could easily provide a "un punto común de partida" [a common starting point] for "esa mercancía intelectual" [that intellectual merchandise] (243). Again, he underscored that this idea was merely a sensible solution to a geographical challenge. And, bearing in mind the reactions to his first editorial, de Torre insisted that this suggestion had no hegemonic implications. Logistically, the Spanish capital would simply provide "una medida de interés cultural y de eficacia económica, dadas las mejores condiciones en que España se encuentra para esa labor difusora" [a measure for cultural interest and economic efficiency, given the better conditions for distribution in Spain] (243). As such, the city could merely function as a "centro bibliográfico en Europa de toda la producción Americana" [European bibliographic centre for all American production] (243). Framing the idea as a favour to Latin America, de Torre clarified that Madrid would only play this role temporarily. Of course, the Spanish capital had much to gain from so generously funnelling Latin America's literary exports throughout Europe. More than a bibliographic centre as an editorial hub, Madrid would have a say in publication and distribution of Latin American texts within Europe and Latin America, thus imbuing the former empire with economic and cultural control over Latin America. As a result, de Torre's proposal more closely resembles the export age relationship between Europe and Latin America. Just as Latin America exported its raw materials to Europe in exchange for industrialized products, de Torre and *La Gaceta Literaria*'s proposal equates Latin American literature with raw materials to be industrialized in Spain and then sold back to the former colonies, replicating colonial asymmetry.

Guillermo de Torre further addressed the idea of making Madrid a centre for literary publication and distribution in a series of interviews with Argentine and Spanish publishers. These interviews were part of *La Gaceta Literaria*'s promotional campaign leading up to the 1928 "Exposición del libro argentino-uruguayo en Madrid." De Torre connected with Argentines Samuel Glusberg (also a *Martín Fierro* editor), Manuel Gleizer, Juan Roldán, and Jacobo Samet, and two Spanish editors: Pedro García, whose publishing house was in Buenos Aires, and Julián Urgoiti, Espasa-Calpe's representative in the Argentine capital. Responses from the Argentine editors regarding the idea of a Madrid centre for literary distribution were mixed. Glusberg told de Torre that, economically, entering the Spanish book market was not lucrative for his Editorial Babel. Yet, de Torre recounted that, "sin pestañear" [without blinking], Glusberg stated that his interest in selling his books in Spain stemmed from "razones de conquista espiritual" [reasons pertaining to a spiritual conquest], thus suggesting, and here I borrow Alejandro Mejías López's term, an "inverted conquest" (249).[28] Gleizer held the same view and Roldán (Juan Roldán y Compañía) dismissed the proposal, maintaining that readership needed to increase before the creation of a publication hub could even be considered. Samet, however, agreed with de Torre that a reciprocal venture would be beneficial to both parties. As might be expected, Spanish editors García and Urgoiti also endorsed de Torre's enterprise, but García pointed out that in practice, it would be very difficult to accomplish.

Evaluating the *polémica del meridiano intelectual*, and *La Gaceta Literaria*'s *americanismo* for that matter, in light of the Exposición del libro argentino-uruguayo en Madrid," further illustrates that the Madrid journal's overtures towards cultural reciprocity were motivated by a desire to claim a space in the literary industry. De Torre and *La Gaceta Literaria* were well aware of Buenos Aires's burgeoning literary scene and growing publishing industry. Marrying Jorge Luis Borges's sister, Norah Borges, de Torre had moved to Buenos Aires where he became co-editor of *La Gaceta Literaria*'s "Gaceta Americana" [American Gazette] (Benjamín Jarnés was co-editor in Madrid).[29] As a result, he was very well acquainted with Argentina's literary market. While foreign companies still dominated the Argentine publishing industry, French, Italian, German, and, to a lesser degree, Spanish, national publishers such as Gleizer, Glusberg, and Samet, were substantially developing the industry during the 1920s (De Diego 59). Events that mark this significant growth include the "Primera Exposición Nacional del Libro" [First National Book Expo] organized by Samuel Glusberg in Mar del Plata (March 1928), and the "Exposición Nacional del Libro," which took place six months later in Buenos Aires (September 1928), also coordinated by Glusberg, along with Ricardo Rojas, Arturo Capdevila, and many other prominent Argentine writers and intellectuals (De Diego 60).[30] However, despite their national success, as Peruvian thinker José Carlos Mariátegui observed in "La batalla del libro" [The Book Battle], his review of the "Primera Exposición Nacional del Libro" [First National Book Expo] in Mar del Plata, "[e]n lo que concierne a su abastecimiento de libros, los países de Sudamérica continúan siendo colonias españolas" [in terms of book supply, South American countries continue to be Spanish colonies] (140).[31] He thus maintained that, in terms of book distribution, "los escritores de *La Gaceta Literaria* (sic) estaban en lo cierto cuando declaraban a Madrid meridiano literario de Hispano-América" [*La Gaceta Literaria* writers were correct when they declared Madrid Spanish-America's literary meridian] (140). Yet, the Peruvian thinker did clarify that, of all Latin American countries, Argentina "es el que más ha avanzado hacia su emancipación" [is the one that has made most progress towards emancipation] (140). As a result, although France, Germany, Italy, and Spain dominated the Argentine book industry, rapid national growth during the 1920s could jeopardize European control, which further explains de Torre's interest in promoting Madrid as a "meridian" or "bibliographic centre." Having a centre for book distribution for all Spanish and Latin American books in Madrid would accomplish two goals for Spain by first divesting other European countries from their dominance of the Latin American market and simultaneously preventing the Argentine book industry from expanding and potentially gaining control of it. Organizing an "Exposición del libro Argentino-Uruguayo en Madrid" was therefore an instrumental first step in achieving this outcome.

Conclusions

La Gaceta Literaria's content and format illustrates an undeniable attempt to achieve objectives of being American and Iberian. The journal's main shortcoming, however, was the disconnect between the altruistic, selfless rhetoric it employed to cross borders and overcome boundaries, and its underlying intent to become a key player in transatlantic and Iberian book distribution. As a result, *La Gaceta Literaria*'s otherwise commendable efforts appear deceitful. Another pitfall was the Madrid journal's inability to surrender an unmistakably Castilian-centred perspective. Yet, at the same time, the bombastic exchanges it incited earned *La Gaceta Literaria* a position of prestige in both the transatlantic and Iberian fields, which, in turn, enabled its successful book fairs. Moreover, within and beyond its own borders, the journal generated trans-Iberian, transatlantic, and trans-European interactions that successfully transgressed geographical and national boundaries, generating discussions and mobilizing key cultural stakeholders, including, authors, publishers, and booksellers. Unlike other little magazines, *La Gaceta Literaria* also managed to withstand the test of time without sacrificing the quality, quantity, and the diversity material it published.

Arguably, this success was, in part, owing to its contradictory *americanismo* and *iberismo*. Placating financial backers and investing in the literary market allowed it the monetary means to maintain its strong voice in print for longer than most publications of its kind.

La Gaceta Literaria's trajectory in shaping its *americanismo* and *iberismo* exemplifies how print culture can inform Hispanism's approaches to literary historiography, such as Iberian and Transatlantic Studies. Its very form, the placement of articles, the space they occupy, and their linguistic plurality provide a unique visual account of an Iberian and Transatlantic enterprise. Additionally, the Madrid journal's effort opened a space for dialogue and debate on topics such as regionalism, nationalism, language, translation, culture, and empire. Mapping these discussions enables current scholars to more precisely situate texts when evaluating literary historiography. *La Gaceta Literaria*'s linguistic inclusivity and overall coverage of Iberia and American nations provided a space where empire could be debated on the printed page, thereby visually charting the tensions and challenges that have, and continue to, arise in defining Iberian and Transatlantic Studies. At the same time, the journal's inability to "shake empire" encourages scholarship to account for empire's looming lens in shaping Iberian and Transatlantic research practices. Finally, akin to *Gaceta Literaria*'s conflicting relationship between conceptual *iberismo* and *americanismo* and the very tangible literary market that kept it afloat, Iberian and Transatlantic Studies must meet the challenge of aligning abstract, pluralistic visions with very concrete realities such as institutional organization, departmental divisions, curricula, and the job market students must navigate.

Chapter Four

Vying for Aesthetic Capital

La existencia de la literatura se marca por las polémicas que suscita [Literature's existence is made evident by the polemics it incites].

Salvador Novo, *El Universal Ilustrado*, 22 January 1925

If, as Mexican avant-garde poet and novelist Salvador Novo asserted, literature's existence is made evident according to the polemics it creates, then, by hosting and often initiating contentious exchanges, journals, magazines, and newspapers play a crucial role in literature's development. A brief review of a work of literature appearing in a journal, magazine, or newspaper, might seem insignificant and ephemeral. However, as this chapter will illustrate, such fragmentary writings impact literary aesthetic developments both within national boundaries and across borders. For example, in November 1920 Spanish playwright and critic Cipriano Rivas Cherif reviewed Alfonso Reyes's collection of stories *El plano oblicuo* [The Oblique Plane] (1920) for Madrid's *La Pluma* (1920–4). Rather than focusing on Reyes's writing, however, Rivas Cherif commented on the poet and diplomat's position as a prominent figure within Spanish letters, underscoring his equanimity. This admirable quality, according to Rivas Cherif, made Reyes less like Latin Americans and more like "los españoles de hoy, menguados herederos de la castiza sobriedad de espíritu" [today's Spaniards, diminished heirs to Castilian spiritual sobriety] (283).[1] Using Reyes's figure as a starting point, Rivas Cherif then questioned the current state of Spanish letters, and, two decades after *modernismo* had claimed Latin American aesthetic independence, asserted that it was, "la participación española en el concierto europeo" [Spain's participation in Europe's concert] (283). Unable to relinquish empire, the Spanish intellectual proposed that *modernismo* was a Spanish aesthetic development that had actually strengthened

Spain and Latin America's relationship. Similarly, "Alfonso Reyes, escritor en quien se cumplen verdaderamente las afinidades electivas hispanoamericanas, tan gastadas en las salvas oficiales" (283) [Alfonso Reyes, [is] a writer who truly fulfils Latin American elected affinities, which are so overused in official salutes]. According to Rivas Cherif, just like *modernismo*, Reyes, although coming from Latin America, was worthy of being considered "españoles de hoy" [today's Spaniards]. Appearing towards the end of the *La Pluma* issue, and surrounded by other writings of its kind, Rivas Cherif's seemingly inconsequential review of Reyes's *El plano oblicuo* (which barely remarks on the Mexican poet's anthology) was loaded with unresolved postcolonial tension. As the examples centring poetry and prose described in this chapter demonstrate, Latin American independent nations struggled to establish their cultural autonomy and defend hard-won national identities while Spain attempted to erase borders and maintain cultural dominance over their former colonies. Print culture maps this transatlantic tug of war in which both sides claimed authorship and ownership of literary movements and styles.

While Reyes did not directly respond to Rivas Cherif's articles, he did engage the Spanish critic's commentary in his own contribution to *La Pluma*, "Valle-Inclán y América" [Valle-Inclán and America] (*La Pluma* January 1923), part of a special issue dedicated to Spanish *modernista* Ramón del Valle Inclán. Articles in this issue praised Valle Inclán's dexterity in multiple genres, such as prose, poetry, and theatre. Alfonso Reyes penned the only contribution by a Latin American author. Pointing out that Mexico had shaped Valle Inclán's *modernismo*, Reyes countered Rivas Cherif's view that there was no relationship between literature and nationalism. Taking his point a step further, Reyes described Valle Inclán's novels as a positive result of transatlantic exchange. The Mexican poet and diplomat credited Latin America's cultural and geographic diversity for its role in the advent of new aesthetic forms that were both Spanish and Latin American. Thus contrasting Rivas Cherif's review, Reyes's article evokes reciprocity between equals. Valle Inclán's *modernista* writings were neither Spanish nor Latin American, but rather part of one field of cultural production that traversed the Atlantic in both directions. Akin to this perspective, this chapter argues that, as print culture plainly reveals, Hispanic avant-garde poetry and prose are transnational and transatlantic, the result of extensive dialogues (and often contentious debates) between Spanish and Latin American intellectuals.

The first part of this chapter details polemical exchanges between Spanish poet and *La Gaceta Literaria* editor Guillermo de Torre and multiple Latin American counterparts: Chilean Vicente Huidobro, Argentines Roberto A. Ortelli and Jorge Luis Borges, and Mexican *Contemporáneos* poet Jorge Cuesta. A tug of war in which poets nitpicked over the similarities and origins of poetic styles, *creacionismo* [Creationism] and *ultraísmo* [Ultraism], these debates are concerned with cultural prestige, nationalism, and authorship. The second part of this chapter describes a debate centred on vanguard prose and José Ortega y Gasset's theory on *The Dehumanization of Art* (1925). This dispute over aesthetic imitation and a dehumanized aesthetic between Mexican Jaime Torres Bodet and Spanish Benjamín Jarnés began on journal pages, *El Estudiante* (Salamanca-Madrid 1924–6) and *Valoraciones* (Buenos Aires 1923–7), and culminated in Torres Bodet's novel *Margarita de niebla* [Misty Margarita] (1927). A discussion on *El Estudiante*'s publication of Ramón del Valle Inclán's *Tirano Banderas* [Tyrant Banderas] (1926) as an affirmation of its position-taking within a Spanish American field of cultural production concludes this chapter. Thematically and stylistically, this vanguard prose novel bridges the Atlantic and fully participates in a Spanish American field of cultural production. Just like *El Estudiante*, it endorsed a dialogue intended to do away with outdated imperialist paradigms.

Creation and Imitation: Debating *creacionismo* and *ultraísmo*

Creacionismo [Creationism], a poetic movement developed by Chilean Vicente Huidobro in 1914, called upon poets to stop imitating reality and instead take control of their medium. Employing adjectives and metaphors, poets could create a world of their own with verse. First introducing his movement in Chile in 1914, Huidobro then disseminated his new poetic style in Buenos Aires, Argentina, two years later.[2] Subsequently transporting *creacionismo* to Europe when he moved to Paris in 1916, the Chilean poet further developed his aesthetic as he came into contact with leading cubists and futurists in Parisian avant-garde circles. Huidobro then brought *creacionismo* to Madrid in 1918. That same year, Spanish poets including Guillermo de Torre, Rafael Cansinos-Asséns, and Gerardo Diego, together with Argentine Jorge Luis Borges (then living in Madrid) sought to break with *modernismo* and revolutionize poetry. They created *ultraísmo*, a style that focused the metaphor, poetry's most rudimentary element. Andalusian poet Isaac del Vando Villar's journal *Grecia* (Sevilla 1918–20) published their first *Manifiesto ultraísta* [Ultraist Manifesto] in 1919 and the movement spread across Spain in other short-lived journals, including *Ultra* (Madrid 1921–2).

Ultraism became a transatlantic movement when Borges returned to Argentina in 1921 and plastered the Buenos Aires cityscape with *Revista Mural Prisma*, a large, one-page flyer filled with their poetry. Almost simultaneously, Mexican poet Manuel Maples Arce posted his *Estridentista* Manifesto, *Actual 1*, on Mexico City's walls, which, as de Torre claimed in his *Literaturas europeas de vanguardia* [European Vanguard Literatures] (1925), resembled the Ultraist manifesto *Vertical* [Vertical] he had published in 1920.[3] In fact, as Luis Mario Schneider points out in *El estridentismo: México (1921–1927)* (1985) [Stridentism in Mexico (1921–1927), in *Actual 1* Maples Arce called de Torre his "hermano espiritual" [spiritual brother] (Schneider 43). Moreover, in *El estridentismo o la literatura de estrategia* (1970) [Stridentism or a Strategic Literature], Schneider helps explain the affinity between Ultraism and Maples Arce's Stridentism, noting that Ultraism had reached Mexico through journals like *Ultra* (Madrid 1921–2), *Grecia* (Sevilla-Madrid 1918–20), and *Cosmópolis* (Madrid 1919–22). In addition, in "Manuel Maples Arce: Correspondencia con Guillermo de Torre (1921–1922)" [Manuel Maples Arce: Correspondence with Guillermo de Torre], Carlos García cites exchanges between these intellectuals, which establish de Torre's role acting as an "intellectual meridian" between Borges and Maples Arce. Furthermore, Maples Arce published Borges's poem "Ciudad" [City] (a version that did not make it into *Fervor de Buenos Aires* (1923) in his first *estridentista* journal, *Irradiador* (Mexico 1923), and Borges deemed Maples Arce's poetry collection *Andamios interiores: Poemas radiográficos* [Interior Scaffolding: Radiographic Poems] to be *ultraísta* in "Acotaciones: Eduardo González Lanuza" [Annotations: Eduardo González Lanuza] published in Buenos Aires's *Proa* in August 1924.[4]

Like the historical avant-gardes that emerged during the same period, Creationism, Ultraism, and Stridentism were at once nationalist and transnational. Although these movements identified with their creators' country of origin, in this case Chile, Spain, and Mexico, as the above summary of their trajectories demonstrates, these poetic styles developed within national boundaries, across borders, and the Atlantic. On one hand, their creators travelled and came into contact with each other. And, on the other hand, print culture enabled dialogues, such as the positive interaction between Borges and Maples Arce cited above, that transcended borders. Focusing on perhaps less amical but equally intriguing exchanges, this section will underscore print culture's key role in outlining a Spanish American field of cultural production. Ironically, despite their objective of proving originality and difference, these often-heated exchanges centring on authorship and cultural prestige actually demonstrate the opposite. These poetic movements had much in common precisely because they were part of the same transnational and transatlantic field of cultural production. As a result, evaluating this literary corpus requires considering the national, transnational, and transatlantic context within which it developed.

The first series of intense altercations this section will evaluate took place between Vicente Huidobro and Guillermo de Torre around tensions between Ultraism and Creationism. Spanish poet and critic Guillermo de Torre, already discussed in this book for his role in the *polémica del meridiano intelectual*, disputed the originality of Huidobro's Creationism. De Torre's editorial "Madrid: Meridiano intelectual de Hispanoamérica" instigated the *polémica del meridiano intelectual* because Latin American intellectuals read the article as an attempt to gain control over cultural capital. Likewise, control over cultural capital was the main driver behind the dispute between de Torre and Huidobro. De Torre was the instigator in this series of exchanges as well, and his main goals were to discredit Creationism, and therefore Huidobro's claims to poetic originality, in order to affirm Castilian Ultraism's unique contribution to vanguard aesthetics. The heated squabble between de Torre and Huidobro took place in the Galician journal *Alfar* (La Coruña 1923–7) from September 1923 to April 1924. De Torre opened the debate with "Los verdaderos antecedentes líricos del creacionismo en Vicente Huidobro" [The True Lyrical Antecedents of Vicente Huidobro's Creacionismo] in September 1923. Huidobro retorted in April 1924 with "Al fin se descubre mi maestro" [My Teacher Has Finally Been Discovered] in *Alfar* 39 and de Torre closed the tense interaction with "Rasgos polémicos: Réplica a Vicente Huidobro" [Polemical Features: Response to Vicente Huidobro] in the same issue.

Intentionally triggering discord, de Torre's first article in this series set out to defame Huidobro and mock his claims to having initiated Creationism. He declared that Uruguayan poet Julio Herrera y Reissig was the "genuino e insospechado precreacionista" [genuine and unexpected pre-Creationist] who had significantly influenced "los pretendidos monopolizadores de esta" [this movement's alleged monopolizers] (32). De Torre made his case by painstakingly comparing multiple examples of Herrera y Reissig's and Huidobro's poetry, highlighting their similarities, which, he insisted, denied the Chilean poet authorship of Creationism (32). Not only had de Torre affirmed that Huidobro did not invent Creationism, he had also accused him of imitating a poet whose style the Chilean did not appreciate. Therefore, in his response, Huidobro sardonically thanked de Torre for naming Herrera y Reissig his predecessor: "Gracias a los esfuerzos del sagaz detective Guillermo de Torre se descubre (sic) finalmente los orígenes del Creacionismo"

[Thanks to the efforts of sagacious detective Guillermo de Torre, the origins of *Creacionismo* are finally discovered] (347). Since de Torre had so meticulously compared and contrasted specific examples of Huidobro's and Herrera Reissig's poetry in order to prove his point, the Chilean poet satirized the Spanish critic's methodology by using the same examples. For instance, he ridiculed de Torre for comparing two verses that had only one commonality, the use of the word "astros" [celestial body] (347). Huidobro further compared de Torre's "discovery" of the true origins of Creationism with Christopher Columbus's fortuitous "discovery" of the Americas when he originally set out to reach India, implying that, like Columbus, de Torre didn't "discover" anything. Continuing his parody, Huidobro accused himself of having imitated none other than de Torre. Employing de Torre's technique of juxtaposing Huidobro's and Herrera y Reissig's verses in order to impugn the Chilean for plagiarism, Huidobro compared examples of his poetry to de Torre's, repeatedly admonishing himself for not having predicted what de Torre would write in the future. Moreover, as Huidobro surveyed his poetry in comparison to de Torre's, he facetiously stressed that the Spanish poet's verses were far superior to his own. And, brimming with irony, Huidobro praised de Torre's more sophisticated poetic dexterity and thanked the Spanish poet for reviving his creations.

Rebutting Huidobro's article, de Torre wrote the last piece in this altercation. He first took aim at Huidobro's grammar, accusing him of having "created" his own morphology and chastising evident French influence in his syntax. The Spanish thinker then reproached Huidobro's sarcastic tone, discrediting the Chilean's satire as "fácil humorismo" [simple humour] and snubbed him for "defenderse acusando" [defending himself by accusing] (353). Charging the Chilean of excessive vanity, de Torre explained that Huidobro's enormous ego left him no other choice but to comb through *Hélices* [Propellers] (1923), line by line, in an attempt to refute his allegations. Echoing accusations Huidobro had made against de Torre, the Spanish poet claimed that Huidobro selected verses from *Hélices* that were only loosely related to the Chilean's poetry, because they either used similar vocabulary or employed metaphors in a comparable manner. Thus, as Huidobro had done employing de Torre's own methodology, the Spanish poet deemed the Chilean poet's associations flimsy and incapable of sustaining a valid argument against him.

Despite their brevity and pettiness, these articles in a Galician journal contribute to outlining a field of cultural production and help situate literary works. The fact that they engaged an aesthetic debate in the first place suggests that de Torre and Huidobro were participating in the same field of cultural production. Additionally, both poets' efforts to detail the differences between their poetry actually underscore their similarities and thus provide further evidence of their participation in one transnational and transatlantic field of cultural production. Moreover, their tug of war over authorship and, consequently, cultural capital, can be read as symptomatic of other underlying postcolonial tensions. In this case, as Huidobro's allusion to Columbus suggests, this dispute was more likely connected to negotiating a postcolonial cultural relationship between Spain and Latin America than to subtle differences and similarities between Creationism and Ultraism. From this perspective, de Torre's attempt to discredit Huidobro can more plausibly be understood as an effort to maintain Spanish cultural dominance over its former colonies than as an actual disagreement over poetic form. As the next section details, exchanges over Ultraism between de Torre and Argentine intellectuals further supports this theory.

Ultraísmo(s): De Torre vs. Argentina's "Nueva Generación"

Upon his return from Spain in 1921, Jorge Luis Borges brought Ultraism to Argentina. In December 1921 Alfredo A. Bianchi and Roberto F. Giusti's journal *Nosotros* (Buenos Aires 1907–43) published his *manifiesto ultraísta* [Ultraist Manifesto], and the *Revista Mural Prisma* graced Buenos Aires's façades announcing the new poetic movement.[5] Signed by de Torre and Argentines Eduardo González Lanuza, Guillermo Juan, and Borges, *Mural Prisma* proclaimed Ultraism's intent to "desanquilosar el arte" [deossify art] and surpass "esas martingalas de siempre i [*sic*] descubrir facetas insospechadas al mundo" [those worn artifices and reveal unexpected dimensions to the world] (Schwartz 140). The poetic movement's arrival in Buenos Aires thus represented a significant break with past aesthetic tendencies and helped consolidate Argentina's new generation of intellectuals. A 1923 *Nosotros* survey, "Nuestra encuesta sobre la nueva generación literaria" [Our survey about the new literary generation] further defined Argentina's "nueva generación" [New Generation] and affirmed Ultraism as its aesthetic; thereby linking the movement to nationalism and the generational shift detailed in chapter 2.

Ultraism's incorporation into Buenos Aires's avant-garde circles, however, was not without controversy. Unsurprisingly, in its first issue (October 1923) the militant and rebellious *Inicial: Revista de la nueva generación* (Buenos Aires 1923–7), discussed in chapter 2, critiqued none other than the movement's founders Jorge Luis Borges and, of course, de Torre. On one hand, Roberto A. Ortelli's article "Dos poetas de la nueva generación" [Two New Generation Poets], affirmed *Inicial*'s allegiance to the movement, but on the other hand, it deemed Borges's and de Torre's recent publications to be insufficiently Ultraist. Ortelli assessed that Borges's *Fervor de Buenos Aires* [Buenos Aires Fervor] (1923) included an array of themes and poetic styles that did not correspond to Ultraism. Since Borges had introduced Buenos Aires to the poetic style, Ortelli expected that the poet's work would best illustrate the new aesthetic, but instead, his collection only vaguely alluded to the technique he had so exuberantly circulated in *Revista Mural Prisma*. Yet, if Ortelli had deemed *Fervor* insufficiently Ultraist, he was even more frustrated with de Torre's *Hélices*. He conceded that de Torre was "un escritor de talento" [a talented writer], but considered his collection a "selva inextricable" [inextricable jungle] and a "libro prismático" [prismatic book] in which too many contradictory literary tendencies converged (91). Revealing his own conservative notion of poetry, Ortelli particularly despised de Torre's "prosaísmo" [prosaism] and argued that poetry should neither attempt to resemble prose nor lack rhyme and rhythm. Ortelli's negative perception of *Fervor de Buenos Aires* and *Hélices* can be attributed both to narrow-minded taste as well as to misunderstanding the Ultraist style. In fact, in a letter to de Torre, Borges suggested that Ortelli's position on Ultraism was due to his limited interpretation of the aesthetic style that only considered the movement's emphasis on the metaphor (García 95).[6]

True to form, de Torre engaged Ortelli's critique of his work by responding in a letter published in *Inicial* as "Una curiosa epístola" [A Curious Letter] (December 1923). The letter consisted of a series of diatribes that refuted Ortelli's negative review of *Hélices* and disparaged the Argentine writer's character. However, Ortelli's parenthetical notations in his transcription of the letter humorously interrupted de Torre's angry tone and denoted the Argentine's contempt for the Spanish poet's defensive reply:

> Me limitarę, empero a advertirle – todavía amigablemente – (¡gracias!) que no es ese tono falso, ridículamente definidor y arribista (!!!) el que más le conviene. Ya que es usted, y sus amigos, los necesitados de amabilidades y benevolencias comprensivas (¡pobre!) como indubitables epígonos (!) del ultraísmo castellano, y no ninguno de nosotros, los iniciadores [I will limit myself, however, to warn you – amicably still – (thank you!) that that false defining and opportunistic (!!!) tone is not the best suited for you. Since you, and your friends, are the ones that need understanding amiability and benevolence (poor dear!) like indubitable epigones (!) of Castilian *ultraísmo*, and not any of us, the founders]. (207)

De Torre thus claimed authorship by underscoring his role as an originator of Ultraism and also defined it as Castilian. In a response he included at the end of the article, Ortelli lamented de Torre's need to ascribe such importance to Ultraism's origins: "El señor De Torre [*sic*] habla de la creación de una tendencia estética como del invento de un específico convenientemente registrado en el Departamento de Marcas y Patentes" [Mr. De Torre [*sic*] speaks of the creation of an aesthetic tendency as though it were something specific conveniently registered in the Department of Trademarks and Patents] (209). Additionally, he postulated that Argentines were creating their own art "al margen de la pedantería europea" [on the fringes of European pedantry] and did not need to either imitate or claim authorship of Ultraism (209). Nevertheless, as Ortelli chided de Torre for his insistence on claiming authorship and national prestige with regard to the creation of Ultraism, his own retort similarly cited Argentine cultural innovation as a sign of national esteem.

Despite his, perhaps narrow, view of Ultraism, Ortelli's article does point to a rivallry between Spanish and Argentine poets and Ultraism, one that illustrates the tensions between national identities and participation in a cosmopolitan field. Adding to this altercation, just as de Torre and Huidobro disputed the similarities between Creationism and Ultraism in order to assert cultural authority, intellectuals on each side of the Atlantic endorsed supposedly different versions of Ultraism. In August 1924 Borges published "Acotaciones" [Annotations] in the first issue of *Proa* (second series), a review of Argentine poet Eduardo González Lanuza's *Prismas* [Prisms] (1924). Framing his argument by first establishing a distinction between Ultraism in Spain and Ultraism in Argentina, Borges posited González Lanuza as the most accomplished Ultraist, the "arquetipo de una generación" [the paragon of a generation] (31). According to Borges, in Spain the movement was a bold effort to bring Spanish letters into the present by transforming poetic language to reflect the latest technology. In Argentina, the movement called for an aesthetic overhaul that broke with previous literary traditions. While Borges pointed to both Huidobro's and French poet Guillaume Apollinaire's influence on Spanish Ultraism, he cited Spanish Golden Age poet Garcilaso de la Vega as a model for Argentine Ultraism. For him, this distinction implied that, while Spanish Ultraism followed novel aesthetic currents initiated by contemporary poets, Argentine Ultraism was fashioned after a more enduring archetype.

Going back to González Lanuza, Borges underscored his involvement with Ultraism in Buenos Aires dating back to 1921, when he contributed to *Prisma* (31). Three years later, González Lanuza had managed to fully develop "nuestro gesto de entonces, tan espontáneo y fácil" [our gesture from back then, so spontaneous and simple] in a collection that comprised "[t]odos los motivos del ultraísmo" [all off Ultraism's motifs] (31). Evaluating González Lanuza's poetry alongside contemporary publications, which included de Torre's *Hélices*, Mexican Manuel Maples Arce's *Andamios interiores* (1922), Chilean Santiago Reyes's *Barco ebrio* [Drunken Ship] (1922), Spanish poet Gerardo Diego's *Imagen* [Image] (1922), Argentine poet Francisco Luis Bernárdez's *Kindergarten* (1924), Uruguayan Fernán Silva Valés's *Agua del tiempo* [Time's Water] (1921), and his own *Fervor de Buenos Aires*, Borges affirmed *Prismas* was "el libro ejemplar del ultraísmo" [Ultraism's exemplary book] (31).[7] Thus, in Borges's estimation, Gonález Lanuza's Ultraist poetry had not only distinguished itself in Buenos Aires but had also managed to surpass transnational and transatlantic efforts to develop the poetic style. As a result, Borges affirmed that González Lanuza had "logrado el libro nuestro, el de nuestra hazaña en el tiempo y el de nuestra derrota en lo absoluto" [achieved our book, the one about our accomplishment in time and the one about our absolute defeat] (31). Thus, in Borges's estimation cultural prestige with regard to Ultraism belonged to Argentina.

Not surprisingly, de Torre strongly disputed Borges's perspective. In February 1925 the Spanish poet responded to Borges's position on Ultraism from the short-lived Spanish journal *Plural* (Madrid 1925). His review of Argentine poet Norah Lange's *La calle de la tarde* [Afternoon Street] (1925) contended that her poetry exemplified an *ultraísta* aesthetic that was the same on both sides of the Atlantic. Characteristics of Lange's poetry such as a "[p]esquisa de metáforas y desdoblamiento de imágenes" [an inquiry into metaphor and unfolding of imagery], "[e]spejamiento dinámico o reducción elíptica de sensaciones múltiples" [dynamic mirroring or elliptical reduction of multiple sensations], were present in both Spanish and Argentine versions of Ultraism (27). Responding to Borges, de Torre insisted that Ultraism was one and the same in Spain and Argentina, "dos ramas gemelas del árbol ultráico" [two twin branches of the Ultraist tree] (27). If Borges had argued that González Lanuza's *Prismas* proved that Spanish and Argentine Ultraism were different, de Torre proposed that Lange's *La calle de la tarde* confirmed the opposite. Replying to Borges's claims, de Torre affirmed that, at once modern and enduring, Lange's *La calle de la tarde* reflected the "voluntad de renuevo" [will for renewal] that Borges had attributed to Spanish Ultraism, while simultaneously emulating the "arte absoluto" [absolute art] that, according to Borges, Argentine Ultraism envisioned (27). Although he was not as explicit in this article, by denying the existence of an Argentine Ultraism, de Torre was reaffirming the same argument he maintained concerning Ortelli, that Ultraism was Castilian. Argentina could have its own branch, but the core and roots were decidedly Spanish.

Just like de Torre's exchanges with Huidobro concerning Creationism, authorship and cultural prestige were at stake in the disputes he had with Ortelli and Borges over Ultraism. From de Torre's perspective, not only was he the initiator of the poetic style that Huidobro claimed as Creationism and Borges contended had an Argentine variant, but cultural prestige for the aesthetic innovation belonged to Spain. As a result, although these brief and seemingly ephemeral disputes across journals, magazines, and newspapers could seem insignificant, together, they tell a nuanced story of aesthetic development and socio-political tension within which works must be situated when analysed. In this particular case, these struggles over authorship and cultural capital offer unique contextual background into larger polemics, such as the *polémica del meridiano intelectual* discussed in chapter 3 that took place only a few years later. Additionally, as the next section details, frictions akin to those that emerged in these altercations over poetry also surfaced around prose.

Margarita de niebla (1927) and "The Dehumanization of Art"[8]

On 1 October 1927, the Spanish literary critic Esteban Salazar y Chapela reviewed Mexican Jaime Torres Bodet's novel *Margarita de niebla* (1927) for Madrid's daily newspaper *El Sol* (1917–39) in "Jaime Torres Bodet: *Margarita de niebla*" (2).[9] Casting the young novelist as a disciple of Spaniard Benjamín Jarnés, Salazar y Chapela affirmed that *Margarita de niebla* was an imitation of the Aragonese writer's *El profesor inútil* [The Useless Professor] (1926) (2). Unsurprisingly, this review spawned an acrimonious exchange across the Atlantic when the Mexican literary journal *Ulises* (1927–8) published the unsigned "*Margarita de niebla* y Benjamín Jarnés" in November 1927. Disputing the accusation that Torres Bodet had imitated Jarnés, the Mexican journal attributed similarities between the texts to what it termed an "epochal shift," equally palpable in Europe and Latin America. Despite its use of the vague term "epochal shift," *Ulises* argued more precisely that, like Spain, Mexico was contributing to a cosmopolitan literary dialogue seeking to break with the previous generation's aesthetic style, namely, *modernismo*.

Modernist journals like *Ulises* along with newspapers such as *El Sol* provided a forum in which intellectuals experimented with aesthetics and debated their ideas. Tracing such interactions across journal pages outlines the cosmopolitan dialogue that *Ulises* described and thus offers keen insight into a Spanish American literary field during the Hispanic Modernist era. This section focuses a 1926 altercation between Torres Bodet and Jarnés that shows how seemingly minor exchanges in journals actually played an important role in Modernist aesthetic developments both within national boundaries and across the Atlantic. Connections between Torres Bodet and Spanish philosopher José Ortega y Gasset's *Revista de Occidente* (Madrid 1923–36) circle, which included Jarnés, have been well documented by scholars including Domingo Ródenas de Moya, Guillermo Sheridan, and Pérez Firmat.[10] Thus thematic and stylistic affinities between Jarnés's *El profesor inútil* and Torres Bodet's *Margarita de niebla* are unsurprising and intimate a dialogue between the novelists.[11] Uncovering a more concrete connection, however, this section traces a textual relationship back to journal pages, underscoring print culture's crucial role in the development of the Hispanic Vanguard Novel.

Jarnés's and Torres Bodet's contribution to the development of a transnational and transatlantic vanguard aesthetic were certainly attributable to an "epochal shift," as described in *Ulises*. However, journals, magazines, and newspapers offer explicit evidence that connections between these authors and their novels were even more concrete. This section posits that *Margarita de niebla* was actually a metafictional response to a debate between Jarnés and Torres Bodet centred on Spanish philosopher José Ortega y Gasset's essay "The Dehumanization of Art." Writing in Argentina's *Valoraciones* (La Plata 1923–7), Torres Bodet critiqued José Ortega y Gasset's *La deshumanización del arte* (1925) and Jarnés responded in *El Estudiante* (Salamanca-Madrid 1925–6).[12] Torres Bodet maintained that Ortega's Eurocentric description of modern art failed to properly take Latin American cultural production into account. Jarnés, in turn, condescendingly underscored that the Mexican had misunderstood the concept of dehumanization. Following the initial exchange, Torres Bodet extended this discussion beyond the journals when he metafictionally addressed it in his in his novel *Margarita de niebla*.

Most likely published in either Mexico's *El Universal* (1916–present) or *Excélsior* (1917–present) first, Torres Bodet's "La deshumanización del arte" [The Dehumanization of Art] appeared in two Argentine journals, *Nosotros* (Buenos Aires 1907–34) and *Valoraciones* (La Plata 1923–7) in March 1926.[13] The Mexican novelist later republished "La deshumanización del arte" in his collection of essays entitled *Contemporáneos* (1928), which is more often cited by scholars.[14] However, the republication of Torres Bodet's article in La Plata's *Valoraciones* is particularly relevant because this journal had a history of exchanges (1925–6) with

Madrid's *El Estudiante*, the journal that published Benjamín Jarnés's response to Torres Bodet's essay, "La deshumanización del arte: Carta al poeta Torres Bodet." Additionally, as discussed in chapter 2, university students created both journals and their relationship came to be when *Valoraciones* ardently supported *El Estudiante*'s call for solidarity between young Spanish and Latin American intellectuals around the issue of educational reform. And, as chapter 2 narrates in detail, *Valoraciones* based much of its platform on Ortega's theories from *El tema de nuestro tiempo* (1923) [The Modern Theme] and had engaged in a dialogue (1923–4) with the Spanish philosopher, who responded from his "pulpit" at Buenos Aires's *La Nación* (Buenos Aires 1870–present).[15] Thus the journal's publication of an article that contested Ortega is notable, suggesting that *Valoraciones*'s views on the Spanish thinker might have evolved throughout the 1920s.

In his well-known essay entitled "The Dehumanization of Art," Ortega employed the term "dehumanization" to describe an aesthetic shift taking place across Europe during the early twentieth century. Artists relocated focus from the object depicted in a work of art to the means of artistic representation. He illustrated this phenomenon with his now classic "windowpane/garden" metaphor. If one looks through a windowpane to see a garden, one does not pay attention to the windowpane. Conversely, if focus is shifted away from the garden onto the windowpane, one loses sight of the garden. For Ortega, this metaphor articulated the ways in which new art emphasized style, technique, and medium – the windowpane – rather than the reality – the garden – depicted.[16] Torres Bodet, as Vicky Unruh has pointed out, primarily disagreed with Ortega's notion that creating art required a "triumph over the human" (25). She explains that the Mexican novelist believed that "[a]rt … should always make contact in some way with the 'disorderly humanity' that Ortega believed modernity had exiled from the work of art" (25). In fact, reflecting on this essay in his 1955 memoir *Tiempo de arena* [Sand Time], Torres Bodet continued to insist that "el poeta no empieza donde el hombre acaba" [the poet does not begin where the human ends] (226).

Beyond conflicting aesthetic views, Torres Bodet condemned Ortega's Eurocentric perspective.[17] The Spanish philosopher's exclusion of Mexico and Latin America from his theoretical scope incensed Torres Bodet: "¿y América? ¿Por qué olvidar las posibilidades de arte nuevo, las reservas de ingenuidad que esconde nuestra América?" [What about America? Why dismiss the possibilities for new art, the reserves of ingenuity that our America conceals?] ("La deshumanización del arte" 246) [The Dehumanization of Art]. However, the Mexican novelist also critiqued Latin America's young intellectuals for carelessly believing in Ortega's "orientación más retórica que filosófica" [more rhetorical than philosophical orientation] and appropriating concepts that did not address their reality ("La deshumanización del arte" [The Dehumanization of Art] 247). Deeming *The Dehumanization of Art* "un libro europeo, con datos europeos, escrito para europeos" [a European book, with European data, written for Europeans], Torres Bodet contended that Ortega's theory inhibited Latin Americans from imagining their own autochthonous aesthetic, one that took their own cultures into account ("La deshumanización del arte" [The Dehumanization of Art] 246). Instead of reconstructing European modes in order to fit their reality, Torres Bodet emphasized that Latin Americans, and particularly Mexicans in their post-revolutionary moment, needed to develop their own artistic trends: "exigiremos al arte nuevo modalidades autóctonas y no postizas actitudes como las que ahora asume" [we will require from new art autochthonous modalities and not phony attitudes like the ones it currently appropriates] ("La deshumanización del arte" [The Dehumanization of Art] 247). Yet, as we shall see in *Margarita de niebla,* Torres Bodet's position on exactly how to reconcile "autochthonous modalities" and "new art" is ambiguous and expressed in gendered terms.

Although Ortega did not respond to Torres Bodet's article, Benjamín Jarnés, whose novels were deemed exemplary of a dehumanized aesthetic, did contest the Mexican's essay.[18] Continuing the Spanish journal's dialogue with *Valoraciones,* Jarnés wrote "La deshumanización del arte: Carta al poeta Torres Bodet" [The Dehumanization of Art: Letter to the Poet Torres Bodet] in *El Estudiante*'s May 1926 issue. Calling Torres Bodet a "leal camarada de un equipo opuesto" [loyal comrade from an opposing team] from the outset, Jarnés pronounced his disagreement with the Mexican writer's article (10).[19] Yet his argument against Torres Bodet's essay centred on stylistic discrepancies and ignored the Mexican's nationalist stance. Jarnés primarily addressed Torres Bodet's opposition to the idea of "el triunfo sobre lo humano" [the triumph over the human], explaining that Ortega's aesthetic perspective did not eliminate the human element (10). The Spanish novelist, however, did concur with Torres Bodet that art could not exist without "materia humana" [human matter] and asserted that "[s]i el arte nuevo estuviese totalmente evadido de lo humano, no sería la suya una actividad dinámica, sino de reposo, y en el arte no vale descansar" [[i]f new art were completely removed from the human, rather than a dynamic activity, it would be one of repose, and resting has no place in art] (10). Nevertheless, he indicated that the Mexican novelist contradicted himself by first disputing Ortega's notion of dehumanization and then pronouncing that "no hay arte sin materia humana que estilizar" [there is no art without human matter to stylize] because "[e]stilizar implica deshumanizar" [stylization implies dehumanization] (10).[20] If Torres Bodet acknowledged that art stylized the human element, he could not oppose dehumanization since the term referred to new modes of artistic stylization. As a result, Jarnés rebuked Torres Bodet for either misunderstanding Ortega or carelessly reading his essay: "si es difícil hallar conclusiones más diáfanas, también lo es hallar otras tan turbiamente comprendidas. Quiero creer en las lecturas precipitadas. Ver la diferencia entre realidad humana y realidad artística, es algo de que no puede eximirse ninguna mirada sincera de hoy" [if it is difficult to find clearer conclusions, it is also a challenge to find others that are so turbidly understood. I want to believe in careless reading. Any sincere perspective today cannot be exempt from seeing the difference between human reality and artistic reality] (10). Thus deeming his view a misinterpretation, Jarnés dismissed Torres Bodet's perspective without engaging the Mexican writer's key objection to Ortega's theory, that it did not take Latin America into account.

Torres Bodet did not respond to Jarnés in an article either in *El Estudiante* or in *Valoraciones*, but his novel *Margarita de niebla* continued the debate metafictionally.[21] Two scenes in particular underscore the Mexican novelist's objections to the Spanish philosopher's theory and to Jarnés's article. In the first scene, the protagonist Carlos Borja shaves in front of a mirror and describes the reflected images he sees: "Por el hueco de la ventana abierta se instala junto a mi rostro, en el fondo del espejo al que me aproximo, un paisaje todavía frágil, embalado por la niebla. Sólo la sombra de mi barba, crecida durante la noche, rompe la claridad de esta acuarela" [Through the open window and in the mirror I am facing, a fragile scenery, still embalmed in fog, gleams alongside my countenance. Only my beard's shadow, grown overnight, breaks this watercolor's clarity] (55). Vicky Unruh suggests that in this scene Torres Bodet directly addresses the windowpane metaphor Ortega used to illustrate his theory of dehumanization and compounds it by incorporating the mirror's multiple reflections (72). While Borja shaves and looks at himself in the mirror, he simultaneously sees the window and the landscape behind him reflected by the mirror. Furthermore, Unruh notes that, as the sun rises, the new lighting continuously changes Borja's perception of the landscape (72). As a result, if Ortega's original metaphor suggests that focusing on the windowpane rather than on the garden illustrates dehumanized art, Unruh points out that Torres Bodet complicates the metaphor as Borja "focuses on the interaction between the framing process and its raw material, that is, between art and life, as well as on the position and activity of the human subject who constructs the interaction" (72). Therefore, Borja engages with art both as an observer and as an image within the artistic representation. Torres Bodet thus proposes that art can represent the tension between art and humanity as a work of art in itself, a point he made in his *Valoraciones* article, which Jarnés took to mean that the Mexican had not understood Ortega.

Another scene that engages dehumanization is a dialogue on music between Borja and Margarita's mother, Señora Millers, who considers Wagner more of an artist, and Beethoven, more "human." Borja asks her, "¿Se ha enterado usted de la teoría que algunos formulan, según la cual Beethoven podría ser considerado como el primero de los *músicos puros*, es decir como el primero de los músicos deshumanizados?" [Have you heard the theory some are proposing, that Beethoven could be considered the first *pure musician*, meaning the first *dehumanized musician*?] (22). Incensed, Señora Millers rejects the idea that Beethoven could be considered dehumanized: "Qué tiene Beethoven que no sea humano? Busque una página en toda su obra que alguien no pueda sentir" [What does Beethoven have that is not human? Find a single page in his work that someone cannot feel] (22). Beethoven, according to Señora Millers, could not be considered dehumanized because his music incited feelings and empathy. Señora Millers further states that she and her husband had tried to appreciate "música pura" [pure music] to no avail (22). Although entertaining, in their estimation, modern music, by composers such as Erik Satie and Igor Stravinsky, could not be taken seriously (22). The Millers' rejection of modern aesthetic tendencies is consistent with their outdated aristocratic way of life. Adorned with "baratijas sentimentales" [sentimental trinkets] like porcelain vases, paintings, and photographs from past trips, their home is a nostalgic gallery of mementos (20). The Millers thus represent an Old World order, one that Borja, at least in this scene, renounced. Advocating a modern attitude and a new world order, Borja responds, insisting that "no podemos seguir siendo devotos de una música que corresponde a una manera espiritual que ya no es nuestra, a la sensibilidad de un mundo desaparecido" [we can no longer continue to be devoted to a music corresponding to a spiritual manner that is no longer ours, to a sensibility that no longer exists] (22). Borja speaks in favour of the new aesthetic practices that Ortega y Gasset characterized as dehumanized. At the same time, his words echo Torres Bodet's insistence that Latin America, and more precisely its youth, could no longer blindly follow antiquated European tendencies did not account for a Latin American reality. Yet, Torres Bodet does not reject Europe, just its outdated Europeans like the Millers, who could not embrace modernity. He thus advocates the conscious creation of an aesthetic that was *nuestra*, whether Mexican or Latin American, one that incorporated "autochthonous modalities" into "new art."

While the scenes discussed above rearticulate the position Torres Bodet had taken in his *Valoraciones* article – first that the human element was essential in artistic stylization and second, that Latin American art needed to be at once modern and autochthonous – the opposition between Margarita and Paloma in the novel further accentuates his view. Throughout *Margarita de niebla*, Torres Bodet contrasts Margarita with her best friend Paloma in order to illustrate the complexity of incorporating "autochthonous modalities" and "new art" into one national aesthetic.[22] Margarita Millers, the daughter of wealthy German aristocrats – which is not a coincidence since Ortega was a well-known Germanophile – represents a dated European aesthetic, while Paloma Le Franc, the daughter of a French immigrant who grew up in Mexico, stands for a modern aesthetic that is also Mexican. Contrasting Margarita's traditional German upbringing, Paloma's French heritage intimates that she would have a more contemporary outlook, since France, and Paris in particular, was a bustling centre for cultural innovation. Borja is perplexed by two types of women: Margarita, who, as Pérez Firmat has noted, serves as a blank canvas for his artistic reflection, and her friend, a stronger character who baffles him: "Frente a Paloma soy todo edad y torpeza" [In Paloma's presence I am all age and ineptitude] (75).[23] While Margarita is amorphous, Paloma is precise, "[e]n contra de lo que esperaba, es más alta que Margarita. Sus cabellos, cortados a la Bob [*sic*], no tienen esa facilidad sentimental que deshace – fatiga anticipada – las trenzas de su amiga" [[c]ontrary to what I was expecting, she is taller than Margarita. Her bob cut lacks the sentimentality that – anticipating weariness – unravels her friend's braids] (39).

Paloma is Mexican and from a small town from the "interior," a self-made woman who becomes a French teacher in Mexico City (41). Being from the interior, she is presumably well acquainted with a more authentic Mexican culture. Yet, Paloma's ability to speak French enables her upward mobility, allowing her to embrace modernity in the capital. Paloma is an independent, cosmopolitan professional, while Margarita is still a student, bound by her parents' decisions, and has a more traditional demeanour (Borja describes Margarita's classic attire at length when she is at her parents' home as well as her domestic activities, such as baking, when preparing for his visits). Moreover, in contrast to his uncertain feelings towards Margarita, Borja admits to a more definite connection with Paloma: "me comprendería mejor que nadie porque, inteligente y buena, el don de perder ha adquirido en ella las proporciones especiales, la técnica de una sabiduría" [[she] would understand me better than anyone because, intelligent and good, the gift of losing has given her, in unique proportions, the skill of knowledge] (73). Nevertheless, Borja wavers. Despite his forceful rejection of an Old World order in his discussion with Señora Millers, he is still drawn to Margarita, himself unable to fully come to terms with modernity.

Borja's dilemma over modern Paloma and traditional Margarita comes to a head when Margarita's parents announce their return to Germany. Propelled by her imminent departure, Borja hastily decides to marry Margarita and leave Mexico. Yet, he cannot bring himself to consummate their marriage and, on their way to Europe, Borja belatedly regrets his decision. At breakfast with Margarita and her family, he notices that the Mexican family sitting next to them also comprises parents and newlyweds: "una familia mexicana nos reproduce en moreno como la copia de un espejo inteligente que no tomara de la realidad sino los elementos esenciales" [a Mexican family duplicates us, a brown version, like the copy in an intelligent mirror that takes only from reality the essential elements] (99). Borja realizes that he and the groom share the same race: "Él, como yo, es un criollo de rasgos insignificantes y de hablar contenido y pretencioso" [He, like me, is a creole with insignificant features and a pretentious and reserved way of speaking] (99). The bride, however, bears a likeness to Paloma, not Margarita: "Ella se parece a Paloma tan visiblemente que Margarita se cree en el caso de tener que darle la espalda" [She resembles Paloma so visibly that Margarita feels the need to turn her back to her] (99). Seeing this family, Borja recognizes that marrying a foreigner had been a mistake:

> al comparar este grupo con el nuestro, la copia me parece superior al original. Es posible que el padre de la desconocida no tenga el hábil criterio comercial del señor Millers. Es seguro que la madre no interprete a Beethoven ... Pero ¡con qué delicadeza se han hecho a un lado de la vida de sus hijos! ¡Cómo se advierten esas virtudes de silencio y de inteligente modestia que son las de mi raza, las de Paloma, acaso también las mías! [as I compare this group to ours, the copy seems superior to the original. The unknown bride's father may not have Señor Miller's clever commercial judgment. The mother certainly cannot interpret Beethoven ... But with what delicacy they have created a life alongside their children! How apparent are their virtues of silence and intelligent modesty, virtues that characterize my race, Paloma's virtues, perhaps mine as well!] (100)

In marrying Margarita, Borja admits he had underestimated his own culture and sacrificed his race. Despite being from a humbler background, Paloma is Mexican and modern, a self-made woman. As Rosa García Gutiérrez describes her, Paloma embodies "a Mexican culture, recently initiated, almost anxious to build itself."[24] Like Paloma, Mexico was a young, self-made country that had achieved independence from Spain and overcome a devastating revolution. Thus, in dismissing Paloma in favour of Margarita's supposed sophistication and pedigree, Borja also betrayed himself when he chose an obsolete European model. Borja's regret thereby recalls Torres Bodet's appeal to Latin America's youth in "La deshumanización del arte"; a new Mexican aesthetic needed to connect autochthonous modalities and a modern sensibility while dismissing Margarita's Old World attitudes that no longer suited their reality. For Torres Bodet, post-revolutionary Mexico should assimilate modernity without losing sight of its authentic culture, simultaneously crossing borders while respecting national boundaries.

Conclusions: *El Estudiante*'s Aesthetic Position-Taking[25]

Chapter 2 details how the modernist journals *Valoraciones* and *El Estudiante* came together in solidarity surrounding educational reform and *iberoamericanismo*. Yet, as hospitable spaces that hosted transnational contributions and became forums for discussion, they would also act as conduits for the contentious exchange between Jarnés and Torres Bodet described above. As a result, in hosting these polemics, journals, magazines, and newspapers offer a nuanced view of artistic production and play a critical role in shaping cultural fields. Moreover, evaluating the debate over the dehumanization of art alongside other controversies taking place across print culture, such as the debates over Creationism and Ultraism described earlier in this chapter, allows unique insight into and, most important, proves the existence of a broader field of cultural production that must be considered when evaluating literary texts. Notably, parallel topics emerged in both cases: 1) similar aesthetic styles led to accusations of imitation and even plagiarism, and 2) postcolonial tensions surrounding Latin America's cultural independence were also at the forefront. Therefore, despite their polemical tone, these debates and exchanges actually trace a transatlantic dialogue within one Spanish American field.

Although *El Estudiante* did not further partake in the dispute between Jarnés and Torres Bodet, its repeated publication of Don Ramón del Valle Inclán's *Tirano Banderas* (1926) [Tyrant Banderas] seems to echo Torres Bodet's perspective that an avant-garde aesthetic should be both cosmopolitan and socially engaged. Moreover, the novel endorses one Spanish American field of cultural production that crosses borders while acknowledging national boundaries and therefore supersedes postcolonial tensions present in the debates over poetry and prose described in this chapter. Thus, in a sense, *El Estudiante*'s publication of this novel offers a resolution of sorts to arguments over authorship and cultural prestige that, as print culture illustrates, regularly surfaced between Spain and Latin America during the 1920s.

El Estudiante featured selections from Ramón del Valle Inclán's *Tirano Banderas* in sixteen of twenty-five issues. In fact, when the journal moved from Salamanca to Madrid on 6 December 1925, *El Estudiante* made it a point to re-publish selections that had appeared in Salamanca issues:

> De esta novela que don Ramón del Valle-Inclán nos entregó para su publicación en *El Estudiante* apareció ya, en números anteriores, su primer capítulo. Como en esta reaparición cuenta nuestra Revista [*sic*] con una suma de lectores muy superior a la que antes disfrutaba, hemos decidido dar la hermosa novela de don Ramón desde un principio, seguros de que acertamos a satisfacer con tal determinación los deseos de nuestros lectores [From this novel, that Don Ramón del Valle-Inclán has given us for publication in *El Estudiante*, we have published the first chapter in a previous issue. Since, upon our reappearance, our journal now has a superior readership, we have decided to once again publish Don Ramón's splendid novel from the beginning, certain that we will satisfy our readers' wishes]. (6)

First, *Tirano Banderas* echoes *El Estudiante*'s socio-political platform on political oppression, an anti-imperialist stance against Spain and the United States, and *iberoamericanismo*. Set in Santa Fe de Tierra Firme,[26] an undisclosed area in a presumably Latin American country, *Tirano Banderas* narrates the twenty-four-hour period leading to a revolution that overthrows (and murders) dictator Santos Banderas. Mirroring *El Estudiante*'s views on Spanish oligarch Miguel Primo de Rivera described in chapter 2, the revolution in the novel stands against the dictator's political and economic oppression. At the same time, this revolution, demanding land rights for oppressed populations and a more egalitarian society, is strikingly similar to Mexican history (namely, the revolution in 1910–17).

Simultaneously engaging multiple fields of cultural production, and thereby respecting national boundaries, the novel speaks to Spanish, Mexican, and Argentine fields. In doing so, just like *El*

Estudiante, Tirano Banderas thus participates in a transatlantic Spanish American field. For instance, recalling autocrats such as Porfirio Díaz in Mexico, Juan Manuel de Rosas in Argentina, and Miguel Primo de Rivera in Spain, the grotesque and authoritarian protagonist Santos Banderas speaks to specific cultural contexts. Yet, this character also represents the novel's universal stance against political oppression. Moreover, *Tirano Banderas*'s anti-colonialist position that critiques Spain's involvement in Tierra Firme's national affairs and also condemns the United States' economic infiltration in the territory, could apply to either individual Latin American countries or to the region as a whole. Furthermore, language in the novel depicts multiple dialects of Castilian from countries such as Spain, Mexico, and Argentina. Thus conflating histories and linguistic variances from multiple Latin American countries and Spain, the novel speaks to one Spanish American culture, which supports the notion of *iberoamericanismo* that *El Estudiante* advocated. However, as Dru Dougherty has noted, Valle Inclán's depiction of *iberoamericanismo* in the novel was also critical (214).[27] Tied to his anti-colonialist perspective, Valle Inclán stood against purely rhetorical *hispano-* and *iberoamericanismo*, championing, like *El Estudiante*, concrete dialogues that could 1) effect real change on both sides of the Atlantic and 2) establish a new postcolonial relationship, defined by solidarity and equanimity, that could transcend centuries of tension.

If *Tirano Banderas* reflects *El Estudiante*'s socio-political position in the cultural field, the novel also affirms the Spanish journal's views on the avant-garde. Socially engaged, Valle Inclán's text also employs avant-garde stylistic tendencies. Narrative style, termed *Esperpento* by Valle Inclán himself, is fragmented (recalling Impressionism, Expressionism, and Cubism) and plot development is not chronological. In *Esperpento*, distorted descriptions emphasize society's ills. As result, this novel that, despite being stylistically "dehumanized," connects with a "disorderly humanity" in its indisputable socio-political stance, corresponds with Jaime Torres Bodet's perspective on a modern aesthetic. Thus, by publishing so many selections of *Tirano Banderas*, *El Estudiante* ultimately promoted an avant-garde aesthetic that was also socially engaged, thereby taking a position that was more aligned with the Mexican novelist's point of view in his debate with Jarnés.[28] Therefore, socio-politically and aesthetically, *El Estudiante*'s publication of *Tirano Banderas* can be read as representative of the journal's position-taking in the Spanish American cultural field throughout its twenty-five issues spanning from May 1925 to May 1926. Conversely, reading Valle Inclán's text within the context of the journal underscores its role as an agent seeking to effect change across multiple fields of cultural production. *El Estudiante*'s unrelenting effort to bridge the Atlantic endorsing a dialogue within one Spanish American field of cultural production that could reconfigure outdated imperialist paradigms is thus one small example of print culture's pivotal role in shaping literary historiography.

Epilogue

Reflecting on a Medium, a Process, and a Path Forward

América ha dado un paso adelante; y es innegable que también la otra persona del diálogo, Europa, ha dado el suyo hacia nosotros.

[America has taken a step forward; and it is undeniable that the other interlocutor in this dialogue, Europe, has taken one towards us.]

Alfonso Reyes, "Un paso de América," *Sur*

Printed in the first issue of Victoria Ocampo's *Sur* (Buenos Aires 1931–92), the above-cited article by Alfonso Reyes would appear to respond to this book's opening anecdote, Ernesto Giménez Caballero's "Un gran romance mexicano" [A Great Mexican Romance], published four years earlier in *La Gaceta Literaria* (Madrid 1927–31). If Giménez Caballero had condescendingly praised Mexican Mariano Azuela's *Los de abajo* [The Underdogs] (1915) for evoking the exotic qualities that Europe craved from America, Reyes argued that America has taken a step forward and surpassed "este género de literatura, mediocre en sí mismo" [this literary genre, mediocre in itself] (151). In fact, the Mexican diplomat posited that real writers from America actually fled from "la peste de todo abuso llamado 'color local'" [the stench of all abuse called "local colour"] (Reyes 151). Instead, echoing Mexican novelist Jaime Torres Bodet's perspective that Mexican literature needed to reflect both nationalism and cosmopolitanism, Reyes maintained that writers across America had managed to bridge an autochthonous aesthetic and a universal style. They had outlined national boundaries while simultaneously crossing borders to participate in a cosmopolitan field of cultural production. Offering examples, Reyes points to "peruano universal" [universal Peruvian] Ventura García Calderón's *La venganza del condor* (1924) [The Condor's Revenge], Argentine Ricardo Güiraldes's

Don Segundo Sombra (1926) [Mr. Segundo Sombra], "un monumento de valor más que nacional" [a monument surpassing national value], and Colombian José Eustasio Rivera's *La vorágine* (1924) [The Vortex]. He then underscores that, exhibiting the same qualities, fellow Mexicans Martín Luis Guzmán and Mariano Azuela's novels *El águila y la serpiente* (1928) [The Eagle and the Snake] and *Los de abajo* (1915), respectively, had overcome the Pyrenees through French translation, effectively gaining Mexico's participation in what Cipriano Rivas Cherif, cited in chapter 4, had described as "Europe's concert" (Reyes 151–2).

Reyes goes on to describe a series of "fatalidades concentrícas" [concentric fatalities] that had historically undermined Americans' own confidence in their identity(ies), such as Spain's lack of understanding of *hispanoamericanismo*, a controversy addressed most directly in chapter 1 (154). He explains, however, that America had largely overcome these obstacles and cites José Ortega y Gasset's acknowledgment of "mayoría de edad para los hispanoamericanos" [coming of age for Spanish Americans] as proof (155). Reyes was most likely referring to the Spanish philosopher's comments in *El Espectador* (1917) [The Spectator], described in chapter 2, that his ideas were more readily understood in Argentina than in Europe. Of course, as the journals, magazines, and newspapers evaluated in this book evidence, empire's presence loomed large, and Latin America's struggle for cultural independence from Spain during the 1920s was not so easily resolved. Although Reyes does concede that European ignorance of American, cultures, nations, and identities was still prevalent, he closes his reflection nevertheless emphasizing that, "ya no se puede hablar de América a tontas y a locas. América tiene ya mayoría, tiene ya personería jurídica, y cada vez que se le nombre ha de acudir al juicio" [it is no longer permissible to speak of America willy-nilly. America has already come of age, it has legal personhood, and every time it is named, sound judgment must be employed] (158).

Reyes's reflection speaks to a shift in Latin America's prestige within a Spanish American field of cultural production in the early twentieth century. Emancipating themselves from a colonial paradigm, Latin American writers had not only achieved distinction within their national contexts but had managed to intervene in a transatlantic cultural field on their own terms. This book underscores the importance of journals, magazines, and newspapers as a medium that tangibly maps the process through which America reached its "legal personhood." Print media helped define and strengthen national identities while crossing borders and engaging transcultural dialogues that played a role in shaping fields of cultural production. As a result, it is a resource that scholarship necessarily needs to consider when evaluating literary production.

On the one hand, this book has offered examples of how debates across journals, magazines, and newspapers directly impacted literary production, such as the debate between Benjamín Jarnés and Jaime Torres Bodet surrounding José Ortega y Gasset's *The Dehumanization of Art* (1925) that began on journal pages and culminated in *Margarita de niebla* (1927). On the other hand, debates on *hispano/iberoamericanismo* outlined in this book, encourage Hispanism to reconsider artificial dichotomies, namely, Latin Americanism vs. Peninsularism, that shape the field and categorize the literary production it evaluates. Similarly, Hispanism can draw lessons from *La Gaceta Literaria*'s brand of Americanism and Iberianism. In as much as the journal did break barriers by promoting Iberian and Transatlantic exchanges as well as plurilingualism, its efforts were nevertheless driven and shaped by empire. As Hispanism continues to debate how to define and employ Iberian Studies and Transatlantic Studies, we should be mindful of inadvertently replicating empire's purview through a different lens. At the same time, despite its empire-centred intent, and perhaps paradoxically, *La Gaceta Literaria* helped shape Transatlantic and Iberian fields of cultural production that de-centred empire.

In his contribution to the volume *Transatlantic Studies: Latin America, Iberia, and Africa* (2020), "Alfonso Reyes, Hispanist Praxis, and the Critique of Transatlantic Reason," Ignacio Sánchez Prado explains that Alfonso Reyes understood "the Atlantic as a space not reducible to the relationship between Spain and Latin America" (377). Thus evaluating the progression in Alfonso Reyes's reasoning throughout his career, Sánchez Prado finds that it "proves important to thinking the category of the 'Atlantic' for Hispanic Studies without falling back on a reductionist view based on the politics of academic knowledge. His work understands both Spain and Latin America to be part of richer circuits and networks" (378). In line with this perspective, this book has shown that print media proves invaluable in helping Hispanists explore and understand these "richer circuits and networks" in order to transcend the limiting paradigm that has structured the field for so long. Outlining and traversing borders, print culture offers a more nuanced perspective of the complex postcolonial relationship between Spain and Latin America that shaped aesthetic production within and beyond national boundaries. Debates and exchanges taking place across journals map an intricate network that forces us to re-evaluate Hispanic literary historiography by moving beyond the Atlantic.

Intrigued by Gustavo Pérez Firmat's use of print culture to discuss the Hispanic Vanguard novel in *Idle Fictions: The Hispanic Vanguard Novel 1926–34* (1993), I first embarked upon this study in fall 2009. I found the medium fascinating and decided to make it the object of my doctoral work, which was well received at my institution, the University of California, Los Angeles. Finding a committee chair, however, required some creativity, given the department's division across the Atlantic. The expectation was that I would either be a Latin Americanist or a Peninsularist, and my work did not fully ascribe to either category. Fortunately, Michelle Clayton and Roberta Lee Johnson had the vision to support my work and share the committee chair role. More than a decade later, Hispanism has moved forward in this regard. Tenure track positions for transatlantic scholars have become more common. Yet, many are still structured within the Latin Americanist–Peninsularist dichotomy. At San José State University, for instance, I was hired as a Peninsularist whose work is transatlantic. Within a Department of World Languages and Literatures, our Spanish program (undergraduate and graduate) is still divided by the Atlantic. This means that although I am supported in teaching my research, it is within courses designated either Peninsular or Latin American. Even as I teach graduate seminars such as "Decolonizing Borderlands: Breaking with Empire in Hispanism," in which we explore why the Atlantic Ocean divides Hispanism into the study of Peninsular literature and Latin American literature, in 2024, I remain a transatlantic scholar navigating the confines of an outdated structure.

In the past two decades Hispanist scholarship has certainly advanced in explorations of Iberian Studies and Transatlantic Studies. For instance, Alejandro Mejías López's *The Inverted Conquest: The Myth of Modernity and the Transatlantic Onset of Modernism* (2009) articulates the existence of a Spanish American field of cultural production and Akiko Tsuchiya and William G. Acree Jr.'s volume *Empire's End: Transnational Connections in the Hispanic World* (2016) probes empire's legacy in shaping Hispanism. Fernando Degiovanni's *Vernacular Latin Americanisms: War, the Market, and the Making of a Discipline* (2018) details how the Spanish and US empires shaped Latin Americanism provides a more accurate narrative of the field's formation. Yet, more recently, Cecilia Enjuto-Rangel, Sebastiaan Faber, Pedro García Caro, and Robert Patrick Newcomb's volume *Transatlantic Studies: Latin America, Iberia, and Africa* (2020), illustrates that there continues to be a lack of consensus around defining and practising Iberian and Transatlantic Studies. My hope is that this volume, in calling attention to the blueprint that debates and exchanges in journals, magazines, and newspapers provide Hispanists, will encourage scholars to make use of this invaluable medium in their research as we forge a path forward that, like 1920s print culture, defines and defies borders to transcend the Atlantic.

Appendix

Argentine, Mexican, and Spanish Journals

Argentine Journals

Nosotros *(Buenos Aires, 1907–34)*

Nosotros "Revista mensual de letras, arte, historia, filosofía y ciencias sociales" [*Us* monthly journal of Letters, Art, History, Philosophy, and Social Sciences] was founded by Alfredo A. Bianchi and Roberto F. Giusti. As it published a variety of subjects from authors of multiple inclinations, generations, nationalities, and views, it endured four decades earning a prominent space in Argentine letters. As La Fleur, Provenzano, and Alonso put it, "al hablar de la revista *Nosotros* se está nombrando al documento más importante de la vida intelectual argentina de las primeras cuatro décadas del siglo" [when mentioning the journal *Nosotros*, one is naming the most important document of Argentine intellectual life during the century's first four decades]. (La Fleur, Provenzano, Alonso 59). *Nosotros*'s relative longevity was in part owing to its openness to provide a space where a variety of socio-political and artistic tendencies could coexist. Additionally, *Nosotros* published national and transnational content, noting developments in other Latin American countries, Europe, and the United States. Most important, however, was the journal's ability to evolve. *Nosotros* first embraced *modernismo* and the so-called Spanish Generation of '98, but, during the twenties and thirties, the Argentine journal published emerging literary trends such as Jorge Luis Borges's Ultraist Manifesto (December 1921),[1] as well as the "Encuesta de la Nueva Generación" [New Generation's Survey] that asked young writers to share their views on the current state of literature in Argentina and gave them the label "Nueva Generación."[2]

Valoraciones *(La Plata, 1923–8)*

In September 1923, the University of La Plata's "Grupo Renovación" [Renovation Group] published Valoraciones [Valuations], directed by Carlos Américo Amaya. *Valoraciones* participated in the *Reforma universitaria* [University Reform], but it played host to a plurality of concerns in each issue. Affirming that elevating culture could attain social change, the journal maintained that art, literature, and socio-political issues were inextricably linked. Combining politics, history, philosophy, and the arts, this sophisticated journal aimed to "provocar batalla en el campo de las ideas" [provoke battles in the field of ideas] in order to precipitate reform (*Valoraciones* 1 September 1923). "Grupo Renovación" stood for university reform, opposing archaic values, and arguing that universities had a vital social role. Pronouncing that the university had become a degenerated institution, they believed that, by elevating culture, their journal could inspire students to participate in reconfiguring higher education. Moreover, "Grupo Renovación" proposed that politics, history, philosophy, and aesthetics needed to converge in order to attain reform. *Valoraciones* paid close attention to Argentine intellectuals but also attempted to cover the broadest range of national and foreign events, publishing contributions from French, German, Spanish, and Mexican thinkers.

Sagitario: Revista de Humanidades *(La Plata, 1925–7)*

Carlos Américo Amaya, Julio V. González, and Carlos Sánchez Viamonte founded *Sagitario* [Saggitarius] in June 1925. Its striking similarities in form and content to *Valoraciones* are not coincidental. As La Fleur, Provenzano, and Alonso explain, Amaya directed *Valoraciones*'s first six issues and founded *Sagitario* when he broke with the *Valoraciones* group. Like *Valoraciones, Sagitario* was a journal of Argentina's "Nueva Generación" that sought to continue "el gran movimiento de reconstrucción" [the great movement of reconstruction] that began with the University Reform movement (9).[3] While *Valoraciones*'s goal was to inspire reform by elevating culture, going one step further, *Sagitario* would, perhaps more boldly, be a "registro de las más modernas tendencias que van de la filosofía a la historia y de las matemáticas al arte y la biología" [register the most modern tendencies, from Philosophy to History, and from Mathematics to Art and Biology] (9). Each issue was divided into four main sections: 1) main articles on topics including philosophy, literature, science, and math; 2) a book review section entitled "Bibliografía"; 3) a "Comentarios" section detailing news on University Reform; and 4) a "Noticias" section.

Inicial (Buenos Aires, 1923–7)

Brandán Caraffa, Homero Guglielmini, Roberto Smith, and Roberto A. Ortelli first published *Inicial: Revista de la nueva generación* [Initial: Journal of the New Generation] in October 1923. Firmly entrenched in the *Reforma Universitaria* movement, this boisterous, aggressive journal stood for radical socio-political changes and published the latest aesthetic tendencies.[4] In its first issue (October 1923), *Inicial* affirmed its intent to provide a space where the world's problems could be openly discussed. *Inicial* primarily engaged philosophy, politics, nationalism, Latin Americanism, and educational reform. However, articles pertaining to aesthetics – poetry, art, dance, and theatre – were included within *Inicial*'s agenda to promote social change within Argentina and across Latin America. *Inicial* also published French, Spanish, Russian, and Latin American intellectuals and participated in transnational and transatlantic dialogues. In each issue, *Inicial* published introductory essays that addressed the journal's vision for the "Nueva Generación" and its right to break with past generations' socio-political and aesthetic perspectives.[5] Finally, the recurring section "Protestamos" [We Protest] lists various cultural and political matters that the journal's editors adamantly rejected, such as governmental infringements upon workers' rights. This section's combative tone is in keeping with *Inicial*'s overall aggressive stance.

Proa *(Buenos Aires, 1924–6)*

Resulting from a rift between Brandán Caraffa and *Inicial* collaborators Homero Guglielmini, Roberto Smith, and Vicente Ruiz de Gallarreta, "cuatro escritores jóvenes formados en distintos ambientes" [four young writers shaped in different environments] – Jorge Luis Borges, Brandán Caraffa, Ricardo Güiraldes, and Pablo Rojas Paz – first published *Proa* in August 1925 (3).[6] This small journal, adorned with brightly coloured covers, echoed some of *Inicial*'s perspectives in its first issue. *Proa* announced that, having witnessed the First World War and having participated in university reform, Argentina's new generation was ready to create a journal that was at once cosmopolitan and distinctly Argentinean: "Jamás nuestro país ha vivido tan intensamente como ahora la vida del espíritu. La alta cultura que hasta hoy había sido patrimonio exclusivo de Europa y de los pocos americanos que habían bebido en ella, empieza a trasuntarse ... como producto esencial de nuestra civilización [Never has our country lived the spirit's life as intensely as now. High culture, which, until today, had exclusively belonged to Europeans and the few Americans able to taste it, begins to appear as an essential product of our civilization] (3). Unlike *Inicial* and *Valoraciones*, however, *Proa* did not engage socio-political topics. Instead, the journal features prose, poetry, literary criticism, art, and art criticism. While Argentine writers' and artists' presence in *Proa* far surpassed that of intellectuals from other nationalities, *Proa* also attempted to maintain an international scope. Contributions from French writers and artists are the most notable, along with significant publications on or by Latin American poets and writers. In addition, *Proa* also published Austrian Symbolist painter Gustav Klimt, Irish Modernist James Joyce, Indian thinker Rabindranath Tagore, and Persian philosopher Omar Khayyam within its spectrum of international contributions. Interestingly, similarities between *Proa* and *Plural* [Plural] suggest that the Spanish journal may have been modelled after its Argentine predecessor.

Martín Fierro *(Buenos Aires, 1924–7)*

Martín Fierro [Martín Iron] appeared in February 1924, championing international vanguard aesthetics while harnessing the distinctly Argentinean symbol, *Martín Fierro* (1872), José Hernández's late nineteenth-century epic poem about a gaucho [cowboy]. Seeking reform in Buenos Aires's cultural scene and, breaking with *modernista* aesthetics, Évar Méndez and Samuel Glusberg published the first issue of the vanguard literary magazine *Martín Fierro* in February 1924.[7] Sardonically outlining the explosive journal's positions, the "Manifiesto *Martín Fierro*" [*Martín Fierro* Manifesto] penned by Oliverio Girondo, appeared in the fourth issue (May 1924). Girondo's text emulated other vanguard manifestoes, such as Mexican Maples Arce's *Actual 1* and Marinetti's Futurist Manifesto. However, the "Manifiesto *Martín Fierro*" mocked the need for self-definition and the expectation among Argentine intellectuals that the journal take a position on nationalism.

Regular contributors to *Martín Fierro*, referred to as *martinfierristas*, included avant-garde poet Oliverio Girondo, essayist and poet Pablo Rojas Paz, historian Ernesto Palacio, journalist Conrado Nalé Roxlo, writer Luis Franco, and poet Córdova Iturburu.[8] Formatted like a newspaper, *Martín Fierro*'s bi-weekly, eight- to twelve-page issues published Argentine vanguard writers, including Borges; Girondo; Rojas Paz; experimental novelists Macedonio Fernández, Ricardo Güiraldes, and Eduardo Mallea; and artists Norah Borges, Emilio Petorutti,

Pedro Figari, and Alberto Prebisch. The journal's international scope included French, Spanish, Portuguese, Italian, Brazilian, and Latin American contributions, although the French presence in *Martín Fierro* was the most significant. This satirical and consciously disruptive vanguard publication featured poetry, prose, theatre, and criticism (literary and artistic). Often adorned with humorous caricatures, *Martín Fierro* merged cutting-edge vanguard aesthetics with issues concerning the "Nueva Generación" [New Generation], effectively bridging nationalism and cosmopolitanism. However, the journal's haphazard format was meant to provide just a glimpse into issues more thoroughly addressed in *Proa*, *Inicial*, and *Valoraciones*.[9]

Síntesis *(Buenos Aires, 1927–30)*

In June 1927, the same year that *Martín Fierro* ceased publication, the more elegant and formal *Síntesis* [Synthesis] appeared. Directed by Galician immigrant Xavier Bóveda, the editorial board also featured Jorge Luis Borges and Argentine poet Arturo Capdevila and would eventually welcome Spanish poet and critic Guillermo de Torre upon his arrival in Buenos Aires in 1928. Purely a literary journal, *Síntesis* promoted "una cultura hispano-americana" [a Hispanic American culture] by publishing primarily Argentine and Spanish writers and intellectuals. Like *Revista de Occidente* [Journal of the West], *Síntesis* published lengthier texts, such as entire novel chapters. In addition, essays on social issues, such as education, philosophy, art, and literary criticism, regularly appeared in *Síntesis*. Moreover, *Síntesis* included an extensive bibliographic section with detailed reviews of books, other journals, and current events taking place in the literary world.

Mexican Journals

La Antorcha *(Mexico, 1924–5)*

José Vasconcelos's journal *La Antorcha* [The Torch], subtitled *Letras, Arte, Ciencia, Industria: Semanario de José Vasconcelos* [Letters, Art, Science; José Vasconcelos's Weekly], is a cross between a newspaper and a literary supplement that offers insight into Mexico's cultural and socio-political climate during the 1920s. Aspiring to be "un órgano de pensamiento libre" [a medium for free thought] (Announcement in *La Antorcha* 1, 4 October 1924, 35), *La Antorcha* engaged a variety of topics, such as economics, agriculture, politics, science, literature, art, film, theatre, music, education, health, folklore, sports, fashion, humour, and even surveys on the readership's favourite car. Moreover, Vasconcelos's journal included a vast array of international contributions from Latin America, Europe, the United States, and Asia. Each weekly issue included an editorial introduction by José Vasconcelos that either addressed a theme that loosely framed the issue or commented on an important current event, most often relating to either Mexico or Latin America. For instance, in the first issue, published on 4 October 1924, Vasconcelos affirmed that his journal would strive to make sense of Mexico's current "épocas caóticas" [chaotic times] (1).

Irradiador *(Mexico, 1923)*

Manuel Maples Arce and Fermín Revueltas published the first *estridentista* [Stridentist] journal, *Irradiador: Revista de vanguardia, proyector internacional de nueva estética* [Irradiator: Vanguard Journal, International New Aesthetic Projector] in September 1923. Reminiscent of Spanish Ultraist journals, every aspect of *Irradiador*'s content, structure, and format was designed to represent a Stridentist aesthetic. Bright, bold colours and vanguard illustrations that recall cubist and futurist designs adorn the journal's front and back covers. Each of *Irradiador*'s three issues illustrated Stridentism's primary goals: 1) avant-garde artistic and poetic forms that embraced modernity and technology and 2) a concern with social movements. For instance, Revueltas's "El Restorán" [The Restaurant] which appeared in the first issue, is a black-and-white cubist drawing, while muralist Diego Rivera's "Los mineros" [The Miners] (October 1923) is a more realist representation of mine workers. Each *Irradiador* issue published art, poetry, and articles on current events. Artists such as Jean Charlot, Guillermo Ruiz, and Leopoldo Méndez illustrated the journal alongside poems by Germán List Arzubide, Salvador Gallardo, and Kyn Taniya. Notably, José Juan Tablada, originally a *modernista* also published avant-garde poetry in *Irradiador*. A "Proyector Internacional," *Irradiador* also published Swiss poet Gestón Dinner, Spanish poet Humberto Rivas, and Argentine Jorge Luis Borges.

Horizonte *(Xalapa, 1926–7)*

Three years later, Germán List Arzubide published *Horizonte* [Horizon], the second Stridentist journal. Like *Irradiador*, *Horizonte*'s front covers were printed in colour, featuring *estridentista* paintings by Ramón Alva de la Canal and Leopoldo Méndez. While some covers were abstract works of art, other paintings illustrated workers, peasants, and Indigenous figures. Subtitled "Revista mensual de actividad contemporánea"

[Monthly Journal of Contemporary Activity], *Horizonte* published prose, poetry, art, photography, and literary criticism, as well as essays on politics (most often concerning Xalapa, Veracruz), education, science, agriculture, and technology. As the front covers indicate, *Horizonte* also paid close attention to the labour movement and workers' rights. Echoing Vasconcelos's assertion that *La Antorcha* would strive to make sense of Mexico's chaotic times, *Horizonte* set out to guide Mexico through its time of crisis ("Propósito" [Purpose] April 1926, 1). A space where modern political, social, philosophical, and aesthetic thought could converge, *Horizonte* aimed to broaden its readership's "horizons." For example, *Horizonte* called on Mexico's young intellectuals to become leaders in making revolutionary ideals a reality. In "Se necesita juventud" [Youth Is Needed] (April 1926, 4) *Horizonte* proclaimed that Argentine intellectuals had already managed to effect change in their country and that Mexicans needed to do the same. *Horizonte* also participated in continental social and political movements, such as the University Reform.

Contemporáneos's *Journals*

In contrast to the Stridentists, the group of Mexican novelists, poets, and chroniclers, including Jorge Cuesta, Jaime Torres Bodet, Carlos Pellicer, Salvador Novo, and Xavier Villaurrutia, that identified themselves as the *Contemporáneos* [Contemporaries] did not create a specific aesthetic movement nor were they politically engaged in the same manner. Yet, the *Contemporáneos* were equally invested in reforming Mexico's cultural scene. Famously called a "grupo sin grupo" [group without a group] by poet and novelist Xavier Villaurrutia, the *Contemporáneos* came together because they shared a similar vision for Mexican aesthetics, one that was at once Mexican and cosmopolitan. However, despite their shared values, diverging views within the group were evident in their literary journals: *La Falange* (1922–3) [The Phalanx], *Ulises* (1927–8), and *Contemporáneos* (1928–31). *La Falange* and *Contemporáneos*, directed by Torres Bodet and Bernardo Ortiz de Montellano, are more sober than Novo and Villaurrutia's more daring *Ulises* [Ulysses]. Yet, as compared to Stridentist publications, *Contemporáneos*'s journals rarely addressed socio-political issues.

Ulises *(Mexico, 1927–8)*

As its title proclaims, *Ulises* [Ulysses] embarked upon countless journeys to satisfy its "curiosidad" [curiosity], which often entailed participating in contentious debates, such as the *polémica del meridiano intelectual*, detailed in chapter 3.[10] Directed by Xavier Villaurrutia and Salvador Novo, *Ulises*'s adventures also included poetry, philosophy, essays, art, and vanguard prose. Mexican philosopher Antonio Caso was often featured in *Ulises*. Members of the *Contemporáneos*, such as Jorge Cuesta and Gilberto Owen authored most of the prose and poetry published in *Ulises*, although the journal did feature French poets such as Max Jacob and Italian writers such as Massimo Bontempelli. *Ulises* also paid close attention to Spanish intellectuals, commenting regularly on vanguard prose writers such as Antonio Espina and Benjamín Jarnés, whose novels were part of *Revista de Occidente*'s "Nova novorum" series. *Ulises*'s layout was simple, and the journal's cover only included its name and issue number, depicted in large, bold-coloured print. The journal published prose, poetry, and essays, followed by a closing section entitled "Notas" [Notes]. "Notas" was often divided into smaller sections, including the recurring "El curioso impertinente" [The Impertinent Curious [one]] where the journal published some of its more polemical pieces, such as its contribution to the *polémica del meridiano intelectual*.

Spanish Journals

La Pluma *(Madrid, 1920–4)*

Writer, politician, and president of the Second Republic (1936–9) Manuel Azaña, together with playwright Cipriano Rivas Cherif, founded *La Pluma* [The Quill] with the intent of providing "un refugio donde la vocación literaria pueda vivir en la plenitud de su independencia, sin transigir con el ambiente" [a refuge where literary vocation can live independently, without having to accommodate to the environment] (*La Pluma* June 1920, 2). Opposing the exclusivity of movements such as Ultraism, *La Pluma* was meant to be a more open space for writers who, while not affiliated with any specific group, could come together around a "hostilidad a los agentes de corrupción del gusto y propenden a encontrarse dentro del mismo giro del pensamiento contemporáneo" [hostility towards agents who corrupt taste and tend to find themselves within similar currents of contemporary thought] (*La Pluma* June 1920, 2). Despite its aversion to Ultraism, which Rivas Cherif considered a weak imitation of other European vanguard movements, *La Pluma* was in fact open to many literary genres, including Rámon Gómez de la Serna's vanguard prose, and Ramón del Valle Inclán's experimental theatre, which he called *esperpento*.[11] *La Pluma* published prose, poetry, and theatre, and it included two recurring columns – "El paseante en corte" [The stroller at court] and "La dame de coeur" [The Lady of Heart] – that focused on life in Madrid. Most issues also concluded with a final section entitled "Gacetilla" [Little Gazette], a list of isolated comments on heterogeneous subjects.

During its four years of publication, *La Pluma* made a significant effort to include literature from other European countries and Latin America in recurring sections such as "Letras Francesas" [French Letters], "Letras Portuguesas" [Portuguese Letters], "Letras Alemanas" [German Letters], "Letras Inglesas" [English Letters], and "Letras Italianas" [Italian Letters]. An intergenerational publication, *La Pluma* published writers from the Generation of '98, including Miguel de Unamuno and Antonio Machado, Latin American *modernistas* such as Rubén Darío (Nicaragua) and Manuel Gutiérrez Nájera (Mexico), and Generation of '14 writers such as Ramón Pérez de Ayala. The journal also provided a space for younger Generation of '27 writers such as Federico García Lorca, Antonio Espina, Pedro Salinas, and Jorge Guillén. In spite of its professed openness to multiple genres and writers from different nationalities, *La Pluma* did engage in controversial transatlantic debates, such as an exchange over *modernismo* between Rivas Cherif and Mexican *ateneísta* [Athenaeum Member], writer and diplomat Alfonso Reyes.

Alfar *(La Coruña, 1923–7)*

Emerging from the chrysalis of some earlier ventures, and existing under different names from 1920 through 1922, in 1923 the elegant journal *Alfar* [Pottery] finally became the official name of Casa América Galicia's publication. In contrast to other Galician journals, which were published either in Galician or in Galician and Castilian, *Alfar* was published entirely in Castilian. It was directed by Uruguayan diplomat in Galicia Julio J. Casal, who had previously worked on the literary journal *Vida* [Life] (La Coruña 1920).[12] Both displayed Casal's efforts to create a publication in which various forms of aesthetic expression by authors from different generations and nationalities could coexist.[13] *Alfar* combined Casal's penchant for fostering connections and exchanges between artists and genres with Casa América Galicia's goals of strengthening political and economic ties between Spain and Latin America. As a result, journal issues mentioned economic updates or topics related to trade between Latin America and Galicia, while publishing visual arts (art criticism, illustrations, and music criticism) and literature (prose, poetry, and literary criticism) from Spain, Europe, and Latin America. Principally preoccupied with vanguard aesthetic movements, *Alfar* published essays, art criticism, and reproductions of paintings by painters such as Uruguayan Rafael Barradas and Spanish Surrealist Salvador Dalí. Spanish vanguard prose novelist Benjamín Jarnés frequently appeared in *Alfar*, as did Ramón Gómez de la Serna. Moreover, Generation '27 poets such as Rafael Alberti and Gerardo Diego were often featured in the Galician journal. As compared to contributions from other Latin American nationalities, Argentine intellectuals such as *ultraístas* Jorge Luis Borges and Eduardo González Lanuza most frequently appeared in *Alfar*. However, Latin Americans from other countries, such as Mexican Alfonso Reyes, Chilean poet Vicente Huidobro, and Peruvian poet César Vallejo, also published their work in *Alfar*. *Alfar*'s last issue was published in 1927, but the journal's most successful period only lasted until 1926 when it was published in La Coruña. The journal's quality and consistency suffered greatly when Julio J. Casal transferred it to Uruguay.

Revista de Occidente *(Madrid, 1923–36)*

Perhaps the most prominent Spanish literary journal of the 1920s, José Ortega y Gasset's *Revista de Occidente* [Journal of the West] appeared in the culturally rich period between the First World War and the Spanish Civil War. Ortega had a very clear vision for his publication, which he had outlined in the first issue in "Propósitos" [Purposes] (*RDO* July 1923). *Revista de Occidente* was to be a cultural journal that published philosophical, scientific, and literary texts of the highest quality. In order to further enrich cosmopolitanism in the Western world, *Revista de Occidente* promoted transnational and transatlantic exchanges by accepting contributions from a variety of authors (*RDO* "Propósitos" [Purposes] July 1923, 3). Ortega's journal published Spanish, Latin American, French, American, German, and British intellectuals (the latter four in Spanish translation). Among foreign contributors, however, French and German intellectuals were most often featured in *Revista de Occidente*.[14] Unlike many journals at the time that were often published irregularly, there were no lapses in *Revista de Occidente*'s monthly issues between 1923 and 1936. Given its consistency and superb calibre, *Revista de Occidente* was widely read in Latin America, where Ortega y Gasset had gained much popularity among young intellectuals with *España invertebrada* (1921) [Invertebrate Spain], *El tema de nuestro tiempo* (1923) [The Modern Theme], and *La deshumanización del arte* (1925) [The Dehumanization of Art].[15]

Plural *(Madrid, 1925)*

Novelists Benjamín Jarnés and Valentín Andrés Álvarez, along with Guillermo de Torre, created *Plural* [Plural] in 1925. Their journal was to be "el punto de fusión o convergencia de varios escritores jóvenes … que, habiendo partido, en su mayor parte, del mismo foco, después de ramificarse en surcos individuales, vuelven a encontrarse en un punto meridiano de cruce común" [the point of fusion or convergence of various young writers … whose majority, having emerged from the same focal point and then branched off on individual paths, to now come back together, intersecting on one meridian] (*Plural* January 1925, 1).[16] Publishing prose, poetry, and reviews, *Plural* did not promote a particular aesthetic movement, although it was aligned with European vanguard aesthetics. In addition to Spanish contributors, *Plural*'s two issues included French and Latin American articles on literature, visual arts, and music. Yet, like most vanguard journals during the 1920s, *Plural*'s international scope privileged French intellectuals. Despite its brief period of publication, *Plural* is significant for its efforts to engage in a transatlantic dialogue with Latin American intellectuals, especially from Argentina.

El Estudiante *(Salamanca and Madrid, 1925–6)*

A group of students from the University of Salamanca first published *El Estudiante: Semanario de la juventud escolar española* (1925–6) [The Student: Spanish School Aged Youth's Weekly] in May 1925. Their goal was to initiate a student movement that would counter Spain's cultural decay. As students of the University of Salamanca, an institution that represented Spain's past, they wanted to be the first to revise their country's educational system in order to achieve more substantial political reform, which implied a resistance to Miguel Primo de Rivera's dictatorship. To do so, they boldly reached across the Atlantic, seeking solidarity from Latin American peers. Socio-political and educational reforms were its primary focus, but *El Estudiante* also published literary criticism and novel fragments. Transnational and transatlantic in its scope, *El Estudiante* published contributions from French and Latin American intellectuals. Although short-lived, *El Estudiante*'s initiative to invert the postcolonial paradigm in a Spanish American field of cultural production is unparalleled by any journal of its kind during the 1920s.

La Gaceta Literaria *(Madrid, 1927–32)*

Ernesto Giménez Caballero's *La Gaceta Literaria* [The Literary Gazette] was first published in January 1927. *La Gaceta Literaria* picked up where

Alfar left off in 1926 when the latter's director, Julio J. Casal, moved the journal to Uruguay.[17] However, Giménez Caballero's vision was broader than Julio J. Casals's. Professing to be "Ibérica, Americana e Internacional" [Iberian, American, and International] *La Gaceta Literaria* published European, Latin American, Russian, and North American contributions. Formatted like a newspaper and in the same category as the French *Les Nouvelles Litteraires* (Paris 1922–85) [The New Literatures] and the Italian *La Fiera Letteraria: lettere, scienze, arti* (Milano 1925–7) [The Literary Fair: Letters, Sciences, Arts], *La Gaceta Literaria* published essays, reviews, poetry, prose, and criticism. Moreover, this interdisciplinary journal also paid close attention to art, film, and architecture. In order to bring "peripheral" literatures to the Spanish capital, *La Gaceta Literaria* sponsored book fairs (Catalan, Portuguese, and Argentine). Catalan, Latin American, and Portuguese literature and art were regularly reviewed and published in *La Gaceta Literaria* from its inception and would eventually earn their own supplemental "gacetas" [gazettes], such as *La Gaceta Americana* edited by Benjamín Jarnés in Madrid and Guillermo de Torre in Buenos Aires.

Notes

Introduction

1 See Eric Bulson, *Little Magazine, World Form,* and Aránzazu Ascunce Arenas *Barcelona and Madrid: Social Networks fo the Avant-Garde* for further discussion on Giménez Caballero's "Carteles."
2 I briefly discuss this article in "Discord and Solidarity: Spain, Argentina, and Mexico in *El Estudiante* (Salamanca, Madrid 1924–26)" *Pierre Bourdieu and Hispanic Studies,* edited by Ignacio M. Sánchez Prado, Palgrave, March 2018, p. 225–48.
3 The idea of Latin America itself, as Walter Mignolo has well noted, stems from "the process of European colonial history and the consolidation and expansion of the Western world view and institutions" (2).
4 Studies on Spanish journals, magazines, and newspapers include Andrés Soria Olmedo's *Vanguardismo y crítica literaria* and María del Rosario Rojo Martín's *Evolución del movimiento vanguardista. Estudio basado en La Gaceta Literaria (1927–1932),* which trace avant-garde developments in Spain through literary and avant-garde magazines; César Antonio Molina's *Medio siglo de prensa literaria española (1900–1950),* which surveys literary periodicals by movement and region; and Rafael Osuna's *Revistas de la vanguardia española* and *Las revistas españolas entre dos dictaduras: 1931–1939,* which provide comprehensive lists that evaluate each publication chronologically. Studies on specific journals include: *La "Revista de Occidente" y la formación de minorías (1923–1926)* by Evelyn López Campillo and *Litoral: La revista de una generación* by Julio Neira. Finally, Manuel José Ramos Ortega's *Revistas literarias españolas del siglo XX 1919–1975* is a detailed index that includes literary magazines published between 1919 and 1975.
5 Granados's book is a compilation of papers given at a conference in Mexico City in 2011, sponsored by UAM Cuajimalpa. In 1968, Boyd G.

Carter was one of the first scholars to use journals in order to construct literary historiography in Latin America.

6 Hector René LaFleur, Sergio D. Provenzano, and Pedro Alonso published *Las revistas literarias argentinas: (1893–1960)* and Nélida Salvador's *Revistas argentinas de vanguardia (1920–1930)*. Nélida Salvador and Elena Adrissone published *Bibliografía de tres revistas de vanguardia: Prisma (1921–22), Proa (1922–23) y Proa (1924–26)*, which provides indexes of these particular journals ordered by authors and topics. John King's *A Study of the Argentine Literary Journal and Its Role in the Development of a Culture: 1931–1970*, Nora Pasternac's *Sur, una revista en la tormenta: Los años de formación 1931–1944*, and Rosalie Sitman's *Victoria Ocampo y Sur* are also significant contributions.

7 Fernando Curiel, Carlos Ramírez, and Antonio Sierra recently published their *Índice de las revistas culturales del siglo XX (Ciudad de México)*. Another important contribution is *Las revistas literarias de México*, published by the Instituto Nacional de Bellas Artes in 1963. It is a two-volume collection of conference presentations on Mexican literary magazines from the late nineteenth and early twentieth centuries. However, these presentations are anecdotal accounts by figures who were directly involved, in one capacity or another, with the production of these magazines in order to provide "un examen histórico-crítico de aquellas publicaciones a través de las cuales halló expresión el desenvolvimiento de las letras en el país" (11). The Universidad Autónoma Metropolitana in Mexico has also published *Irradiador*, the first *estridentista* journal, directed by Manuel Maples Arce.

8 See Guillermo Sheridan's *Índices de Contemporáneos: Revista mexicana de cultura: 1928–1931* (1988) and *Los Contemporáneos ayer* (2003), Luis Mario Schneider's *El estridentismo: Una literatura de la estrategia* (1970) and *El estridentismo: México 1921–1927* (1985) and Pedro Ángel Palou's *La casa del silencio: Aproximación en tres tiempos a Contemporáneos* (1997).

9 Other examples of recently published transatlantic correspondence between Latin America and Spain include: *Preciadas cartas (1932–1979): Correspondencia entre Gabriela Mistral, Victoria Ocampo y Victoria Kent*, Sevilla, Renacimiento, 2019. *Alfonso Reyes: Max Aub: Epistolario 1940–1959: escribo conforme voy viviendo*, Fundación Max Aub, 2007. *Queridos todos: El intercambio epistolar entre escritores hispanoamericanos y españoles del siglo XX*, edited by Ana Gallego Cuiñas, and Erika Martínez Cabrera.

10 See Alejandro Mejías López, *The Inverted Conquest*, Fernando Rosenberg's *The Avant Garde and Geopolitics in Latin America* (2006), Mariano Siskind's *Cosmopolitan Desires: Modernity and World Literature in Latin America* (2014), and Ericka Beckman's *Capital Fictions: The Literature of Latin America's Export Age* (2013).

1 Surpassing Colonialism: Negotiating Nationalism and Empire in Print Culture

1 Unless otherwise noted, translations are my own.
2 Throughout this book I use the term "Latin American" for consistency and clarity.
3 Javier Krauel offers a clear summary of Unamuno's evaluation of *casticismo* in *Imperial Emotions: Cultural Responses to the Myths of Empire in Fin-de-Siècle Spain* (Liverpool 2013). He explains that Unamuno "identifies the main components of this *castizo* core, which include psychological traits (such as dogmatism, intransigence, and individualism), political characteristics (such as the spirit of conquest and expansionism, unitarism, and blind submission to authority), cultural features (such as isolation from the main currents of European thought) and economic elements (such as the aversion to work and endemic poverty). He then analyzes the ways in which *castizo* values have manifested themselves in major works of the Spanish literary canon" (86).
4 However, Unamuno clarifies that Castille's dominance, which he terms "ordenancismo" was neither absolutist nor despotic (Unamuno *En torno* II n/p).
5 Unpacking *intrahistoria* further, Krauel notes that "membership of the intrahistoric Spanish political community has a paradoxical quality in that it is simultaneously a matter of unreasoned attachment (a primordial condition) and a matter of principled choice (a reasoned, political commitment) … Unamuno chooses to privilege the (permanent, primordial) cultural component of *intrahistoria* over its (ongoing, principled) political counterpart" (97).
6 Despite his call for Latin American unity, as Fernando Degiovanni points out in *Vernacular Latin Americanisms*, the Uruguayan thinker did not envision the formation of a Latin American literature, "Although Rodó defends literature's cultural authority in the construction of a disciplined citizenship (which must stand up against Americanization), he nonetheless questions the value of Latin American literary production in such a role" (53).
7 For a more thorough evaluation of Reyes in this light, see Ignacio Sánchez Prado's contribution to Enjuto Rangel et al. *Transatlantic Studies: Latin America, Iberia, and Africa* (2020), "Alfonso Reyes, Hispanist Praxis, and the Critique of Transatlantic Reason."
8 In 1918 Spanish poets, including Guillermo de Torre, Rafael Cansinos-Asséns, and Gerardo Diego, together with Argentine Jorge Luis Borges (then living in Madrid), sought to break with *modernista* aesthetics and transform poetry. Influenced by Futurism, they created *ultraísmo*, a

style that reduced poetry to its most basic element, the metaphor. They published their first *Manifiesto ultraísta* in Andalusian poet Isaac del Vando Villar's journal *Grecia* (Sevilla 1918–20) in 1919. *Ultraísmo* spread to Argentina when Borges returned to Buenos Aires in 1921 and had much in common with the Mexican vanguard movement *estridentismo*, which also began in 1921.

9 I came to this article when reading Gayle Rogers's *Incomparable Empires: Modernism and the Translation of Spanish and American Literature*.

10 While I cite the digitized versions of the original articles available at filosofía.org, Mariátegui's articles in *El Mundial* are also reprinted in *Temas de nuestra América. Obras completas*, volume 12.

11 I cite reprinted, digitized versions of these articles available at filosofía.org.

12 Luis Araquistáin also addressed Lugones's militaristic stance in "Lo explicable y lo inexplicable del Sr. Lugones" (*El Sol* 18 April 1925, 1). The speech that Mariátegui referenced was published in *La Nación* on 14 January 1925. Lugones affirmed his support for "militares" instead of "politicos" in Chile and then said that "[e]l pacifismo no es más que el culto del miedo o una añagaza de la conquista roja" ("Lo inexplicable" 1).

13 In Puerto Rico for example, as part of the 1902 Foracker Act, English was imposed as the language of instruction in schools.

14 Vasconcelos's article was most likely originally published in Mexico's *Excelsior*. I reference the 1926 book *Poetas y bufones* that reprinted this article and is available at filosofía.org. This site offers a broader index of articles and publications that participated in this extensive debate: http://www.filosofia.org/bol/bib/nb059.htm

15 Included in *Poetas y bufones* (1926).

16 A note on the translation: "Licenciado" in English translates to "licenced"; however, in this case, Santos Chocano is referring to the fact that Vasconcelos has a degree in higher education. Such a way of addressing a person would normally imply respect. However, Santos Chocano is being facetious.

17 This article was first published in Peru, but later reprinted in *Horizonte*'s first issue in April 1926.

18 For Santos Chocano's version of the events, see his *El libro de mi proceso*, published in Lima in 1927 and in Madrid in 1931. The anthology *Poetas y bufones*, compiled by José María Rodríguez, also includes other texts related to the polemic.

19 Fernando Degiovanni's *Vernacular Latin Americanisms: War, the Market, and the Making of a Discipline* (2018) offers unique insight into how the concept of a Latin American literature emerged within US academia and Latin America.

2 Transcultural Solidarity: Generational Shifts and Social Reform in Print Culture

1 A very summarized version of this material appears in chapter 9, "Discord and Solidarity: Spain, Argentina, and Mexico in *El Estudiante* (Salamanca, Madrid, 1924–1926)" in *Pierre Bourdieu in Hispanic Literature and Culture,* edited by Ignacio M. Sánchez Prado (Palgrave Macmillan 2018).
2 Ortega's writings also reached Latin America through *Revista de Occidente;* in addition, his articles were published in Mexico's *El Universal* and Buenos Aires's *La Nación.*
3 These ideas are aligned with Spain's Institución Libre de Enseñanza, founded by Francisco Giner de los Ríos in 1876.
4 *Inicial*'s patriarchal perspective is clear.
5 *Inicial*'s anti-Semitism is also evident.
6 In *Ortega y Gasset en La Nación,* Marta M. Campomar offers an evaluation of Ortega's relationship with Argentina and his dialogue with Argentina's younger generation in *La Nación.* She explains that Ortega had intended for his articles responding to *Valoraciones* and *Inicial* to be entitled "Para dos revistas argentinas" (Campomar 93).
7 I cite these articles compiled in *Los escritos de Ortega y Gasset en La Nación 1923–1952.*
8 Natalio R. Botana explains that Ortega wrote this article in support of young Argentine intellectuals who had adopted his philosophy and who were being criticized for their rejection of the previous generation's values by older intellectuals like Adolfo Posada (Spain), who was a regular contributor to *La Nación.* Marta M. Campomar also describes this debate over generations.
9 Marta M. Campomar makes this point in the cover art for her book *Ortega y Gasset en* La Nación; the image depicts Ortega pontificating.
10 For an interesting discussion on *Reforma universitaria* and its role in the formation of Latin American literature as a discipline, see Fernando Degiovanni's *Vernacular Latin Americanisms: War, the Market, and the Making of a Discipline* (Pittsburgh 2018).
11 Material in this section has previously been published as part of chapter 9, "Discord and Solidarity: Spain, Argentina, and Mexico in *El Estudiante* (Salamanca, Madrid, 1924–1926)" in *Pierre Bourdieu in Hispanic Literature and Culture,* edited by Ignacio M. Sánchez Prado (Palgrave Macmillan 2018).

3 *La Gaceta Literaria* (1927–31): Postcolonial Networks, Cultural Capital, and the Literary Market

1 "No hay más delicado placer para quien un día ha pespunteado un intinerario ideal sobre papel transparente que ir otro día cercano

recubriendo con trozos rojos y reales aquellos ilusorios caminos (sangre en la arteria vacía). Este placer está gozando *La Gaceta Literaria* desde poco después de su fundación. Su formal tripartición orientadora – tres flechas, tres caminos – de *ibérica, americana e internacional*, ha ido rellenándose de contenido, de hechos y de verdad" [There is no (greater) pleasure for he/she who one day stitched an ideal itinerary on transparent paper than to shortly thereafter be covering those illusory paths (blood in an empty artery) with real and red pieces. *La Gaceta Literaria* is enjoying this pleasure not long after its founding. Its formal tripartite orientation – three arrows, three paths – Iberian, American, and International, has been filling itself with factual and truthful content] (1).

2 In *Madrid's Forgotten Avant Garde: Between Essentialism and Modernity*, Silvina Schammah-Gesser points out that "A significant innovation, *La Gaceta* presented itself as an Iberian, American, and International journal designed to sponsor all peninsular languages – Spanish, Catalan, Galician and Portuguese – strengthening the idea of a global Iberian union where the emerging avant-gardes could communicate to broader audiences" (108)

3 Antonio Sáez Delgado offers a comprehensive evaluation of *La Gaceta Literaria*'s imperialist, and ultimately fascist, Iberianism in his article "Madrid, meridiano intelectual ibérico (la polémica peninsular de *La Gaceta Literaria*)."

4 In *La Gaceta Literaria (1927–1932): Biografía y Valoración*, Miguel Ángel Hernando suggests the opposite, that the journal's Madrid location actually frees it from regionalism, "su misma ubicación en Madrid, le libera de conseciones regionalistas en colaboradores y contenido" (14)

5 Gayle Rogers's *Modernism and the New Spain Britain, Cosmopolitan Europe, and Literary History* explores how other journals, such as José Ortega y Gasset's *Revista de Occidente*, also managed to "cuajar ese hueco ibérico" by collaborating with British counterparts.

6 In *La Gaceta Literaria: Biografía y Valoración*, Miguel Ángel Hernando explains that these similar journals are *Les Nouvelles Litterarires* in France, *La Fiera Letteraria* in Italy, *Die Literarasche-Welt* in Germany, and England's *Times Literary Supplement* (11).

7 For more on *La Gaceta Literaria* as a journal of the avant-garde and how it evolved due to Ernesto Giménez Caballero's finances and political views, see Lucy Tandy's *Giménez Caballero y "La Gaceta Literaria" [O la Generación del 27]*, M. Ángeles Vázquez's "Las vanguardias en nuestras revistas: Otras revistas de vanguardia en España," Luis Moreno-Caballud's "Las relaciones interartísticas de vanguardia ante lo político. Un estudio sobre *La Gaceta Literaria* (1927–32), Fernando García de Cortazar's "Nacionalismo y vanguardia en 'La Gaceta Literaria,'" María Sferrazza's *Ernesto Giménez*

Caballero en la Literatura española: De la dictadura a la república, Miguel Ángel Hernando's *La Gaceta Literaria: Biografía y Valoración*, and Silvina Schammah-Gesser's *Madrid's Forgotten Avant-Garde: Between Essentialism and Modernity*.

8 The majority of the featured authors are, unsurprisingly, men, but there is one "Mapa en Rosa" [Pink Map] that showcases poetry by women poets (Concha Mendez Cuesta, Pilar de Valderrama, María Luisa Muñoz, María Teresa Vernet).

9 For instance, the first issue includes an article in French on science, "Scientistes o cientifics?" by A. Pi Suñer.

10 On 15 February 1928, for example, the journal dedicated an entire "Letras" section to Italy.

11 De Torre revealed his authorship when he republished the article in Costa Rica's *Repertorio Americano* in April 1927.

12 See Juan E. de Castro, *The Spaces of Latin American Literature: Tradition, Globalization, and Cultural Production* and Alejandrina Falcón, "El idioma de los libros: antecedentes y proyecciones de la polémica 'Madrid, meridiano 'editorial' de Hispanoamérica."

13 See Carmen Alemany Bay's anthology of the debate, *La polémica del meridiano intelectual de Hispanoamérica (1927): Estudios y textos* for the majority of the articles that participated in the polemic. For a blow-by-blow account of the debtate, see my dissertation: "A Transatlantitc Dialogue: Argentina, Mexico, Spain and the Literary Magazines that Bridged the Atlantic (1920–1930)" (2013).

14 See José del Valle, "Linguistic Histories and the Role of Transatlanticity in *Transatlantic Studies: Latin America, Iberia, and Africa*, Enjuto Rangel, Sebastiaan Faber, Pedro García Caro, and Robert Patrick Newcomb, eds.

15 I cite Carmen Alemany Bay's anthology of the debate, *La polémica del meridiano intelectual de Hispanoamérica (1927): Estudios y textos* and from now on abbreviate citations for this text with AB.

16 For instance, "tú eres" becomes "vos sos."

17 Ericka Beckman notes that in Domingo Faustino Sarmiento's *Facundo: Civilización y Barbarie* (1845), "The terms 'barbarism' and 'civilization' were themselves invoked to differentiate modes of production on a global scale, with European commercial societies representing the pinnacle of civilization, and the rest of the world still mired in barbarism" (*Capital Fictions* 12). *Martinfierristas*'s position regarding Spain's backwardness in the *polémica del meridiano intelectual* inverts this nineteenth-century paradigm.

18 In this article, Mariátegui confessed to not having seen eye to eye with *Martín Fierro* when it was first published, but supported their adamant opposition to Spain in this polemic. Moreover, their reaction to the polemic

actually encouraged him to appreciate their role within Latin American letters.

19 Alejo Carpentier "Sobre el meridiano intelectual de nuestra América," *Diario de la Marina* on 12 September 1927, reprinted in Carmen Alemany Bay *La polémica del meridiano intelectual de Hispanoamérica (1927): Estudios y textos*.

20 Torres Bodet's article was initially published in *Excelsior* and later reprinted in Costa Rica's *Repertorio Americano* on 3 December 1927. I cite from the *Repertorio Americano* publication of the article because *Excelsior* microfilm proved difficult to read. I found this article thanks to Celina Manzoni's reference "La polemica del meridiano intelectual."

21 Spanish historian and writer Salvador Madariaga also contributed an article in *El Sol* that commented on *La Gaceta Literaria*'s editorial on 22 October 1927.

22 The topic is discussed in María Fernández Moya's "Editoriales españolas en América Latina. Un proceso de internacionalización secular" and Alejandrina Falcón's "El idioma de los libros: antecedents y proyecciones de la polemica 'Madrid, meridiano 'editorial' de Hispanoamérica."

23 Carmen Alemany Bay's compilation of the 1927 polemic is the most complete thus far. However, it does not include the articles from the Buenos Aires journal *Síntesis* that I discuss.

24 On 1 August 1927, *La Gaceta Literaria* published a brief editorial commenting on Xavier Bóveda's visit to Madrid to collect articles from Spanish intellectuals for *Síntesis*. The Spanish journal praised Bóveda for endorsing the spiritual ties between Spain and Latin America.

25 This article has not been included in either Marcela Croce's or Carmen Alemany Bay's anthologies of the debate.

26 For a more detailed account of this intriguing debate, see *Barcelona and Madrid: Social Networks of the Avant-Garde* by Aránzazu Ascunce Arenas.

27 These talks are available in their entirety in the volume *Cataluña Ante España*.

28 Alejandro Mejías López, *The Inverted Conquest: The Myth of Modernity and the Transatlantic Onset of Modernism.*

29 In particular, de Torre's series of "Escaparate de libros" articles, published between 1 June and 15 July. For instance, in his "Primer escaparate de libros" (*La Gaceta Literaria* 1 June 1928), to his great dismay, he observes that many Spanish books for sale in Buenos Aires are pirated. And, legitimate Spanish books, "aun disfrutando de una hegemonía incuestionable," had fierce international competition in the capital's bookstores (219). Other topics he addressed include *Martín Fierro*'s demise.

30 I thank Guido Herzovich for recommending José Luis de Diego's *Editores y políticas editoriales en Argentina, 1880–2000.*

31 I reference this article in connection to this topic thanks to Juan E. de Castro's observations. The article was first published in Lima's *Mundial* in March 1928.

4 Vying for Aesthetic Capital

1 I previously published some of this material in "Discord and Solidarity: Spain, Argentina, and Mexico in *El Estudiante* (Salamanca, Madrid 1924–26)" in *Pierre Bourdieu and Hispanic Studies*, edited by Ignacio M. Sánchez Prado, Palgrave, March 2018, p. 225–48.
2 Grünfeld, Mihai. *Antología de la poesía latinoamericana de vanguardia 1916–1935*.
3 Noted by Carlos García in his article "Manuel Maples Arce: Correspondencia con Guillermo de Torre, 1921–1922."
4 Rose Corral Jorda points to connections between Borges and Maples Arce in "Un poema de Borges en la revista 'Irradiador' (1923)."
5 *Ultraísmo* was also published in the Buenos Aires journal in *Los Raros*, where in 1920 Bartolomé Galíndez provided a lengthy overview of European vanguard movements and dedicated much space to *ultraísmo*, publishing poems as examples. In "Periferias ultraístas: Guillermo de Torre y Roberto A. Ortelli (1923)," Carlos García considers Ortelli's position most likely linked to a 1920 polemic that ensued when Spanish poet Isaac del Vando-Villar disputed *ultraísmo* with Uruguayan Ildefonso Pereda Valdés. Vando-Villar accused the Latin American writer of having misunderstood *ultraísmo*, citing the distance across the Atlantic as the reason why Latin Americans "incurrían en grandes errores confundiendo las cosas de una manera lamentable" (98). In addition, García suggests that Ortelli's reaction was in keeping with *Inicial*'s program to liberate Argentine culture from European hegemony (98).
6 García also notes that Borges had encouraged de Torre to give Ortelli a copy of *Hélices* so that he could review it for *Nosotros*, where he was an administrator. However, Ortelli left his position in *Nosotros* and became one of *Inicial*'s editors, which is why the review appeared in *Inicial* (94).
7 In *Inquisiciones* (1925), Borges includes a more complete review of Maples Arce's *Andamios interiores* (1922) in which he explains that he critiques the Mexican poet because he admires his work (129–32).
8 I previously published some of this material in "From Journal Debate to Novelistic Form: The Case of *Margarita de niebla* (1927)" *Journal of Modern Periodical Studies* 8.1, 2017, pp. 81–99.
9 Jaime Torres Bodet was a well-known Mexican poet and novelist who participated in the avant-garde group *Contemporáneos* and published the journal with the same name, *Contemporáneos* (1928–31).

10 See Domingo Ródenas de Moya, *Contemporáneos: Prosa* (Madrid: FSCH, 2004); Guillermo Sheridan, *Los contemporáneos ayer* (Mexico City: FCE, 2003); Gustavo Pérez Firmat, *Idle Fictions: The Hispanic Vanguard Novel, 1926–1934* (Durham, NC: Duke UP, 1982).

11 Jarnés, Benjamín, "El profesor inútil" in *Elogio de la impureza: Invenciones e intervenciones* (Madrid: FSCH, 2007), pp. 10–58.

12 Jaime Torres Bodet "La deshumanización del arte," *Valoraciones* 9 (March 1926), 245–9; Benjamín Jarnés, "La deshumanización del arte: Carta al poeta Torres Bodet," *El Estudiante* 2.14 (1926), pp. 10–11.

13 Jaime Torres Bodet "La deshumanización del arte," *Valoraciones* 9 (March 1926), 245–9; "La deshumanización del arte," *Nosotros* 202 (March 1926), 251–6. Despite its presence in Argentine journals, Patricia Artundo underscores that Torres Bodet's essay was grounded in a Mexican context and did not represent an Argentine perspective on Ortega's theory. Patricia Artundo, "La flecha en el blanco: José Ortega y Gasset y La deshumanización del arte," *Estudios e investigaciones* 6 (1996), 73–100.

14 Jaime Torres Bodet, *Contemporáneos,notas de crítica* (Mexico: Herrero, 1928).

15 See Marta Campomar, *Ortega y Gasset en La Nación* (Buenos Aires: Elefante Blanco, 2003).

16 Ortega y Gasset, *The Dehumanization of Art*.

17 Years later, Jaime Torres Bodet conceded that he had perhaps been too critical of Ortega: "Al reconocer en esas manifestaciones las pruebas de una voluntad europea de deshumanización artística, Ortega no hacía sino definir – y definir admirablemente, el fenómeno que enjuiciaba" in *Tiempo de arena* (Mexico City: FCE, 2002), p. 225.

18 An editor of Ortega y Gasset's *Revista de Occidente* (1923–6) Jarnés was also very much a part of Ortega's circle in Madrid.

19 In *Tiempo de arena* Torres Bodet deems Jarnés's response "severa pero amistosa" *Tiempo de arena* (Mexico City: FCE, 2002), p. 228.

20 Torres Bodet points out that despite his opposition in this article, Jarnés's literary production actually supported the Mexican's perspective, *Tiempo de arena* (Mexico City: FCE, 2002), p. 228.

21 In *Tiempo de arena*, Torres Bodet reveals that he wrote *Margarita de niebla* in order to "afrontar … las supuestas dificultades del estilo 'moderno' de aquellos días." *Tiempo de arena* (Mexico City: FCE, 2002), p. 229.

22 Torres Bodet notes that Margarita, the heroine, was meant to entice the protagonist narrator's "pedantería romántica," while "las simpatías del autor" were inclined towards Paloma, *Tiempo de arena* (Mexico City: FCE, 2002), p. 232.

23 Gustavo Pérez Firmat, *Idle Fictions: The Hispanic Vanguard Novel, 1926–1934*, Duke, 1982.

24 "La cultura Mexicana, recién iniciada, casi ansiosa por construirse." Rosa García Gutiérrez 337 *Contemporáneos: La otra novela de la Revolución Mexicana* (Huelva: Universidad de Huelva, 1999).
25 I previously published some of this material in "Discord and Solidarity: Spain, Argentina, and Mexico in *El Estudiante* (Salamanca, Madrid 1924–26)" in *Pierre Bourdieu and Hispanic Studies*, edited by Ignacio M. Sánchez Prado, Palgrave, March 2018, pp. 225–48.
26 The title ironically recalls the Spanish conquest of the Americas.
27 Dru Dougherty, *Guía para caminantes en Santa Fe de Tierra Firme* (Valencia: Pre-Textos, 1999), 214.
28 Whether an avant-garde aesthetic should be socio-politically engaged was widely debated across Spain and Latin America during the 1920s. In Mexico, for example, it emerged as a 1925 polemic over the feminization of literature and in Spain José Díaz Fernández's 1930 essay "El nuevo romanticismo" (*Prosas*, Madrid: Fundación Santander Central Hispano, 2006) would consolidate a theory in which vanguard prose should also be politically engaged. Thus, in publishing *Tirano Banderas, El Estudiante* was assuming a clear position across a transatlantic Spanish American field and multiple national fields of cultural production.

Appendix: Argentine, Mexican, and Spanish Journals

1 Ultraísmo was also published in Buenos Aires in *Los Raros*, where in 1920 Bartolomé Galíndez provided a lengthy overview of European vanguard movements and dedicated much space to ultraísmo, publishing poems as examples. Carlos García makes reference to Galíndez in his article, stating that Galíndez's description of the movement makes clear that he did not understand it.
2 As noted by Nélida Salvador in"*Prisma* y *Proa*, Hacia una nueva definición estética" *Letras* 2nda época #3 Julio 2004 Buenos Aires pp. 44–8, Borges's *Mural Prisma* appeared plastered on Buenos Aires's streets at the same time.
3 "Las flechas del carcax" (*Sagitario* 1, pp. 5–9) functions as the journal's manifesto.
4 I reference Fernando Diego Rodríguez's introduction to the facsimile version of *Inicial* published by the Universidad Nacional de Quilmes.
5 Topics addressed in *Inicial*'s opening editorials include "La nueva mentalidad de occidente" (*Inicial* 4 January–February–March 1924), "Kant y la juventud" (*Inicial* 5 May 1924), "La nueva generación argentina en la perspectiva histórica" (*Inicial* 7 December 1924), "El problema de la cultura y la nueva mentalidad argentina" (*Inicial* 7 December 1924), and "Oswald Spengler y la nueva generación" (*Inicial* 9 January 1926).

6 For further information about the rift in *Inicial* that led to the creation of *Proa*, see Patricia Artundo's "Punto de convergencia: *Inicial* y *Proa* en 1924," in *Bibliografía y antología crítica de las vanguardias literarias: Argentina, Uruguay, Paraguay.*

7 Sarlo, Beatriz. "Vanguardia y criollismo: La Aventura de *Martín Fierro*" in *Ensayos argentinos: De Sarmiento a la vanguardia.*

8 For a detailed account on the creation of *Martín Fierro*, see La Fleur, Provenzano, and Alonzo, *Las revistas literarias argentinas (1893–1967).*

9 As noted by La Fleur, Provenzano, and Alonzo in *Las revistas literarias argentinas (1893–1967)*, *Martín Fierro* provoked a "revuelo" in the Argentine capital's "mundillo literario," but lacked the transcendence of a journal like *Proa* (La Fleur, Provenzano, Alonzo 102).

10 See Guillermo Sheridan *Los Contemporáneos ayer*, pp. 280–1.

11 Cipriano Rivas Cherif wrote a scathing review of Guillermo de Torre's *ultraísmo* in December 1920, "Guillermo de Torre *Manifiesto Vertical.*"

12 In "*Alfar*: Historia de dos revistas literarias," Víctor G. de la Concha details the continuity between *Vida* and *Alfar* given Julio J. Casal's salient presence in both publications. As described by de la Concha, *Vida* was a spirited literary journal that aimed at illustrating the aesthetic and social preoccupations of its editors. It published a broad variety of topics such as art criticism, theatre, and prose fiction, along with essays on science, medicine, local criticism, and music (de la Concha 501).

13 César Antonio Molina's fifth chapter in *La revista literaria Alfar y la prensa literaria de su época (1920–1930)* provides a more thorough description of this topic.

14 Evelyn López Campillo offers a detailed account of foreign contributions to *Revista de Occidente* in *Revista de Occidente y la formación de minorías.*

15 Before being published as books, Ortega y Gasset published many of his essays in Madrid's *El Sol*, which were often reproduced in Mexico's *El Universal* and Buenos Aires's *La Nación*. Ortega also published regularly in *La Nación.*

16 *Plural* does not list its directors, but in *Revistas de la vanguardia española* Rafael Osuna cites Francisco Arias Solís, who affirmed that Benjamín Jarnés, Guillermo de Torre, and Valentín Andrés Álvarez founded *Plural* (262).

17 In *La Gaceta Literaria (1927–1932): Biografía y valoración*, Miguel Ángel Hernando cites Ortega y Gasset's "Sobre un periódico de letras" (*LGL* 1 January 1927) and notes that the philosopher most likely considered *La Gaceta Literaria* to be in a different category from *Alfar*.

Works Cited

Alemany Bay, Carmen. *La polémica del meridiano intelectual de Hispanoamérica (1927): Estudios y textos*. Universidad de Alicante, 1998.

Altamirano, Carlos, and Beatriz Sarlo. *Ensayos argentinos de Sarmiento a la vanguardia*. Centro Editor de América Latina, 1983.

"América." *El Estudiante*, vol. 2, 25 May 1925, p. 9.

Américo Amaya, Carlos. "José Ortega y Gasset: *España invertebrada, Bosquejo de algunos pensamientos históricos*." *Valoraciones*, vol. 1, Sept. 1923, pp. 43–6.

– "José Ortega y Gasset: *El tema de nuestro tiempo*." *Valoraciones*, vol. 4, Jul. 1924, pp. 77–82.

Anderson, Benedict. *Imagined Communities: Reflections on the Origin and Spread of Nationalism*. Verso, 1991.

Araquistáin, Luis. "Un congreso de escritores." *El Sol*, 21 Nov. 1924, p. 1.

– "Una carta desconsoladora." *El Sol*, 17 Apr. 1925, p. 5.

– "Lo explicable y lo inexplicable del Sr. Lugones." *El Sol*, 18 Apr. 1925, p. 1.

– "Organización de la cultura hispánica." *El Sol*, 20 Apr. 1925, p. 1.

Artiles Rodríguez, Jenaro. "El precio de los libros de ocasión." *La Gaceta Literaria*, vol. 26, 15 Jan. 1928, p. 6.

Artundo, Patricia M. "La flecha en el blanco: José Ortega y Gasset y La deshumanización del arte." *Estudios e investigaciones*, vol. 6, 1996, pp. 73–100.

– "Punto de convergencia: *Inicial* y *Proa* en 1924." *Bibliografía y antología de las vanguardias literarias: Argentina, Uruguay, Paraguay*, edited by Carlos García and Dieter Reichardt, Vervuert-Iberoamericana, 2004, pp. 253–66.

Ascunce Arenas, Aránzazu. *Barcelona and Madrid: Social Networks of the Avant-Garde*. Bucknell UP, 2012.

Beckman, Ericka. *Capital Fictions: The Literature of Latin America's Export Age*. U Minnesota P, 2013.

Borges, Jorge Luis. "Acotaciones: Eduardo González Lanuza." *Proa*, vol. 1, Aug. 1924, pp. 30–2.

– *Inquisiciones*. Seix Barral, 1993.

Botana, Natalio R. Prologue. *Los escritos de Ortega y Gasset en La Nación 1923–1952*. La Nación, 2005.
Bradbury, Malcolm, and James Walter McFarlane. *Modernism: 1890–1930*. Penguin, 1976.
Bulson, Eric. *Little Magazine, World Form*. Columbia UP, 2016.
Campomar, Marta M. *Ortega y Gasset en La Nación*. Elefante Blanco, 2003.
Capdevila, Arturo. "La prodigiosa y díscola ciudad del idioma común." *Síntesis*, vol. 2, Jul. 1927, pp. 117–18.
Caraffa, Brandan. "Voces de Castilla." *Proa*, vol. 2, Sept. 1924, pp. 39–49.
Carter, Boyd G. *Historia de la literatura hispanoamericana a través de sus revistas*. De Andrea, 1968.
Cataluña Ante España. La Gaceta Literaria Ed. Madrid, *La Gaceta Literaria*, 1930, memoriademadrid.es. Accessed 10 Nov. 2020.
Corral, Rose. "Un poema de Borges en la revista estridentista 'Irradiador'(1923)." *Hispamérica*, vol. 104, Aug. 2006, pp. 63–8.
Croce, Marcela, comp. *Polémicas intelectuales en América Latina*. Simurg, 2006.
Cruz, Anne J. "American Hispanism(s)." *South Atlantic Review*, vol. 73, no. 4, Fall 2008, pp. 86–106. Accessed 16 Apr. 2016.
Curiel, Fernando, et al. *Índice de las revistas culturales del siglo XX (Ciudad de México)*. UNAM, 2007.
De Araujo, Norberto. "Duas obras notaveis." *La Gaceta Literaria*, vol. 45, 1 Nov. 1928, p. 3.
De Castro, Juan E. *The Spaces of Latin American Literature: Tradition, Globalization, and Cultural Production*. Palgrave Macmillan, 2008.
De Diego, José Luis, editors. *Editores y políticas editoriales en Argentina, 1880–2000*. Fondo de Cultura Económica, 2006.
Degiovanni, Fernando. *Vernacular Latin Americanisms: War, the Market, and the Making of a Discipline*. U Pittsburgh P, 2018.
De la Concha, Víctor. "*Alfar*: Historia de dos revistas literarias: 1920–1927." *Cuadernos Hispanoamericanos*, vol. 254, Feb. 1971, pp. 500–39.
"De la España joven." *Valoraciones*, vol. 6, Jun. 1925, pp. 315–16.
De la Vega, J. Lasso. "Guía de la exposición." *La Gaceta Literaria*, vol. 45, 1 Nov. 1928, p. 1.
Del Valle, José. *Linguistic Histories and the Role of Transatlanticity*. Edited by Cecilia Enjuto Rangel, Sebastiaan Faber, Pedro García Caro, and Robert Patrick Newcomb, 2020, pp. 118–25.
Del Valle Inclán, Ramón. "Tirano Banderas: El jueguito de la rana." *El Estudiante*, vol. 2, no. 1, Dec. 1925, p. 6.
De Torre, Guillermo. "Rasgos polémicos: Réplica a Vicente Huidobro." facsm. ed. *Alfar*, vol. 39, Apr. 1924, pp. 352–6.
– "*La calle de la tarde*, poemas por Norah Lange." *Plural*, vol. 2, Feb. 1925, p. 27.

– "Carta abierta a Évar Méndez." facsm. ed. *Martín Fierro*, vol. 18, 26 Jun. 1925, p. 120.
– "Carta abierta a Évar Méndez." facsm. ed. *Martín Fierro*, vol. 19, 18 Jul. 1925, p. 136.
– "Nuevos poetas mexicanos." *La Gaceta Literaria*, vol. 6, 15 Mar. 1927, p. 2.
– "Madrid, Meridiano intelectual de Hispanoamérica." facsm. ed. *La Gaceta Literaria*, vol. 8, 15 Apr. 1927, p. 43.
– "Primer escaparate de libros." *La Gaceta Literaria*, vol. 35, 1 June 1928, p. 1.
– "Modelos de estación." *Síntesis*, vol. 14, July 1928, pp. 229–35.
– "Ante la exposición del libro argentino y uruguayo en Madrid." facsm. ed. *La Gaceta Literaria*, vol. 39, 1 Aug. 1928, p. 243.
– "Ante la exposición del libro argentino y uruguayo. Lo que dicen los editores bonaerenses: Samuel Glusberg, director de la editorial Babel." facsm. ed. *La Gaceta Literaria*, vol. 40, 15 Aug. 1928, p. 249.
– "Ante la exposición del libro argentino y uruguayo. Lo que dicen los editores bonaerenses: El editor Manuel Gleizer." facsm. ed. *La Gaceta Literaria*, vol. 41, 1 Sept. 1928, p. 255.
– "Ante la exposición del libro argentino y uruguayo. Lo que dicen los editores bonaerenses: El editor Pedro García." facsm. ed. *La Gaceta Literaria*, vol. 44, 15 Oct. 1928, p. 277.
– "Ante la exposición del libro argentino y uruguayo. Lo que dicen los editores bonaerenses: El editor Juan Roldán y Compañía." facsm. ed. *La Gaceta Literaria*, vol. 49, 1 Jan. 1929, p. 318.
– "Ante la exposición del libro argentino y uruguayo. Lo que dicen los editores bonaerenses: El editor Jacobo Samet." facsm. ed. *La Gaceta Literaria*, vol. 54, 15 Mar. 1929, p. 359.
– "A través de las revistas." *Síntesis*, vol. 23, Apr. 1929, pp. 229–38.
– "Ante la exposición del libro argentino y uruguayo. Lo que dice un editor español en Buenos Aires: Julián Urgoiti delegado de Espasa Calpe." facsm. ed. *La Gaceta Literaria*, vol. 55, 1 Apr. 1929, p. 365.
– *Literaturas europeas de vanguardia*. Renacimiento, 2001.
Díaz Fernández, José. *Prosas*. Fundación Santander Central Hispano, 2006.
Diego Rodríguez, Fernando. "Foreword." *Inicial: Revista de la nueva generación (1923–1927)*. facsm, edited by Buenos Aires, Universidad Nacional de Quilmes, 2003.
Dougherty, Dru. *Guía para caminantes en Santa Fe de Tierra Firme*. Pre-Textos, 1999.
"Edwin Elmore." *El Estudiante*, vol. 2, no. 1, 6 Dec. 1925, p. 5.
"El espíritu de América: Cartas entre Romain Rolland y Vasconcelos." *Valoraciones*, 3 Apr. 1924, pp. 263–6.
Elmore, Edwin. "Un nuevo ibero-americanismo." facsm. ed. *Horizonte*, vol. 1, Apr. 1926, pp. 27–8.

El Universal Ilustrado. "Existe una literatura mexicana moderna?" *El Universal Ilustrado*, vol. 8, no. 402, 22 Jan. 1925, pp. 30–1.

"El verdadero meridiano de Hispanoamérica: La traducción." facsm. ed. *La Gaceta Literaria*, vol. 17, 1 Sept. 1927, p. 99.

Enjuto-Rangel, Cecila, et al., editors. *Transatlantic Studies: Latin America, Iberia, and Africa*. Liverpool UP, 2019.

"Entrevista con Alejo Carrera: El libro español en Portugal." *La Gaceta Literaria*, vol. 45, 1 Nov. 1928, p. 7.

Esterlich, Juan. "Respuesta de Juan Esterlich." *Cataluña ante España*, edited by La Gaceta Literaria, La Gaceta Literaria, 1930.

"Exposición del libro portugués." *La Gaceta Literaria*, vol. 28, 15 Feb. 1928, p. 1.

Faber, Sebastiaan. "Economies of Prestige." *Hispanic Research Journal*, vol. 9, no. 1, 2008, pp. 7–32.

– "Fantasmas hispanistas y otros retos transatlánticos." *Cultura y cambio social en América Latina*, edited by Mabel Moraña, Iberoamericana Vervuert, 2008, pp. 315–45.

– "Hispanism, Transatlantic Studies, and the Problem of Cultural History." *Empire's End*, edited by Akiko Tsuchiya and William G. Acree, Vanderbilt UP, 2016, pp. 17–33.

Falcón, Alejandrina. "El idioma de los libros: antecedentes y proyecciones de la polémica 'Madrid, meridiano "editorial" de Hispanoamérica'." *Iberoamericana*, vol. 10, no. 37, 2010, pp. 39–58.

Fernández, James D. "'Longfellow's Law': The Place of Latin America and Spain in U.S. Hispanism, Circa 1915." *Spain in America: The Origins of Hispanism in the United States*, edited by Richard L. Kagan, U Illinois P, 2002.

Fernández, Vanessa Marie. *A Transatlantic Dialogue: Argentina, Mexico, Spain, and the Literary Magazines that Bridged the Atlantic (1920–1930)*. 2013. U California P, PhD dissertation.

– "From Journal Debate to Novelistic Form: The Case of *Margarita de niebla* (1927)." *Journal of Modern Periodical Studies*, vol. 8, no. 1, 2017, pp. 81–99.

– "Discord and Solidarity: Spain, Argentina, and Mexico in *El Estudiante* (Salamanca, Madrid 1924–26)." *Pierre Bourdieu and Hispanic Studies*, edited by Ignacio M. Sánchez Prado, Palgrave, Mar. 2018, pp. 225–48.

Fernández Moya, María. "Editoriales españolas en América Latina. Un proceso de internacionalización secular." *ICE*, vol. 849, Jul.–Aug. 2009, pp. 65–77.

Franco, Jean. *An Introduction to Spanish American Literature*. Cambridge UP, 1994.

Fundación Max Aub. *Alfonso Reyes: Max Aub: Epistolario 1940–1959: escribo conforme voy viviendo*. Biblioteca Valenciana, 2007.

Gallego Cuiñas, Ana and Erika Martínez, editors. *Queridos todos: El intercambio epistolar entre escritores hispanoamericanos y españoles del siglo XX*. Peter Lang, 2013.

García, Carlos. "Manuel Maples Arce: Correspondencia con Guillermo de Torre, 1921–1922." *Inicio*, vol. 15, no. 1, 2004, pp. 151–62.
– "Periferias ultraístas: Guillermo de Torre y Roberto A. Ortelli (1923)." *Fragmentos: revista de lingua e literatura estrangeiras*, vol. 35, 2009, pp. 91–106.
García Blanco, M. "Coimbra en alta voz." *La Gaceta Literaria*, vol. 45, 1 Nov. 1928, p. 6.
García de Cortázar, Fernando. "Nacionalismo y vanguardia en 'La Gaceta Literaria'." *ABC*, 30 Jun. 2014, https://www.abc.es/cultura/20140630/abci-gimenez-caballero-gaceta ilustrada-201406291829.html. Accessed 7 May 2018.
García Godoy, Federico. "Hispanoamericanismo literario." *Nosotros*, vol. 171, Aug. 1923, pp. 433–41.
García Gutiérrez, Rosa. "El meridiano intelectual de Hispanoamérica: Una polémica vista desde México." *Modernismo y modernidad en el ámbito hispánico*, edited by Trinidad Barrera, UIA/AEELA, 1998, pp. 291–305.
Giménez Caballero, Ernesto. "Universo de la literatura española contemporánea." *La Gaceta Literaria*, vol. 14, 15 Jul. 1927, p. 4.
– "Un gran romance mejicano." facsm. ed. *La Gaceta Literaria*, vol. 17, 1 Sept. 1927, p. 101.
– "Cartel de la nueva literatura." *La Gaceta Literaria*, vol. 32, 15 Apr. 1928, p. 7.
– "12.302 Kms. Literatura." *La Gaceta Literaria*, vol. 38, 15 Jul. 1928, p. 1.
– "Saludo a Portugal." *La Gaceta Literaria*, vol. 45, 1 Nov. 1928, p. 1.
Gómez Barquero, Eduardo (Andrenio). "Saludo de 'Andrenio'." *Cataluña Ante España*, edited by La Gaceta Literaria, La Gaceta Literaria, 1930.
González, Ariosto D. "España invertebrada." facsm. ed. *Inicial*, vol. 4, Jan.–Feb.–Mar. 1924, pp. 261–8.
Granados, Aimer, coord. *Las revistas en la historia intelectual de América Latina: Redes, política, sociedad y cultura*. UAM, 2012.
Grünfeld, Mihai. *Antología de la poesía latinoamericana de vanguardia 1916–1935*. Hiperión, 1995.
Guglielmini, Homero M. "Algo más sobre Ortega y Gasset." facsm. ed. *Inicial*, vol. 5, May 1924, pp. 376–8.
"Guillermo de Torre." *La Gaceta Literaria*, vol. 16, 15 Aug. 1927, p. 1.
Hernando, Miguel Ángel. *La Gaceta Literaria (1927–1932): Biografía y valoración*. Universidad de Valladolid, 1974.
Hidalgo, Alberto. *Índice de la nueva poesía americana*. El Inca, 1926.
Horizonte. facsm, ed. Fondo de Cultura Económica, Universidad Veracruzana and Museo Casa Estudio Diego Rivera y Frida Kahlo, 2011.
Infante, Ignacio. *After Translation: The Transfer and Circulation of Modern Poetics Across the Atlantic*. Fordham UP, 2013.
"Inicial." *Inicial*, vol. 1, Oct. 1923, pp. 3–6.

Instituto Nacional de Bellas Artes. *Las revistas literarias de México*. Instituto Nacional de Bellas Artes, 1963.
"Intenciones." *Valoraciones*, vol. 1, Sept. 1923, pp. 3–5.
Irradiador, Revista de Vanguardia. facsm. ed. Universidad Autónoma Metropolitana, 2010.
Jarnés, Benjamín. "La deshumanización del arte: Carta al poeta Torres Bodet." *El Estudiante*, vol. 2, no. 14, 1926, pp. 10–11.
– "Revistas nuevas." *Revista de Occidente* , vol. 15, no. 14, Feb. 1927, pp. 263–6.
– "El profesor inútil." *Elogio de la impureza: Invenciones e intervenciones*, edited by Domingo Ródenas de Moya, Fundación Santander Central Hispano, 2007, pp. 10–58.
King, John. *Sur: A Study of the Argentine Literary Journal and its Role in the Development of a Culture, 1931–1970*. Cambridge UP, 1986.
Krauel, Javier. *Imperial Emotions: Cultural Responses to Myths of Empire*. Liverpool UP, 2013.
La Antorcha, vol. 1, Oct. 1924, p. 35.
Lafleur, Héctor R., et al. *Las revistas literarias argentinas (1893–1967)*. El octavo loco, 2006.
"La nueva mentalidad de occidente." facsm. ed. *Inicial*, vol. 4, Jan.–Feb.–Mar. 1924, pp. 221–6.
"La reconquista de América." *Valoraciones*, vol. 9, Mar. 1926, pp. 297–8.
"Las flechas del carcax." *Sagitario*, vol. 1, May–June 1925, pp. 5–9.
"La verbena del meridiano." *La Gaceta Literaria*, vol. 18, 15 Sept. 1927, p. 1.
"Libros portugueses." *La Gaceta Literaria*, vol. 45, 1 Nov. 1928, p. 3.
López Campillo, Evelyne. *La "Revista de Occidente" y la formación de minorías (1923–1936)*. Taurus, 1972.
Lugones, Leopoldo. "Un congreso libre de trabajadores intelectuales." *El Sol*, 16 Apr. 1925, p. 1.
"Madrid, Meridiano intelectual de Hispanoamérica." facsm. ed. *Ulises*, vol. 4, Oct. 1927, pp. 172–3.
Maíz, Claudio. *Constelaciones Unamunianas: Enlaces entre España y América (1898–1920)*. Universidad de Salamanca, 2009.
Marcondes, Clodoaldo M. "Crónica brasileira." *La Gaceta Literaria*, vol. 45, 1 Nov. 1928, p. 6.
"*Margarita de niebla* y Benjamín Jarnés," facsm. ed. *Ulises*, vol. 5, Nov. 1927, pp. 208–10.
Mariátegui, José Carlos. "Un congreso de escritores hispano-americanos." *Mundial*, 1 Jan. 1925, p. 3.
– "¿Existe un pensamiento hispano-americano?" *Mundial*, 1 May 1925, p. 9.
– *Temas de nuestra América, Obras Completas*. Vol. 12. Amauta, 1980.
– "La batalla del libro." *José Carlos Mariátegui: Temas de educación 14*. Biblioteca Amauta, 1986, archivochile.com.

Mejías-López, Alejandro. *The Inverted Conquest: The Myth of Modernity and the Transatlantic Onset of Modernism*. Vanderbilt UP, 2009.
– "Hispanic Studies and the Legacy of Empire." *Empire's End*, edited by Akiko Tsuchiya and William G. Acree, Vanderbilt UP, 2016, pp. 2014–16.
"Mensaje de la Federación universitaria americana a las juventudes de América y España." *La Antorcha*, vol. 15, 10 Jan. 1925, p. 33.
Mignolo, Walter. *The Idea of Latin America*. Blackwell, 2005.
Molina, César Antonio. *Alfar (Revista Casa América-Galicia)*. facsm. ed., Nos, 1984.
– *La revista Alfar y la prensa literaria de su época (1920–1930)*. Nos, 1984.
– *Medio siglo de Prensa literaria española (1900–1950)*. Endymion, 1990.
Mora Galindo, José. "Vasconcelos y el Uruguay." *Valoraciones*, vol. 9, Mar. 1926, pp. 289–97.
Moraña, Mabel. *Ideologies of Hispanism*. Vanderbilt, 2005.
Moreno Caballud, Luis. "Las relaciones interartísticas de vanguardia ante lo político. Un estudio sobre *La Gaceta Literaria (1927–32)*." *Revista de Estudios Hispánicos*, vol. 34, no. 3, Primavera 2010, pp. 429–49.
Neira, Julio. *Litoral: La revista de una generación*. La isla de los ratones, 1978.
Nemesio, Vitorino. "Coimbra e o livro portugués." *La Gaceta Literaria*, vol. 45, 1 Nov. 1928, p. 6.
Newcomb, Robert Patrick. *Iberianism and Crisis: Spain and Portugal at the Turn of the Twentieth Century*. U Toronto P, 2018.
Novillo-Corvalán, Patricia. *Modernism and Latin America: Transnational Networks of Literary Exchange*. Routledge, 2019.
"Nuestra misión." *El Estudiante*, vol. 1, 1 May 1925, p. 1.
"Oliverio Girondo en misión intelectual." facsm. ed. *Martín Fierro*, vol. 5–6, May–June 1924, p. 47.
Ortega y Gasset, José. *El Espectador*. Mayo, 1917.
– "Sobre un periódico de letras." *La Gaceta Literaria*, vol. 1, 1 Jan. 1927, p. 1.
– *The Dehumanization of Art and Other Essays on Art, Culture, and Literature*. Princeton UP, 1972.
– *Obras Completas Tomo III (1917–1925)*. Taurus, 2008.
Ortelli, Roberto A. "Dos poetas de la nueva generación." facsm. ed. *Inicial*, vol. 1, Oct. 1923, pp. 89–93.
– "Una curiosa epístola." facsm. ed. *Inicial*, vol. 3, Dec. 1923, pp. 207–9.
Osuna, Rafael. *Las revistas españolas entre dos dictaduras: 1931–1939*. Pre-Textos, 1986.
– *Las revistas del 27: Litoral, Verso y Prosa, Carmen, Gallo*. Pre-Textos, 1993.
– *Las revistas literarias: un estudio introductorio*. Universidad de Cádiz, 2004.
– *Revistas de la vanguardia española*. Renacimiento, 2005.
– *Semblanzas de revistas durante la República: 1931–1936*. Centro Cultural Generación del 27, 2006.

"Otra vez la voz de América." *El Estudiante*, vol. 9, Jul. 1925, p. 10.
Palacios, Alfredo. "A la juventud universitaria de Iberoamérica." *La Antorcha*, vol. 15, 10 Jan. 1925, p. 9.
– "A los estudiantes españoles." *El Estudiante*, vol. 2, no. 1, 6 Dec. 1925, p. 2.
Palou, Pedro Ángel. *La casa del silencio: Aproximación en tres tiempos a Contemporáneos*. El Colegio de Michoacán, 1997.
Paniagua, Domingo. *Revistas culturales contemporáneas II: Ultraísmo en España*. Punta Europa, 1970.
Pasternac, Nora. *Sur: Una revista en la tormenta: Los años de formación 1931–1944*. Paradiso, 2002.
Pérez de Mendiola, Marina. *Bridging the Atlantic: Toward a Reassessment of Iberian and Latin American Cultural Ties*. State University of New York, 1996.
Pérez Firmat, Gustavo. *Idle Fictions: The Hispanic Vanguard Novel, 1926–1934*. Duke UP, 1982.
Pérez Isasi, Santiago, and Angela Fernandes. *Looking at Iberia: A Comparative European Perspective*. Bern Peter Lang AG, Internationaler Verlag der Wissenschaften, 2013.
Pineda Franco, Adela Eugenia. *Geopolíticas de la cultura finisecular en Buenos Aires, París y México: Las revistas literarias y el modernismo*. Instituto Internacional de Literatura Iberoamericana, 2006.
Pi Suñer, A. "Scientistes o Cientifics?" *La Gaceta Literaria*, 1 Jan. 192, p. 3.
Poetas y bufones: Polémica Vasconcelos-Chocano, El asesinato de Edwin Elmore. Agencia mundial de librería, 1926.
"Postales Ibéricas." *La Gaceta Literaria*, vol. 10, 15 May 1927, p. 2.
Preciadas cartas (1932–1979): Correspondencia entre Gabriela Mistral, Victoria Ocampo y Victoria Kent. Renacimiento, 2019.
"Pretensión." *Plural*, vol. 1, Jan. 1925, pp. 1–3.
Price, Rachel. *The Object of the Atlantic: Concrete Aesthetics in Cuba, Brazil, and Spain, 1868 1968*. Northwestern UP, 2014.
"Proa." *Proa*, vol. 1, Aug. 1924, pp. 3–8.
"Proclama de los Estudiantes e Intelectuales de Costa Rica al Lic. Jose Vasconcelos." *La Antorcha*, vol. 4, 25 Oct. 1924, p. 18.
"Programa." *La Antorcha*, vol. 1, Oct. 1924, p. 1.
"Propósito." *Horizonte*, vol. 1, Apr. 1926, p. 3.
"Propósitos." *Revista de Occidente*, Jul. 1923, pp. 1–3.
"Propósitos: *Dos palabras que no están demás*." *La Pluma*, vol. 1, Jun. 1920, p. 2.
Ramos Ortega, Manuel José, coord. *Revistas literarias españolas del siglo XX (1919–1975)*. Ollero y Ramos, 2005.
"Reaccionarios? Poco definidos?" *Inicial*, 2 Nov. 1923, pp. 3–8.
Reimunde Noreña, María Dolores. *Hispanoamérica en las revistas gallegas (1914–1936)*. 1989. Universidad Complutense, PhD dissertation.

Resina, Joan Ramon. *Iberian Modalities: A Relational Approach to the Study of Culture in the Iberian Peninsula*. Liverpool UP, 2013.
"Revista de Occidente." *Valoraciones*, vol. 2, Jan. 1924, pp. 158–9.
"Revista de Occidente." facsm. ed. *Inicial*, 6 Sept. 1924, pp. 489–90.
Reyes, Alfonso. *Posición de América*. "Valle-Inclán y América." *La Pluma*, vol. 32, Jan. 1923, pp. 30–4.
– "Un paso de América." *Sur*, vol. 1, 1931, pp. 150–8.
Ripa Alberdi, Héctor. "Por la unión moral de América." *Valoraciones*, vol. 2, Jan. 1924, pp. 111–15.
Rivas Cherif, Cipriano. "Alfonso Reyes: *El plano oblicuo*." *La Pluma*, vol. 6, Nov. 1920, p. 283.
– "Guillermo de Torre *Manifiesto Vertical*." *La Pluma*, vol. 1, no. 7, Dec. 1920, p. 335.
Ródenas de Moya, Domingo. *Contemporáneos: Prosa*. Fundación Santander Central Hispano, 2004.
Rodó, José Enrique. *Ariel*. Biblioteca Virtual Universal Editorial del Cardo, 2003, biblioteca.org.ar/libros/70738.pdf. Accessed Jul. 2018.
Rogers, Gayle. *Modernism and the New Spain: Britain, Cosmopolitan Europe, and Literary History*. Oxford UP, 2012.
– *Incomparable Empires: Modernism and the Translation of Spanish and American Literature*. Columbia UP, 2016.
Rojas Paz, Pablo. "Hispanoamericanismo." facsm. ed. *Martín Fierro*, vol. 17, 17 May 1925, p. 112.
Rojo Martín, María del Rosario. *Evolución del movimiento vanguardista. Estudio basado en La Gaceta Literaria (1927–32)*. Juan, Mar. 1982.
Rosenberg, Fernando J. *The Avant-Garde and Geopolitics in Latin America*. U Pittsburgh P, 2006.
Sáez Delgado, Antonio. "Madrid, meridiano intellectual ibérico (la polémica peninsular de *La Gaceta Literaria*)." *Hispanic Review*, vol. 89, no. 4, Autumn 2021, pp. 490–505.
Salaverría, José María. "Estilo de Extremadura." *La Gaceta Literaria*, vol. 3, 1 Feb. 1927, p. 2.
Salazar y Chapela, Esteban. "Jaime Torres Bodet: *Margarita de niebla*." *El Sol*, 1 Oct. 1927, p. 2.
"Saludo a Cataluña." *La Gaceta Literaria*, vol. 23, 1 Dec. 1927, p. 1.
"Saludo a Vasconcelos." *El Estudiante*, vol. 8, June 1925, p. 1.
"Salutación." *La Gaceta Literaria*, vol. 1, 1 Jan. 1927, p. 1.
Salvador, Nélida. *Revistas argentinas de vanguardia (1920–1930)*. UBA, 1962.
– *"Prisma y Proa: Hacia una definición estética." Letras*, vol. 2, no. 3, Jul. 2004, pp. 44–8.
Salvador, Nélida, and Elena Ardissone. *Bibliografía de tres revistas de vanguardia: Prisma (1921–22), Proa (1922–23) y Proa (1924–26)*. UBA, 1983.

Salvador, Nélida, et al. *Revistas literarias argentinas, 1960–1990: aporte para una bibliografía*. Fundación Inca Seguros, 1996.
Sánchez Prado, Ignacio M. *Naciones intelectuales: Las fundaciones de la modernidad literaria Mexicana (1917–1959)*. Purdue UP, 2009.
–, editor. *Pierre Bourdieu in Hispanic Literature and Culture*. Palgrave Macmillan, 2018.
– *Alfonso Reyes, Hispanist Praxis, and the Critique of Transatlantic Reason*. Edited by Cecilia Enjuto Rangel, Sebastiaan Faber, Pedro García Caro, and Robert Patrick Newcomb, 2020, pp. 377–85.
Sarlo, Beatriz. "Intelectuales y revistas: Razones de una práctica." *Le discours cultrurel dans les Revues Latino-américaines (1940–1970)*. Presses de la Sorbonne Nouvelle, 1992.
Schammah-Gesser, Silvina. *Madrid's Forgotten Avant Garde: Between Essentialism and Modernity*. Chicago UP, 2015.
Schneider, Luis Mario. *El estridentismo: Una literatura de la estrategia*. Bellas Artes, 1970.
– *El estridentismo: México 1921–1927*. UNAM, 1985.
Scholes, Robert, and Clifford Wulfman. *Modernism in the Magazines: An Introduction*. Yale UP, 2010.
Schwartz, Jorge. *Las vanguardias latinoamericanas: textos pragmáticos y críticos*. FCE, 2004.
Schwartz, Jorge, and Roxana Patiño. *Revista Iberoamericana: Revistas literarias/ culturales latinoamericanas del siglo XX Núms. 208–209*. Instituto Internacional de Literatura Iberoamericana, 2004.
Sferrazza, Maria. *Ernesto Giménez Caballero en la Literatura Española: De la dictadura a la república*. Turner, 1977.
Sheridan, Guillermo. *Índices de Contemporáneos: Revista mexicana de cultura: 1928–1931*. UNAM, 1988.
– *Los Contemporáneos ayer*. Fondo de Cultura Económica, 2003.
"Significación social de la Argentina." *El Estudiante*, vol. 13, July 1925, pp. 11–12.
Siqueiros, David Alfaro. "Appeals for a Modern Direction to the New Generation of American Painters and Sculptors." *Vida Americana*, vol. 1, 1921.
Siskind, Mariano. *Cosmopolitan Desires: Global Modernity and World Literture in Latin America*. Northwestern UP, 2014.
Sitman, Rosalie. *Victoria Ocampo y Sur: Entre Europa y América*. Lumiere, 2003.
Soria Olmedo, Andrés. *Vanguardismo y crítica literaria en España (1910–1930)*. Istmo, 1988.
Sosnowski, Saúl. *La cultura de un siglo: América latina en sus revistas*. Alianza, 1999.
Tandy, Lucy. *Giménez Caballero y "La Gaceta Literaria" [O la Generación del 27]*. Turner, 1977.
Thacker, Andrew, and Peter Brooker. *The Oxford Critical and Cultural History of Modernist Magazines. Volume 1 Britain and Ireland*, Oxford UP, 2009.

– *The Oxford Critical and Cultural History of Modernist Magazines. Volume 2 North America 1894–1960.* Oxford UP, 2012.
– *The Oxford Critical and Cultural History of Modernist Magazines Volume 3, Europe 1880–1940.* 2 vols, Oxford UP, 2013.
Torres Bodet, Jaime. "La deshumanización del arte." *Valoraciones,* vol. 9, Mar. 1926, pp. 245–9.
– "La geografía intelectual de América, Un meridiano de modestia." *Repertorio americano,* vol. 21, 3 Dec. 1927, pp. 335–6.
– *Contemporáneos: notas de crítica.* Herrero, 1928.
– *Tiempo de arena.* FCE, 2002, p. 225.
– *Margarita de niebla.* UNAM, 2005.
Tsuchiya, Akiko, and William G. Acree, editors. *Empire's End: Transnational Connections in the Hispanic World.* Vanderbilt UP, 2016.
Unamuno, Miguel de. *En torno al casticismo,* cervantesvirtual.com/obra/en-torno-al-casticismo-253798. Accessed 2 Apr. 2018.
– "Hispanidad." *Síntesis,* vol. 6, Nov. 1927, pp. 305–10.
"Una novela de éxito." *La Gaceta Literaria,* vol. 45, 1 Nov. 1928, p. 3.
"Una nueva revista." *El Estudiante,* vol. 10, July 1925, p. 10.
"Un debate apasionado: Campeonato para un meridiano intelectual." *La Gaceta Literaria,* 1 Sept. 1927, p. 3.
"Un filósofo de la nueva generación." *Inicial,* vol. 3, Dec. 1923, pp. 58–63.
Unruh, Vicky. *Latin American Vanguards: The Art of Contentious Encounters.* U California P, 1994.
Vasconcelos, José. "Programa." *La Antorcha,* vol. 1, 4 Oct. 1924, p. 1.
– "Las tres claridades." *La Antorcha,* vol. 4, 25 Oct. 1924, pp. 1–2.
– "Vasconcelos a los estudiantes españoles." *El Estudiante,* vol. 8, June 1925, p. 2.
– "La hermandad lingüística." *La Gaceta Literaria,* vol. 9, 1 May 1927, p. 5.
– *The Cosmic Race: A Bilingual Edition.* Translated by Didier T. Jaén, Johns Hopkins, 1997.
Vázquez, M. Ángeles. "Las vanguardias en nuestras revistas: Otras revistas de vanguardia en España." *Cervantes Virtual,* 16 Feb. 2005, https://cvc.cervantes.es/el_rinconete/anteriores/febrero_05/16022005_02.htm Web. Accessed 3 Feb. 2011.
Villaurrutia, Xavier. "Los caminos de Alfonso Reyes." *Proa,* vol. 10, May 1925, pp. 3–9.
Weinberg, Liliana. "Revistas culturales y formas de sociabilidad intellectual. El caso de la primera época de *Cuadernos Americanos*. La edición de una revista como operación social." Posted on April 29 2014 Blog Universität Augsburg University Spanishsprachige Kulturzeitschriften.
Zuleta, Emilia de. *Relaciones literarias entre España y la Argentina.* Instituto de Cooperación Iberoamericana, 1983.

Index